DATE DUE

The Mystery
of Agatha Christie

The Mystery
of Agatha Christie

Gwen Robyns

DOUBLEDAY & COMPANY, INC.
GARDEN CITY, NEW YORK
1978

Library of Congress Cataloging in Publication Data
Robyns, Gwen.
    The mystery of Agatha Christie.
    Includes index.
    1. Christie, Agatha Miller, Dame, 1891–1976—
Biography. 2. Authors, English—20th century—Biography.
I. Title.
PR6005.H66Z83   823'.9'12[B]

ISBN: 0-385-12623-9
Library of Congress Catalog Card Number 77-76259

To Alasdair Gordon—a wise friend
and kind counselor over many years.

ACKNOWLEDGMENTS

Every biography needs friends—and this one has met with many. When I undertook to write a book about Agatha Christie—reluctantly I must admit—it seemed an impossible task. Due to her paranoiac shyness in public, Dame Agatha lived her life so privately that I wondered how to break through the clichés and find the real woman beneath. My Agatha Christie file may not be complete but after talking to a hundred or so people, I feel I now know something about the Duchess of Death, as she was called.

For legal reasons I have not been able to quote directly from letters written by Dame Agatha Christie which have been lent to me. I have made a précis of their contents and copies of the letters are in my possession.

If I have left anyone out in my thanks I ask them to accept my deepest apologies for without these "friends" this book could never have been written.

Mr. A. F. Herring and Mr. F. J. Baine of the Austral Development, Ltd., Miss Avrid Angers, John Atwell of the Sinodun Players, Mr. and Mrs. G. Brooks of Bristol, Lord Brabourne, Professor Frank Behr of Sweden, Nicholas Bull, Dr. Josephine Bell, Marian Babson, secretary of the Crime Writers' Association, Miss Christianna Brand, Mr. T. J. Binyon of Oxford, the Reverend B. G. Burr, Max Reinhardt of The Bodley Head.

Lord Ritchie Calder of Edinburgh, Peter Cotes, Geoffrey Colville, Mrs. M. Curnow, Mr. Nat Cohen, Mrs. Ada Couch of Torquay, the Marchesa Ray Corsini of New York—whose idea this book was—Mrs. Geri Courtney.

Marshal of the Royal Air Force Sir William Dixon, Richard Dalby of Oxford, Mrs. Gladys Kenward Dobson, Mr. Ernest Dudley, Mr. Wallace Douglas, Mr. Hugh Douglas, Mr. G. A. Heywood, headmaster of the Galmpton Church of England Primary School, Mr. Sebastian Earl, Mr. Charles Gibbs, Mr. and Mrs. G. R. Hatley, Mr. D. Hullah, Information Officer Ealing County Council, Mr. G. W. Matthews, Mr. R. Smith and Mrs. Katie Westbury of the *Herald Express*, Torquay, Mr. R. H. Stockton, editorial director of the Harrogate *Herald*, Miss Elizabeth Jane Howard, and my editor, Miss Louise Gault, of Doubleday and Company, Inc., New York.

Mr. H. R. F. Keating for permission to quote from the anthology *Agatha Christie, First Lady of Crime* (Weidenfeld and Nicolson), the chief librarian of the Kensington and Chelsea Public Library, Miss Mary Law.

Admiral of the Fleet The Earl Mountbatten of Burma, Mrs. Gladys Mitchell, Mr. Nigel Moorland, Miss Ethel Mannin, Professor J. E. Morpurgo, Mr. W. K. Hoenes of the Middlesex County *Press*, Sir Robert Mark, former Commissioner of the Metropolitan Police, Dilys Winn of Murder Ink, of New York, Raymond Mander and Joe Mitchenson, Mr. Ricki Myers, Mr. W. W. Baxter of the Old Swan Hotel and formerly the Harrogate Hydro, Martin Phillips, Frederick Potter of Torquay, and the Reverend Philip Pare of Cholsey.

I would especially like to thank Miss Gwen Petty of Torquay, who gave weeks of her precious time in helping me re-create Agatha Christie's youth. Without her enthusiastic joy this part of the book would not have been written. I am also grateful for the splendid friendship that has developed between us.

Sir Patrick Reilly, the Misses Olive and Gwen Robinson of Dittisham, Mr. Chaim Raphael (Jocelyn Davey), Mr. Tom Roberts, Mr. Robert Rook of Torquay, Mrs. Tania Schmoller, Mrs. R. Schofield of Harrogate, Mr. Julian Symons, president of the Detection Club, the Honorable Lady Sachs of the Harrison Homes, Dr. Anthony Storr of Oxford, Mr. Fred Smith, Mr. L. J. Sills of the South Camden Health District, Lord Snowden.

Mr. John Pike of the Torquay Public Library, Mr. J. M. Evelyn (Michael Underwood), Mrs. Imogen Woollard, Miss Grace Rich of the City of Westminster Public Library, Miss Jennifer Emerton of the Wallingford County Branch Library, Dr. Michael Rhodes of the Westfield College, University of London.

The British Broadcasting Corporation, the British Red Cross, and the Imperial War Museum have all been exceedingly helpful.

And lastly my thanks to the officers of New Scotland Yard, the Surrey Constabulary, the Berkshire Constabulary, and ex-superintendent F. Smith of the Witney Police Force.

CONTENTS

The Mystery
of Agatha Christie

CHAPTER ONE

In st. mary's churchyard, Cholsey, Berkshire, forty-seven miles west of London, lies Lady Mallowan—Dame Agatha Christie—who was known to millions of people throughout the world as the Queen of Crime or, as she preferred, the Duchess of Death.

She chose the site herself ten years before she died in 1976. It is the kind of background that she might have used in any of the ninety-four books she wrote in her lifetime. Dating from A.D. 986 in this ancient churchyard Saxon skulls have been found in the preparation of new graves.

The gray tombstones stained with moss and lichen topple with age in the long grass. Rain and sun have eroded the names on many of the headstones until they are no longer decipherable. At the left-hand side of the oak door of the church is a massive yew tree which is said was planted there by Queen Elizabeth I during a visit to Wallingford.

Far away in the right-hand corner of the churchyard, stark against the skyline, is the headstone of Dame Agatha's grave. Time and the weather will eventually mellow the white stone which now looks desolate and cold in contrast to the old tomb-stones.

The wording is simple giving her name and age and underneath the phrase *Agatha Christie the writer* so that pilgrims will easily recognize the grave in years to come. It is also inscribed with these words that Agatha Christie loved so much. The verse is chosen from Edmund Spenser's epic *The Faerie Queene.*

> Sleep after toil
> Port after stormie seas,
> Ease after warre,
> Death after life,
> Does greatly please.

The grave, which is endowed and thus will be cared for if neces-sary by the church, lies beside two young yew trees overlooking the open Berkshire countryside with its dark brown plowed earth and high, wide sky.

Two small vases at each side hold three rosebuds each and on the grave itself lies a sprig of scarlet polyantha roses—so fresh they must have been morning-picked. One feels her presence near.

Agatha Mary Clarissa Mallowan is not alone. She is surrounded by Englishwomen who have lain there for many a year. There are Sarah and Rosalina, who both died in 1899, and Sarah Pardel, who "departed this life in 1886," Jane who "fell asleep in 1892," and Mary Ann, who was placed there so long ago that the year can no longer be read on the crumbling headstone. They are the kind of women that Dame Agatha Christie would have enjoyed meeting in life. She found much pleasure in talking to simple country people about their daily lives. Despite her wealth and fame she was a plain woman at heart.

The funeral service on January 16, 1976, was just as she had planned—meticulous and well ordered, conventional and correct. At her request it had been kept strictly private and the hordes of photographers and reporters, representing the world's press, were silent and respectful as they waited back at the gates of the church. A sprinkling of the local people of Wallingford, many of whom had worked for Lady Mallowan, as she was known to them, sat at the back of the church.

There was an air of the Edwardian era as the male mourners in the family slowly moved into place wearing full mourning dress and carrying black silk top hats. The central figure was white-haired Sir Max Mallowan, who had been married to Dame Agatha for forty-six glorious years, then Anthony Hicks, her son-in-law, and Mathew Prichard, the grandson she adored. A gleam of two strings of pearls accentuated the black worn by Dame Agatha's daughter Rosalind and in her hand she carried some sprigs of lily of the valley, later to be placed in her mother's grave.

The service was simple and short and was conducted by the Reverend Philip Pare, vicar of St. Mary's, and the Reverend Walter Henry Lofts of Colwinston, South Wales, an old family friend. With her cool logic Dame Agatha had planned her own funeral arrangements down to the last detail including the choice of hymns and readings. She wanted the same Spenser verse to be read as appears now on her tombstone. It expresses the beliefs of this fanatically private woman who disliked anyone prying into her own personal world.

After the service the small family group walked through the frost-covered churchyard to the open grave where Dame Agatha was laid to rest.

These, then, are the people who made up the closely knit family clan and who were also present at most of her important business meetings. They share the major portion of the immense wealth she made over the years making her the most financially rewarded English writer of all time. There are wizards in the City of London who put her fortune as high as £14 million—the gross sum she is reputed to have earned in a lifetime of writing about crime.

Agatha Christie wrote ninety-four books all told and was translated into 103 languages, 14 more than Shakespeare. She wrote eighty-three detective stories, six straight novels (under the pseudonym of Mary Westmacott), one book of reminiscences, two of poems, and her autobiography. Four hundred million copies of her books have already been sold and there is no sign of a decline in sales. Her peak selling period was undoubtedly in the thirties when she wrote seventeen detection novels and six short story collections, and the forties when she wrote her finest books.

The magic and mystery of Agatha Christie is as incomprehensible as the woman herself. There have been more literate women detection writers—Dorothy L. Sayers, Margery Allingham, Ngaio Marsh, and Gladys Mitchell to name a few—but none surpassed her at telling a story with her own peculiar brand of ingenuity and personal charm.

Literary critics have condemned her slapdash grammar and Spartan description of places but undeterred, her readers enjoy romping along, page after page, following her fluent and often comic dialogue.

"I could not put it down" is a phrase that one constantly hears about a new Agatha Christie. With a kind of masochistic pleasure her readers enjoy it as she skillfully ties them in knots until the last explosive pages. They always knew that they could count on a thumping surprise at the end of the book.

Agatha Christie domesticated murder as perhaps no other author had done before or since and transformed it into nothing more perilous than an intriguing game of chess or a satisfactory crossword puzzle. All her life she abhorred violence and blood and constantly confessed that she had no knowledge of the usual implements used for murder. In old age she also admitted that to her knowledge she had never met a murderer.

"I know nothing about pistols and revolvers, which is why I usually kill off my characters with a blunt instrument—or better still with poisons. Besides poisons are neat and clean and really exciting . . . I do not think I could look a really ghastly mangled body in the face. It is the means that I am interested in. I do not usually describe the end, which is often a corpse."

Agatha Christie's personal talent lay in the way she manipulated the basic elements—characters and situations—which make up the formula for a true detection novel as opposed to the aggressive crime thriller. She developed this style of pure puzzle writing with her first book, *The Mysterious Affair at Styles*, in 1920 and continued until her last, *Sleeping Murder* which though written many years before was not published until 1975.

An inveterate traveler, she set her plots in many parts of the world, as well as in the Home Counties, but her technique seldom varied. She had the beguiling gift of using the obvious and she made it perfectly acceptable whether the plot was set in ~~consfield~~ or Baghdad.

Agatha Christie fans are perfectly content to enjoy the story line and if her characters are cardboard or two dimensional it does not matter. All through her sixty-odd years of writing she stayed true to her own métier and never allowed herself to be tempted by the analytical or psychological type of crime with which other writers of her generation experimented. She went on writing just as it pleased her and her fans even accepted with alacrity her equivocal *Passenger to Frankfurt*, which was published to mark her eightieth birthday. The fact that this time she had outstretched herself into the James Bond world of international intrigue was accepted as a brave gesture of defiance at her own advancing years.

A less successful writer might not have been treated quite so kindly by the critics, but as one London bookseller says about Agatha Christie, "All she had to do in those last years was to rewrite a page from a seed catalogue and it would have sold. She had become a legend in her own lifetime."

In a paper that the author Cyril Hare read to the Royal Society of Literature he got as near to unmasking the Christie formula as anyone else. He said: "It resembled one of those connected series of equations by which a mathematician can prove conclusively that nought equals one. Each step in the series is clearly stated and is manifestly correct. The end result is impossible. It is only when you make the closest inspection that you can detect the tiny fallacy which falsifies the equation."

What kind of a woman was Agatha Christie? It was impossible to meet her without instantly liking her. She was everyone's favorite aunt yet she wore her shyness as an armor against anyone penetrating her own private world of the well-bred Englishwoman.

She did not suffer fools gladly and her precision-made mind became easily bored with trivia. At a party she invariably positioned herself away from anyone she suspected might be boring or too inquisitive, yet in her own home she could be vastly entertaining, leaping from one topic of conversation to another with her own private kind of humor. She was never totally at ease when attending public functions.

Even such publicly acclaimed charmers as Admiral of the Fleet The Earl Mountbatten of Burma and Sir Robert Mark, former Commissioner of the Metropolitan Police, found her difficult to talk to unless they hit on a specific subject that interested her. Lesser men have been known to find her positively "crusty." Outside her close circle of family and friends she preferred to speak with men rather than with women. "Men have much clearer brains and are not as cluttered up as women," she said.

Agatha Christie was essentially a modest woman in that she never saw herself as a literary figure but merely as someone with the faculty to amuse. In her quiet chuckly way she used to refer to herself as "a sausage machine. When you cut the string another sausage begins to form. I regard my work as of no importance. I simply set out to entertain. Once I've been dead ten years I'm sure nobody will ever have heard of me."

There are millions of Agatha Christie fans who think differently and believe that her novels will last far into the future. As Sir Robert Mark told me: "She's a storyteller and a great plot maker. I think that the advantage that she enjoys, which perhaps many modern writers will never have, is that she depends for her success on the basic requirements of a storyteller, namely that there should be a story which should be carefully worked out and which should interest the reader.

"In a curious sort of way like Jane Austen or Dickens, all her stories could be set in any period. She is timeless. Among a great many people there is a faint distaste for the abandonment of standards or conventions that they were brought up with—the desire to be reasonably proper and decent. I don't think that Dame Agatha has ever abandoned these standards and therefore she retains an appeal. It is a strong nostalgia for the past which even some of the young are experiencing today."

Agatha Christie was also a social historian of considerable skill. She had the ability to supply accurate information about everyday life in the middle classes over eight decades that have seen so many changes in the British way of life.

One Indian woman was so enthralled by Agatha Christie that she wrote to her saying: "I think you must be a very noble woman." In retelling the story to Edmund Crispin, the detection writer, Agatha Christie remarked wryly: "Now why would she think that I am a noble woman when I have spent most of my life writing about murder."

Dame Agatha carried her craving for privacy to much greater lengths than any other writer of her generation except perhaps the elusive romantic novelist Georgette Heyer. She disliked giving interviews at all and on the few occasions she did there seemed to be little variety in text. No matter how the questions differed she always brought out her stock answers with such authority that the reporter was charmed into thinking that they were specially for him.

Nicholas Bull, formerly of the Torbay *Herald*, was certainly the youngest reporter ever to be given an interview and this was done simply on the basis that he represented a local newspaper in her Home Counties, Devon.

Remembering back to the occasion he says: "She certainly looked a bit horrified when I arrived as I was only twenty-three at the time. She obviously expected a much more mature person. I remember Sir Max Mallowan meeting me and his opening piece was 'Remember this has to be short—half an hour at the most.'

"If anything this helped me to concentrate my mind and I felt I was almost in a race. After half an hour I fully expected him to come in and break up the interview but in fact we went on for an hour. I remember at the critical moment when she was telling me of her love of Devon my fountain pen began to flood. I had to fumble around and find something else to write with. On noting this she was very sweet and understanding."

The interview obviously made a great impression on Nicholas Bull, now in charge of publicity for the city of Exeter, who remembers it vividly.

"Her manner while pleasant was certainly not effusive in any way. She made it quite clear to me that she was doing me a great favor. Even as I talk to you now I feel that she is probably looking down from 'Up There' and saying, 'You rat.' There was no doubt that she had a presence and knew her own value.

"I have always wondered whether this great veil of privacy was not engineered in a sense by those involved around her. Her books were gold and to ensure their continued success I'm wondering whether her publishers, or maybe she herself, wanted her to remain an enigma, an unknown person, if only to stimulate public interest and curiosity. Perhaps the general cloud of mystery that hung over her whole life was deliberately planned."

With the passing of the years her shyness became partly obliterated. What was left instead was a disinclination ever to use the first person singular, a ploy used by some members of the British royal family, which is usually a sign of defensiveness. She invariably spoke of herself as one.

When asked why she gave so few interviews in her life Agatha Christie replied: "One has a very strong feeling that it is not part of an author's life to be in the limelight. If you act, or if you are a member of Parliament, or a public-spirited woman who sits on committees, then you are part of it."

Though she was offered lucrative rewards for lecture tours and television appearances these were all firmly turned down. The BBC has only two short interviews with her in its archives spanning all those long years.

Agatha Christie never curried favor with her readers, publishers, or critics. From the very beginning of her career in 1920 she adopted an aloof take-it-or-leave-it attitude that made her almost a professional recluse.

She would not allow her publishers, William Collins Sons & Co., Ltd., to give any publicity parties for her books, and the small Walter Bird photograph, complete with marcel-waved hair, that was permitted on the back of her books was thirty years out of date. She simply refused to have a new photograph taken to prevent any of her readers from recognizing her in the street.

At semipublic functions whenever a photographer moved into sight she moved out. It was an almost paranoiac dislike of being photographed unawares. In the last year of her life she permitted the Queen's brother-in-law, Lord Snowdon, to take a remarkably frank set of pictures of herself and her husband. They show a frail, immensely old lady, in the surroundings of her home at Wallingford. One suspects that his royal connections pleased her.

All through the picture session she talked frankly and fluently to Lord Snowdon about her work style. The brain was clear and sharp:

"Well I am not an intellectual. I don't really want to study any subject that I can think of much. I might like to have studied astrology, but I wouldn't have been any good. I take an interest in literature, and books that are written and things like that. I mean I love reading Graham Greene's books; they are the sort of books that you can't put down because he writes remarkably well. And I think Elizabeth Bowen is one of the finest female writers we have ever had. Muriel Spark and Ngaio Marsh write a very good detective story but I find Ian Fleming incredibly boring."

She used to give his books to her nephews when they were young as Christmas or birthday presents: "Later they turned to science fiction, which is quite enjoyable, and always seems to make sense and I could quite see why they would be interested in that."

Dame Agatha Christie did not enjoy fine wines or highly sophisticated food but she did have an appreciation of gracious living. When asked what she would like best in life she answered, "A houseful of well-trained servants."

When she discussed her early work with Francis Wyndham she told him: "I am amazed at the number of servants drifting about. And nobody is really doing any work. They're always having tea on the lawn like in the Edwardian novelist, E. F. Benson. It gives one a great nostalgia for the past."

And again to Marcelle Bernstein when she was explaining how she enjoyed doing a little cooking: "I don't want to make grand artistic sweets with cherries and angelica, but it's nice to think up something with shellfish and avocado. Of course one wouldn't want to do it all the time—you rather miss servants. They always had an interesting part to play in books and could be really important characters; you just can't get the same effect with daily helpers. It's rather dull nowadays; you're always in a cement factory or an office—there seems to be less play of drama in surroundings."

Early in her marriage Sir Max Mallowan set out to educate Dame Agatha in the joys of drinking wine so that she could enjoy this pleasure with him just as they shared the same taste for food. With this in mind he set out to teach her—a kind of alcoholic College for One—beginning gently with sweet sauternes and per-

9

severing to claret and finally on to the heady Burgundies. After that he made a more determined effort with tokay, vodka, and absinthe. All to no avail. For the rest of her life, though a generous hostess at her own table, the nearest she came to stimulants were apple juice and cold water.

Nor did he have any better luck with smoking. After their marriage, for six months she steeled herself to have a cigarette after dinner every day. This too proved abortive and after she had choked and spluttered her way through nearly 200 cigarettes she admitted defeat. She never smoked again during her lifetime.

As a royalist Dame Agatha had a high regard for the preservation of tradition. She is recorded as saying that the occasions on which Queen Elizabeth II presented her first with the C.B.E. in 1956 and later with the D.B.E, in 1971 were among "the most satisfactory of my life." Only the knighthood conferred on her husband, Sir Max Mallowan, in 1968 for his services to archaeology gave her greater pleasure.

Peter Saunders, the producer of *The Mousetrap* and a lifelong friend, said in a tribute after her death: "She was as English as Buckingham Palace, the House of Commons, and the Tower of London."

Perhaps the most vivid description of this truly remarkable woman comes from the late Sir Mortimer Wheeler, the eminent archaeologist.

"I think of her at a party as if it might be one of those episodes in her own novels and plays when the characters are assembled and the plot thickens. She is sitting a little to one side of the scene dressed probably in brown with a jewel of old-fashioned style upon her corsage.

"Unlike others she has no wineglass beside her and obviously neither needs the stimulus or the gesture which such provision assures to lesser folk. Beneath her wealth of gray hair she looks upon the world with calm and kindly eyes, observant rather than inquisitive, and always with a twinkle or a smile.

"Her talk is easy and leisurely, enlivened now and then with an anticipated flash of wit but not in the full sense of the term vivacious. She is essentially a shy presence adding her wise geniality to the party rather than noticeably dominating it. This quality of reserve and quiescence seem to me to be an integral quality of her writing."

What changed a lively, friendly little girl into this shy, elusive introvert? As Miss Marple says in the last Christie book, *Sleeping Murder*, "secrets are like bindweed with its roots that go down under-ground a long way."

What then are the secrets of Agatha Christie's life?

CHAPTER TWO

In the beginning of the 1880s Frederick Alvah Miller, formerly of New York, and his English wife, the former Clarissa Margaret Beochmer, with their two children, Marjorie and Louis, settled down to live in Torquay.

Eight years after this event Mrs. Miller had another baby—a girl—who was registered as being born on September 15, 1890, at her parents' home, Ashfield. On November 20, the chubby baby, with fairish red hair, was baptized at All Saints' Church, in the parish of Tormohun, and given the names of Agatha Mary Clarissa.

The baby's sponsors were people of substance—Mrs. W. H. Kitson, whose husband was president of the Torbay Hospital, Master of the Torquay Harriers, and prominent in cricket circles; Mrs. James Sullivan; and Captain the Honorable A. R. Hewitt, Royal Navy, who later became the sixth Viscount Lifford when he succeeded to his brother.

Through my researches for this book I found that Agatha Christie had managed to cover clues to her identity with amazing ingenuity. Her own birth certificate, which would normally have been found in the archives of Somerset House in London, was not there. Instead it lay in the Registrar of Births, Deaths and Marriages offices in Newton Abbot, a small town next to Paignton in Devon.

On her birth certificate and on her marriage certificate to Lieutenant Colonel Christie only the name of her father, Frederick Alvah Miller, appeared, which is not a usual procedure.

During her eighty-five years Dame Agatha Christie kept her family life and its origins to herself. She seldom mentioned her father in public and rarely her mother. Now in her autobiography, published in November 1977 by Collins in England and Dodd, Mead in America, she broke her silence. The book was completed ten years before she died.

Discerning readers of her romantic novels, written under the name of Mary Westmacott, could have found out a great deal about her life. The Miriam of *Unfinished Portrait* was indeed her own mother, Clara, thinly disguised.

One marvels at the detailed conversations in her autobiography that she remembers all those sixty-odd years ago. Are they accurately recalled, or is this the work of a superb storyteller? The answer lies in that it is probably a mixture of both.

Though Agatha Christie does not mention the family name of her grandmother, Beochmer, she does describe how she was left a widow of twenty-seven years when her handsome husband, a captain in the Black Watch, was thrown from his horse and killed. By then she had five children, one of whom had died. Though she was courted by many fellow officers of her husband, Mrs. Beochmer preferred to earn her own living and remained true to her husband's memory. In order to make ends meet she took up fancy sewing and embroidered cushions and other bric-a-brac which was in fashion at the time. She often sat as many as eight hours a day bent over her sewing.

It is interesting to note that when Mrs. Agatha Christie married her second husband, Professor Max Mallowan, it was required in Scotland to give her mother's maiden name. This is recorded as "Beamer."

It was with mixed feelings that Mrs. Beochmer consented to

13

her sister adopting her only daughter, thus leaving her with three boys. This child, Clarissa Margaret, who was known in the family as Clara, was Agatha's mother. Her anguish at having to leave her three brothers behind in Jersey and begin a new life in the cold North of England was to leave its imprint all her life. When she herself married she had a passionate determination that her own children would be given a secure and loving upbringing which she felt had been denied her.

The two Victorian sisters—Auntie-Granny and Granny B as they were called—were to play an important part in Agatha Christie's childhood. Even Clara Beochmer's marriage to her American "cousin" is like a Christie detection novel. Frederick ("Freddy") Miller, her aunt's stepson, was an attractive young man, and, according to Agatha Christie, counted Jenny Jerome, who later became Lady Randolph Churchill, among his flirtations in the social whirl of New York.

Agatha Christie's mother refused Freddy Miller the first time he asked for her hand in marriage simply because she felt that she was too dumpy. This explanation he was fortunately able to overlook, and on the second occasion Clara agreed to marry him.

Frederick Miller was a dandy. According to his daughter Agatha he never did a stroke of work in his life. Why a New York businessman chose to settle down in Torquay was an enigma except that when he visited the town he fell in love with it.

Although the Millers had every intention of returning to America and making their permanent home there, Clara Miller quite obviously had plans of her own. One cannot help but think that it was no accident that while her husband was on a trip to New York she went to Torquay and bought a house called Ashfield from a Quaker woman. Though her husband was somewhat surprised on his return, he did not object. He had already made English friends there, as well as several Americans, who regularly came each winter to "the English Riviera." Besides, he quickly became addicted to English club life.

England, more than any other country in the world, has a club life for men that is unique. It is an escape world where they can play at being emperors or schoolboys and no one is going to give the game away. Quite unabashed business tycoons can be seen in every English club tucking into bread and butter pudding, treacle tart, or steak and kidney pudding. There are the casuals who drop in, when time and inclination suits them, and the regulars who daily build a world of their own, far away from the madding influence of women.

Mr. Miller was a regular. He enjoyed his role as the quiet American. He left the house every morning for the club and returned by cab for luncheon. In the afternoons he returned to the club to play whist. He stayed there until it was time to come back to his home, where he changed for dinner. Once a week at least there was a dinner party at Ashfield and Mr. and Mrs. Miller dined out at least two or three times a week. It was a gratifying existence. Cricket and amateur theatricals were another part of Mr. Miller's life. He was known as a perfect gentleman by everyone who met him, tradesmen and friends alike.

Mrs. Miller was an imposing woman: a woman with presence. She had natural elegance with an innate flair for stylish clothes. Her figure was whalebone straight and her countenance most agreeable. Miss Gwen Petty, a retired schoolmistress with a diamond-bright memory, whose father was the Reverend Harry John Petty, vicar of All Saints' Church, Tormohun, recalls:

"Mrs. Miller was a frequent visitor to the vicarage where she had the habit of calling on Saturday afternoons just when my father was busy in his study preparing the Sunday sermons.

"I was young then, teaching at Sherborne School, but I still remember how impressed I was by her elegance and dignity. She was dressed in the height of fashion for her day in a long black coat of flowing marocain and on her head she wore a wide-brimmed becoming black hat. In her hand she carried a tall, silver-topped ebony stick. She used to walk into the house with her head held high. She was both lively and charming."

Whatever the vicar and his wife were doing at that moment, everything stopped when Mrs. Miller called. She was that kind of person. Tea was immediately served in the drawing room with wafer-thin bread and butter on the top plate in the cake stand, small queen cakes on the second tier, and perhaps a madeira cake lower down.

The Georgian silver teapot and the silver kettle, with its methylated spirit lamp underneath it, gleamed on a Benares tray.

The conversation was varied—about parish affairs, world events, books one had read, and travel that one anticipated. Both the vicar and Mrs. Miller loved people and whereas they began on a purely socially agreeable note they often ended in confidences.

The Millers had three children. Madge was born in Torquay, and son Monty was born in America while Mr. Miller was on a trip to see his grandparents in New England. The third child, also born in Torquay, was called Clarissa after her mother, Mary after her grandmother, and Agatha because a friend of her mother's thought it up on the way to the church for the christening.

Ashfield, where the Miller family lived, was one of the largest villas in Barton Road. It was common talk that Mr. Miller had extensive alterations done before moving in, including the building of a large dining room where 120 people could dance in comfort. The house was white plaster in the Italian style with a conservatory built on one end as was the fashion of the period and was set in a large garden of about two acres.

The Miller family was typical of the other families in the road. They appeared to be extremely comfortably off, though perhaps not excessively rich, and were surrounded by an ambiance that belonged to the gentry of the day.

Sir John Bailey, who lived in the largest house in Barton Road, was a retired educationalist of some fame, having founded Wellington College, and he undoubtedly, as one of the neighbors of the Miller family, would have been interested in Agatha as he was in all children and their upbringing.

Barton Road led off Union Street, which was the ancient turnpike road that ran into Torquay from the 1780s onward. The road had high stone walls on either side of the villas, which were set back in their large gardens to give the maximum privacy.

All the houses had a southerly aspect with the Barton Hills rising behind them to protect them from wind. The views were spectacular, looking out toward Torbay and Berry Head. Barton Road was not community-minded and each household observed the strict etiquette of "calling" and minding its own business. The Miller family were known to have character and carried status within their own select circle but they did not mix freely.

It is this very Englishness which was to form the natural background for Dame Agatha Christie's future writing. When asked once why she so often set her plots within a country house she replied that they had to be set somewhere that would contain the characters naturally.

"I could never manage miners talking in pubs," she said, "because I don't know what miners talk about in pubs."

What she did know about intimately was the behavior of professional people, relationships between mistress and servants, and the essence of genteel living in chintzy country houses. Her details were always meticulously correct and drawn from her childhood memories. The nuances between how the kitchen maid spoke to the cook and the cook to her mistress could not be faulted.

How convenient to make the white-haired village vicar, with his love of poetry, the villain of the piece. But she never did. Church dignitaries were sacrosanct and therefore to be presented in a favorable light. Only once, in *The Murder of Roger Ackroyd*, did she let down the medical profession. It simply was not done to denigrate one's own class.

It was on one of her regular visits to the vicarage, when Agatha Christie was already becoming known as a writer of detection stories, that Mrs. Miller, an avid reader herself, told the Petty family how she had persuaded her small daughter Agatha to write her first story.

The child was in bed with a minor illness and bored with playing with her toys. Mrs. Miller suggested that instead of telling a story, as she usually did, this time she should write it down. When the child remonstrated, her mother replied:

"Of course you can, darling. You just begin *now*." And she did.

Mrs. Miller read the result and knew instantly that her younger daughter was a born storyteller. Agatha Christie did not. "I had no idea that writing would be my career," she remembered many years later.

The house was well run by a staff of four: the cook called Jane, a housemaid, a parlormaid, and a nurse for the children. They were to make a lasting impression on little Agatha. In her autobiography she writes that one of the things that she would have missed most had she been a child of today was servants. They added color and drama to everyday family life and in a family like the Millers were accorded the respect that they deserved.

Agatha Miller's particular friend was "Nursie," and one of her enduring memories of nursery life was the silhouette of her nurse seated by the table, on which an oil lamp burned, mending or sewing. Reassuring, comforting, dependable.

There were the days when Agatha went primrose picking up Shiphay lane with "Nursie" and visited the flower nurseries at the bottom of the hill.

Over seventy years later in a letter sent in 1971 to Francis Doidge, secretary of the Devon Club Cricket Association, who had written to congratulate Agatha Christie on becoming a Dame of the British Empire, she replied that whenever she was in Devon she always took a drive by Chapel Hill. It was here that she used to go for walks with her nurse to see the lambs, before going and looking at the Devon Rosery, which used to run alongside the reservoir.

An imaginative child, Agatha was totally happy in her own company. Given a hoop, it in turn became an engine, a glorious white stallion, a sea monster. There were hours spent as a circus lady on the American rocking horse in the greenhouse or walking tight-rope fashion along the cucumber frame. She was never lonely and was perfectly happy living in her own imaginative world. This was a habit which was to stay with her all her life and enabled her to create the hundreds of characters that she used in her books.

When her father died, Agatha, a child of eleven years, was bewildered to witness the anguish of her mother and see the secure and united family world around her crash.

One of Mr. Miller's influences over his daughter Agatha was to remain with her for the rest of her life.

Every Saturday during the season as a very small girl she used to hold his hand as they walked up Barton Road to the cricket grounds opposite the laundry and dye works. As the official scorer for the Torquay Cricket Club he used to let his young daughter help him keep the score.

"I took it very seriously," she was to say years later.

From this childish pastime stemmed a lifelong interest in cricket. Even fifty years later summer weekend guests to Greenway, Dame Agatha's house on the river Dart, were invariably inveigled into playing family cricket on the homemade pitch and taking a hand at the nets. Despite being a rather heavily built, middle-aged woman she was never shy of "having a go" herself.

It was here on the Greenway pitch that her grandson Mathew put in much leg work as a child improving his cricket, and when he was finally chosen to captain Eton's First XI at the famed Lords Cricket Ground in London, Dame Agatha declared that it was one of the great days of her life.

After Dame Agatha's death few people realized that the tour of the England Young Cricketers Club to the West Indies was in fact mainly financed by Agatha Christie Limited.

The donation was undoubtedly inspired by Mathew Prichard, who with his mother is deeply involved in the running of the Agatha Christie empire, but it must have been done in full knowledge that this would have given great pleasure to his grandmother.

Agatha Christie had herself visited the West Indies in the late fifties and subsequently had written A *Caribbean Mystery* (1964), which was set on the island of St. Honoré and features Miss Marple.

In speaking about her childhood Dame Agatha explained her unusual education: "When it was time for my sister to go to school my mother was just at the stage of believing that children should get the best education. So my sister went to Miss Lawrence's boarding school at Brighton, which was later to become Roedean, and my brother went to Harrow. But, when the time came for me to go my mother's views had changed. She now believed passionately that education destroyed a child's brains and was ruinous to the eyesight. So I never went to school at all."

Mrs. Miller was a woman far ahead of her time. Once she had composed herself after her husband's death, and the overwhelming sense of despair that it left, she may well have felt that there was not sufficient money left for Agatha's education. There is also another reason that it may have been desirable to keep the child at home. Though filled with fun within the seclusion of her own family, Agatha Miller was almost paranoiac in her shyness with strangers. She may not have had the temperament to stand the rigor of an English public school and the jostling on the lacrosse field.

In several of Agatha Christie's books the store the Army and Navy Stores appears. Remember in *Bertram's Hotel* she sends a frail and fluttery Miss Marple there?

Since its formation in 1841 this esteemed London store near Victoria Station was the mainstay of service families in Britain and of those serving abroad.

Every family had a number and the daily mail to the shop came from all over the Empire. "The Gentleman's Relish was not included in last parcel" (Kashmir); "Could we change this sailor's suit to a size larger as my son has grown a lot out here" (Sierra Leone); "I find the water here is not suitable for the delicate flavor of Earl Grey tea, can you suggest something with more body" (Kandy, Ceylon); "Please include six packets of Bath Olivers in our next food parcel" (Nova Scotia).

Every mem-sahib who came home on leave found her way to the Army and Navy to re-equip her family while their made-to-measure tropical uniform department was easily the busiest in England. For the gentry of England it had the same appeal and was just the kind of store that Agatha Christie's grandmother would patronize.

Speaking to Marcelle Bernstein in 1964 for an article in the *Observer* Sunday magazine, Dame Agatha Christie told of her visits there as a child.

"I used to go there with my grandmother. She lived in Ealing and came in a four wheeler because she didn't trust herself in a hansom. She would ensconce herself in the grocery department and listen to the assistant telling her all the medical details about his wife's goitre.

"Then we would go to the confectionary department where we would buy half a pound of coffee creams. Upstairs we would have a splendid lunch, to my mind, and then we'd get another four wheeler and go to the theater.

"My grandmother lived to be ninety-two so she was a great study to the end. I had a great aunt of the same age and a lot of things they approved and disapproved of were representative, and they both contributed to Miss Marple. They worked their servants to the bone but took a lot of care of them if they were ill. If a girl had a rather disorganised baby, granny would go and speak to the young man: "Well, are you going to do the right thing by Harriet?'"

As a girl Agatha Christie worried because she was not talkative. "Writing is a great consolation to anyone who can't express themselves well any other way. I was always bad at that. As a young girl I found dancing so uncomfortable as I never knew what to say."

Mrs. Miller did an expert, if somewhat erratic, job on the education of her younger daughter. Mr. Miller had started her off on arithmetic lessons and Mrs. Miller took over history and the more elusive subject general knowledge. For instance, she insisted that Agatha read newspaper articles essential to a developing mind. The house was filled with books and all the children were encouraged to read. The selection ranged from Jane Austen through the classics to Thackeray, "who I could not get on with." As a child Agatha Miller had read Milton's *Paradise Lost* on which she commented: "Of course I didn't understand it but I loved its sonorous tones."

Discussing her likes and dislikes about her formative reading years later, Dame Agatha commented that with Dickens one could never really tell where the story was going. "I always feel with him he got awfully tired of his characters and dragged in more—but the new ones were just as wonderful.

"*Bleak House* is my favorite, such a good plot. I once tried to write a film version. The amount of characters in that book. I found I had to cut out many of the best ones."

The books that fascinated her most as a teen-ager were Arthur Conan Doyle's detection stories, which introduced her to Sherlock Holmes. These she could read for hours. Perhaps even at that age, suconsciously, the logic of detection plot construction, at which she was to become exceedingly clever, was formulating in her mind.

Early in the 1900s Eden Phillpotts, the perceptive West Country novelist, came into Agatha Christie's life as he lived in Eltham, a house just around the corner from Ashfield. The shy girl used to visit the writer and together they found a sense of intimacy and understanding. Eden Phillpotts, with his timid, elusive manner, was just the right kind of mentor to encourage and guide her reading.

She was to describe him as "like a faun trapped in bricks and mortar but belonging elsewhere," and indeed when the character of Barton Road changed with the building of the South Devon Technical College the noise of the children upset him so much that it drove him to live in seclusion on his beloved Dartmoor where his two great novels, *Sons of the Morning* and *Widecombe Fair*, were set.

He widened her whole conception of reading and introduced her to the vivid vocabulary of De Quincey, the expansive style of Ruskin, and the perception of the travel and adventure writer George Borrow.

And when she herself decided, while still in her mid-teens, to try and write a novel, it was to Eden Phillpotts that she took her handwritten manuscript. Though later she was to describe it as "gloomy, unwieldy with multiplots, and quite unreadable," Eden Phillpotts was filled with encouragement. "Capital. Go on. Excellent dialogue," he said. And then gently, "No need to moralize, let your characters speak for themselves."

Apart from discussing writers and books, Eden Phillpotts and Agatha Miller had so much to tell each other. He used to take her round his garden, which was filled with exotic plants, weaving stories about the lands where they originally came from. Much of her love for trees and gardening stems from these hours they spent together. Dame Agatha's final Devon home, Greenway, is notable for its sweeping areas in the thirty-eight-acre estate devoted to exotic trees from all over the world. Though many had been planted by the previous owner, Tom Williams, Tory Member of Parliament for Torquay, she added considerably to the collection during her twenty-odd years' stay there, especially the many different types of magnolia and rhododendrons.

Despite Mrs. Miller's aversion to education for girls she was nevertheless determined that her daughter should have an all-round tuition as befitted the upper-middle classes. After Mr. Miller died, Agatha was taken to arithmetic classes twice a week and whoever taught her instilled a healthy respect for money into her young head. The accounting departments of the various publishers she had worked for are all familiar with Dame Agatha's tart little notes about her royalty statements.

There were also Swedish exercises, piano, singing, and dancing lessons. Agatha Christie must have had sublime enjoyment when at last she was allowed to wear the accordion-pleated dress allowed the girls when they became the elite of the dancing school.

As Mrs. Miller's own youth in Ealing had been unexciting and uneventful, she was ambitious for her daughter and determined that she should have more fun in her life than she had and that she would be socially accepted wherever she went.

It was the custom in those days for the daughters of the gentry to be sent abroad to be "finished" and this is what Mrs. Miller planned for Agatha when she was sixteen. At that time Paris was filled with small well-established finishing schools run by sisters of a convent or formidable mademoiselles, and they were packed with plump and gauche daughters from the middle-class families of England. Paris invariably left its impression and the English cygnets returned as swans.

At a tea party in London Mrs. Miller met another mother who had already made plans to send her daughter, Dorothy Hamilton-Johnston, to Paris. The two girls, Agatha and Dorothy, were sent off to Miss Dryden's, an expensive finishing school near the Arc de Triomphe. They became inseparable and were to share a large bedroom there during the following two winters. Despite her eighty-five years Mrs. Dorothy Maynard-Hart still remembers Agatha's "beautiful reddish hair and lovely complexion. She was always vivacious, the life and soul of the party and ready for the next adventure." She also recalls how stylishly dressed Agatha was and her complete attachment to her mother.

During the day the girls attended classes in French and German and had lessons in etiquette—in French and English. They were chaperoned on their visits to the Sorbonne for classes in French history. Agatha also took gymnastics and tennis as an extra. After luncheon on Thursday the pupils were taken to a theatrical entertainment or to visit the Louvre and other museums, which was the highlight of the week.

Mrs. Miller went to Paris one Easter to visit her daughter and stayed at the Meurice Hotel. It was from her father that Agatha Miller inherited her lifetime passion for collecting objects such as papier-mâché furniture, boxes and objets d'art made by the thousands of Huguenots when they came to England in the nineteenth century. In Paris Mrs. Miller and the two girls spent some time looking for antique miniatures and silhouettes to add to their English collection.

The friendship between the two girls lasted for many years and Dorothy Hamilton-Johnston was one of the few outsiders invited to Agatha Miller's wedding when she married Lieutenant Colonel Archibald Christie.

Agatha Miller had said during her school days that she wanted to be a nurse but Mrs. Miller had other ideas. She would dearly have loved her daughter to become a concert pianist or a professional singer, perhaps in grand opera. This was unfortunately not to be.

"In those days I would really have liked to be a pianist; I enjoyed it, but I would not have had the nerves for concerts. I was never any good—I was so shy in public that my fingers would not work."

Singing may have been the answer as she had the high pure voice of a young chorister, but again she could not face an audience. "I had a high soprano but it was not strong enough for opera. And you don't only want to sing in your bath."

These were nonchalant words in describing something seventy years later which at the time must have been extremely disappointing and painful, and one suspects that there were many tears of anguish. In the strange modesty that was to be part of Dame Agatha Christie's character it never entered her head as a girl that she was clever, and certainly she had never thought it possible to make even a small career writing novels.

Back home in Torquay after two winters in Paris, Agatha Miller was more poised than before and her shyness partly obliterated and disguised by being exposed to Parisian sophistication. With great determination Mrs. Miller now set about seeing that her favorite daughter would be launched into Torquay's social world. There were tennis and skating parties, clandestine meetings on the pier, and amateur theatricals in which she was invited to join.

Speaking about this period years later Dame Agatha said: "I wasn't sitting writing and writing. I was going about meeting young men and embroidering great bunches of clematis on cushions, and tracing designs from Dresden vases and painting them. We did lots of creative things in those days; perhaps that's why we did not feel the need for careers—when I was sixteen or seventeen only financial disability would have forced you out into the world.

"It's a funny word to use but flirtations meant a lot. You had lots of engagements succeeding each other, you went to all the dances and on your card you'd give three dances to one young man and only two to the other; it made you feel on top of the world. You were a young female, not bad-looking, and they had to please you. Even if you were not allowed more than three dances with one young man, it was quite fun to get hold of him for that time."

House parties were also another place for a young lady to meet a young gentleman and Agatha Miller was frequently asked—much to Mrs. Miller's delight. As Dame Agatha was to recall later: "People went to a lot of trouble arranging things. When you went to a house party there were always three or four young men and nice-looking girls so they all could have a good time. These were very good; your hosts looked after you, not letting you lose money at bridge. You only had a very small dress allowance. Just one new evening dress a year and you had to walk everywhere in pointed-toed patent leather shoes."

Mrs. Joan Millyard describes her at tennis parties at Cockington Court. "Yes, she was tall, very pretty, Scandinavian coloring and a lovely complexion. There was always a quiet shyness about her as though she preferred to look at the world from a distance. But we all liked her very much and several of the boys around at that time found her great fun and exceedingly attractive."

Another lively memory of Agatha Miller during this period of her youth comes from Mrs. Ada Couch, now in her eighties, who still lives nearby in Torquay.

25

"I had come to stay with my auntie and uncle down Tor Park Road as my health was bad, and I remember quite clearly walking up Barton Road behind Agatha and hearing her say to her nanny: 'When I grow up, nanny, we'll build a little cottage inside Ashfield gardens and you and I will live there for *always*.'

"I also remember when the fleet used to put into Torquay Harbor for stores. Whenever a man had died on board he was buried in the cemetery at the top of Barton Road.

"You could hear the boom boom boom of the drums from a long way off in the harbor as they put the coffin on the gun carriage. It was drawn at slow march through the whole town with only the sound of the sailors' feet on the rough stones and the beat of the drums. It was very dramatic and whenever I used to hear the drums coming I used to shout at my auntie, 'It's a funeral. It's a funeral,' and run to the edge of the pavement. All the children did. I remember quite clearly one day Agatha Miller was standing quietly by the fountain at the bottom of Barton Road in her riding habit and Bowler hat as the cortege passed. After it had gone she turned to me and said, 'I am going over to Webbs to get my gee-gee.' Of course she didn't know me, but she was always pleasant. She used to have a horse from the stables in the mews in South Street, which is now the Constitutional Club. She used to ride sidesaddle like all the young ladies of the day. I remember Mrs. Miller but I never recall ever seeing Mr. Miller, even when I was a child."

Ada Couch and Agatha Christie were to meet again years later when the now famous writer brought a reel of film to be developed into the photographic shop where Mrs. Couch worked.

"I recognized her immediately, although thirty years must have passed. When she had gone out of the shop I said to Mrs. Bainbridge, who owned it, 'That's Agatha Christie.'

" 'Oh no,' she said, 'that's Mrs. Mallowan [the name of Agatha Christie's second husband].' Then her nephew Mr. Davidson told me that he thought I had made a mistake.

"She came back again another day and told Mr. Davidson that she wanted a spool to be developed with particular care to be taken of negative number six. Mr. Davidson told her that if it was not too clear he could have it intensified. She was very pleased and said, 'Oh, can you do that?'

"When the spool came back to the office, I found Mr. Davidson holding it to the light and looking at it. He said, 'Mrs. Couch come over here. Look at number six. Whatever is it?'

"I said, 'Oh, Mr. Davidson, that's a sugar hammer,' but he had never heard of one before so I told him my aunt had one. Sugar like salt used to come in a big block in those days and you had to knock off what you needed.

"'Oh,' I said, 'I suppose that is going to be one of her weapons.'

"He said, 'What do you mean by weapons?'

"I replied, 'You know she is an authoress and she is going to murder someone with a sugar hammer.'

"Well, she came back at quarter-past one one day and as I was alone in the office I served her. She gave me the money and I gave her the change and said, 'Thank you, Miss Miller,' without thinking what I was saying. 'Oh, pardon,' I said, 'Mrs. Mallowan.'

"'Yes,' she said, 'but that's rather funny as I was once called Miss Miller.'

I then told her who I was and she said, 'I'm very pleased to meet you because now I've met someone who knew Torquay as I knew it when it was a very nice place indeed. So different from what it is today.'"

A few months later at Christmas Mrs. Couch went to a friend's place and when they were passing out the Christmas presents she was handed a square wrapped parcel.

"'I know you will enjoy that, Ada,' my friend Mrs. Hebbs said. "I opened it and there was a little sugar hammer on the paper cover of the book. It was called *Mrs. McGinty's Dead* and of course was written by Agatha Christie."

All through these dancing and dreaming days of her youth Agatha Miller kept up her writing. She wrote short stories and composed a collection of poems which were later published by Geoffrey Bles in 1925 and called *The Road of Dreams*, which have now been republished by Collins.

The *Poetry Review* also accepted several of Agatha Miller's poems for which they paid the handsome sum of half a guinea.

She also wrote what she was to explain over fifty years later as "one incestuous play which wasn't suitable at the time, but which I am sure would be just the meat now, but would bore me to distraction to write.

"I think you have to get the gloomy side out. I wrote a very gloomy novel that I've got somewhere. I handicapped myself by making the heroine deaf—you can't think how difficult that makes things."

Imperceptibly but undeniably, writing was becoming more than a hobby. It was a way of life.

CHAPTER THREE

WITH MR. MILLER's death there came a startling change in the family's fortunes. For some time before there had been financial difficulties in the family firm and this, combined with Mr. Miller's progressively bad health, may well have been the cause of his early death. Now Mrs. Miller was faced with having to reduce the number of servants and their style of living.

Mrs. Miller had wanted to sell the house and move to a more manageable one near Exeter, a city she had always admired, but the three children were adamant. Madge and Agatha were aghast at the thought of leaving Ashfield and Monty wrote from India violently protesting at the idea. To make the finances a little easier Madge's husband offered to contribute something to Mrs. Miller's reduced income. Ashfield was saved for many years to come and played a considerable part in Agatha Christie's life.

To understand Agatha Christie's character at all it is vital to realize the kind of place Torquay was at the turn of the century when the Millers chose to settle there. The enclaved world of this seaside spa was so exceptional that even for Edwardian England the inhabitants were a rare breed of cosseted gentry. With its reputation for being "Queen of the English Riviera" it had outlived its former description as being "a town for invalids."

Whereas the aristocracy had already discovered the ravishing charm of the French Riviera many of the wealthy middle class were still suspicious of anything foreign. They preferred the established virtues of English domestic life as opposed to the hazards of foreign food, foreign drinking water, and even worse—foreign germs.

Up till 1875 the old narrow-gauge railway line ended at Torre Station but with its standardization and wider gauge it was now possible to transport whole households complete with the family and their domestic chattels for the winter months. By the late 1890s when Agatha Christie was a child the hills were dotted with imposing family houses, each with manicured lawns, raked drives, well-planted trees, two-to-three-acre gardens, and neatly trimmed box hedges shielding off the kitchen garden where such delicacies as strawberries and asparagus grew in abundance.

There would be in residence the family plus the servants—butler, cook, house parlormaid, governess, nannies, and nursery maids. The grooms and garden staff were local. The weekly list of "arrives and departures" at Torre Station in the local newspaper was said at the time to "read like pages from the *Almanack de Gotha*." The town was so prosperous that Walter Savage Landor, the author and wit, had caustically commented, "Torquay is full of fat ugly houses and rich hot looking people."

Torquay, like the city of Rome with its seven hills, was built in Regency days with imposing crescents reminiscent of Bath: Hesketh, overlooking Meadfoot, Lisburne, with its fine view of the harbor, and the Terrace looking out over the Inner Harbour. Behind these came the winding streets of neat houses with wrought-iron balconies and canopied windows. Still further hidden in the lanes were the dwellings of the tradesmen and domestic servants. Steep steps or narrow lanes, often only four feet wide, meandered up and down the hills linking the major roads.

So sheltered was the bay that in the hills above the harbor, semitropical plants and trees flourished in Mediterranean profusion—mimosa, eucalyptus, agapanthus, and grape vines. Today even the names of the roads recall the glory that was—Chestnut Avenue, Oakhill Road, and Ash Hill.

The villas were large and opulent. Sir Lawrence Palk, the fashionable architect of the period, had made the Grand Tour and became so infatuated by Italian architecture that he persuaded the owners of his newly built villas to give them lyrical Italian names. Hidden among the trees around the Warberry and Lincombe hills were pink- or pearl-colored villas capriciously named Villa Borghese, Villa Como, Villa Vomero, Villa Splendido. Some of these remain today and have been turned into apartment houses, private hotels, or homes for the aged gentry.

During the summer months many of them remained closed behind shutters with caretakers living in the basement, but, come November, they came to life in preparation for the arrival of the family. These privileged families came to escape the fog-filled cities of the industrial north, and the dread of pneumonia or bronchitis, which in those days were killers for anyone with a weak chest.

For many years ill health had been "big business" in Torquay. Dr. Radclyffe Hall—grandfather of the novelist Radclyffe Hall—wrote: "When a consumptive invalid, who has suffered from hurried breathing, hot cheeks and hands and restless wakefulness at night has been in Torquay for only two or three days, he usually finds his breathing easier, his restlessness less and his skin softer and cooler in the evening."

An advertisement of the period for the Torquay Medical Baths announced "Massage Douche Aix System . . . debility, sleeplessness, lumbago, sciatica, obesity, diabetes, brain fag, chronic congestion of the liver, stomach, spleen and intestines and many other disorders."

For families like the Millers there was no need to send their daughters to London to "do the season." Whereas in London they may have been lost in the milieu of the rich debutante world, Torquay with its cosmopolitan atmosphere had its own cultural circles and entertainments. The West Country has always

31

been noted for its affluent family life and the young people brought up there had every possibility to enjoy a gay and amusing time.

In 1889 the municipality took over the Bath salons where all kinds of entertainment took place. There were regular lectures— Captain Scott of the Antarctic had the house full—and concerts with such world-established artists as Nellie Melba and Paderewski. In 1907 one of the attractions was the concert given by an orchestra of seventy under the baton of a young conductor, Thomas Beecham. The Miller family were constant patrons of the arts, especially the musical concerts.

There were daily concerts in the spa ballroom where people gathered after treatments or wandered into the glass-enclosed section overlooking the beach and sea below. It was a place for exchanging gossip and enjoying minor flirtations.

A special maple floor had been laid for roller skating at the Bath salons where the elite gathered, while on the Princess Pier the holiday makers used the largest rink in the West of England, which measured 30,000 square feet.

Torquay was also rich in club life and ranged from the exclusive Royal Torbay Yacht Club to the National Women's Society Political Union, whose president in London was Mrs. Emmeline Pankhurst, and the Passive Resistance League.

On the front there were daily band concerts. For one season the town council had accepted the tender of Mr. Karl Kaps to supply a first-class military band of sixteen performers including the conductor for the sum of £56.10 shillings per week. They had played in the glorious Victorian bandstand, which was only removed in recent years after it was found to be beyond repair.

By the end of the nineteenth century sea bathing was strictly organized. In the 1887 bylaws of the town a clause included:

"No bathing whether with or without drawers is allowed between Belgrave and the Imperial and no person of the male sex shall at any time bathe within 50 yards of the ladies' bathing machine." At the turn of the century there were four ladies' bathing sites, two between Livermead Cliff and Corbyn Head, and the others between the public baths and the Imperial Hotel, which was rated among the best hotels of Europe and still is today.

32

By the time the Miller children were old enough to bathe, discreetly chaperoned mixed bathing parties were acceptable. During the summer months in the Miller household all the children and the house guests were piled into a dog cart and regularly taken to the neighboring beach at Anstey's Cove or Paignton, where the shore was lined with gaily striped bathing tents. Picnics were a family tradition that Dame Agatha was to carry on right through her adult life when she was mistress of Ashfield and Greenway. Even as an old lady nothing gave her more pleasure than a picnic with her family on Dartmoor.

Bicycling was never popular in Torquay as in other spas like Cheltenham or Leamington simply because of the hilly surroundings but riding was very much in vogue among families like the Millers. Agatha Miller had only to walk down Barton Road to Row Square to reach well-equipped riding stables. One of the rides that she enjoyed the most was down past All Saints' Church, where she and her family regularly worshiped, entering Old Mill Lane, on through Lower Chelston, and across to the picturesque village of Cockington.

All the young ladies wore long riding habits and Bowler hats and rode sidesaddle. Their bone-polished boots were a matter of great pride and shone like a mirror.

Typical of the advertisements of the period is this one from 1882. "Tailoring and Outfitting Establishment, 39 Fleet Street. W. Montgomery proprietor. Tailor and Habit Maker, Hatter, Hosier, Glover and Shirt Maker."

The Miller family could have done all their shopping right there at Tor in the well-stocked family shops of Coombes the fishmonger, Wicks the furniture shop, Norcombe the grocer and provision merchant, Hill the bootmaker, and Walke's the butcher.

Like all the other residents of Barton Road, Agatha Christie also shopped in the fashionable Strand in Torquay and is remembered today by the owners and staff of Williams where she used to buy clothes, materials and linen. Mr. Nichels, the owner of the Nottingham jewelers, still has her signature on their register from many years back.

All her life Dame Agatha enjoyed shopping and was able to

move among the holiday crowds of Torquay completely unrecognized. Despite her fame she had the kind of homely face that melted into crowds and this is exactly how she wished it.

She used to arrive in the shops casually dressed and knowing exactly what she wanted. She chose with discrimination and care. Among the staff who knew who she was, her arrival created a stir, as they were delighted to serve such a famous character as she had become. She could, however, be aloof and stern when necessary should the taxi ordered to pick her up after a hair appointment be late and if she had her mind on other things.

By 1904 the tramways had opened up the great hills of the borough of Torquay bringing in their wake many more permanent families until the population numbered 30,000.

The social life of Torquay was ritualized by the conventions of calling to leave one's card between 3 and 4:30 P.M. any day of the week, "at homes" on certain days of the month, select luncheon and dinner parties for the more intimate friends, tennis and swimming parties for the young, and dances and balls. And of course the fashionable regatta which the Miller family always attended.

The class distinctions were rigid and inviolable. If you were a professional man you were acceptable but if you were in business, no matter how skilled, intelligent, and attractive, there was a limit to your social life and that of your family.

On Agatha Miller's baptismal certificate Mr. Miller's "rank or profession" was given as "gentleman." Nobody would have dared to pry into such personal matters but there were two versions current at the time as to the origin of his money—one that he dabbled in the stocks and shares market and the other, that he was a retired produce merchant from New York. Both were correct and acceptable in social circles since his money apparently came from America.

There is no doubt that due to the Miller family's status they were totally received into the inner social life of Torquay and counted among their peers the premier family like the Carys, who lived at Torre Abbey, the Mallocks of Cockington Court, and the Shipham Manor owners, while it is extremely doubtful that they ever met Paignton's most sensational residents—the Singer family from America. When bearded Isaac Singer of the sewing machine fame fled to England he asked a local architect called Bridgman to "build me a wigwam, a big wigwam," and a gaunt Victorian yellow-brick mansion suitably called the Wigwam was the result. But it was his third son, Paris, who was to create the flamboyant folly known as Oldway, which still remains today and is owned by the Torbay municipality.

The eastern front was inspired by the Place de la Concorde and the south side by a music pavilion in the grounds of Versailles. The interior was a combination of opulence and vulgarity with the minstrels gallery built as a small replica of the Hall of Mirrors at Versailles. Tennis courts, bowling green, swimming pool, and indoor riding ring completed this astonishing mansion.

For a short period the dancer Isadora Duncan lived there with her lover Paris Singer, by whom she had a son, but the insularity of Paignton and the absence of amusing friends drove her to escape and live on the French Riviera. She was to die there tragically when her scarf was caught in the wheel of the motor car in which she was a passenger.

"Agatha was always fun," Mrs. Joan Millyard said as we talked in her Torquay flat. She is one of the few people left who actually knew Agatha Christie as a girl and, though her memory is impaired, the voice is firm and the eyes are intelligent.

"Oh yes, she was very bright and that sort of thing and seemed all there. She used to come over to Cockington Court to take part in the amateur theatricals my sister organized. I remember the time she played in a burlesque about Bluebeard and they had a photograph taken on the lawn. Oh they had a lot of fun dressing up and it was all good, clean, and wholesome.

"She became a great friend of my sister, who had married a Mallock—the Mallocks succeeded the Carys as the owners of Cockington Court in 1654—and later when my sister's husband was killed in the wars Agatha used to go over regularly to see her and the one surviving twin. My sister was expecting her twins when she was out on the road and was handed a telegram that her husband Charlie Mallock had been killed. The shock was so great to her that while the baby girl lived the boy died. Agatha was very understanding and kind to her in that period."

The one thing that existed in those luxuriant days in Torquay was leisure. Time to develop, time to be gracious, time to expand as a human being.

"One had so much time for leisure," Dame Agatha was to say on one occasion when remembering her youth in Torquay. "The women like my mother had good minds. They read and studied and were exceedingly interesting to talk to. Now people can often only talk about one thing."

And again in an interview with the late Godfrey Winn in the *Daily Mail*, "Personally I feel sorry for the young women of today. Their freedom has become a boomerang. It is too easy for them to have affairs, to become shop soiled. In my day one's parents arranged for us to meet lots of young men. Today a girl seems to 'go steady'—isn't that the expression?—so very early. And then she is trapped.

"If we had no money we had to wait and the waiting often proved salutary. Ardour waned. Today every girl has a career, and if the boy she fancies is still studying and not earning, she is prepared to keep them both."

All through her life at Ashfield, Agatha Christie, a devout Christian, continued her mother's habit of calling at the vicarage. On one occasion she arrived with her secretary and Miss Petty remembers Agatha Miller, as she was then, sitting quietly and letting Miss Fisher do all the talking

"I had the feeling that Agatha Christie was just observing me for a future character in one of her books," she recalls.

Miss Petty remembers: "There was another occasion when she opened the Torre Abbey garden fête. My brother Gerald, then a young medical student, had to run the baby show. Agatha Christie had brought her daughter and they made the grand tour of the fete. My brother looked critically at some of the babies and thought that few qualified for any prize. Someone had the idea that it depended on the number of supporters each child had who should win the prize for the best baby in the show. Mrs. Christie thought it terribly funny as each baby was surrounded by the sisters, cousins, grannies, aunts, and uncles who had all paid an entry fee to ensure that their offspring should bear away the prize."

When in 1929 the Torquay Grammar School's preparatory

school moved to St. Mary's, next door to Ashfield, not only was the peace of the household disturbed but also the number of balls from the children's games wrought havoc with Ashfield's greenhouse. Apologies for the damage were always graciously received, the glass repaired, and peace restored. The greenhouse was badly hit by a storm during this period and when the vicar wrote sympathetically, not only for her loss but the sum of £27 that the repair would cost, Mrs. Christie replied that he was not to worry. She would write a short story to pay for this unexpected expense.

Agatha Christie learned early on in her writing career that if you want your facts right you must go and ask. As she was to say years later about her first novel, *The Mysterious Affair at Styles*: "I wrote a court scene out of my head, which just could never have taken place. I know now there are ways out of this—you ask any barrister and he will tell you with tears in his eyes what you can and you can't do."

On the bookshelf at the vicarage was a copy of *Murder in Three Acts*, inscribed "To Mr. Petty from Agatha Christie." This was her way of thanking the vicar for advising her on ecclesiastical facts such as how long it takes a deacon to become a priest. In this way her details were almost always correct and few of her readers could ever fault her on facts.

CHAPTER FOUR

Aᴌᴛᴇʀ ʜᴇʀ ʜᴜsʙᴀɴᴅ's death Mrs. Miller's health declined. When doctors failed to diagnose what was wrong with her, this formidable lady decided to take things into her own hands. What could be more agreeable than to take her younger daughter for a three-month stay in Egypt where the sun was warm and Cairo was swarming with eligible young men?

Daughter Madge had "come out" in New York and was now happily settled in a well-to-do marriage. With the family finances as they were, after Mr. Miller's death, a London debut was out of the question for Agatha.

Suitable tenants were found for Ashfield and mother and daughter set out by boat for Alexandria with high hopes. With her trousseau of three silk evening dresses and a mane of reddish-gold hair, which she could sit on, Agatha Miller was like nectar for the homesick young subalterns. As for Agatha, any traces of gaucherie that Paris had not been able to remove were effectively dealt with in Cairo. With three months of sight-seeing, picnics, polo matches, dancing every night, and scores of flirtations, mother and daughter returned home both considerably better for the trip.

Later in her life Agatha Christie confessed to having narrowly escaped marriage twice during these months. Reggie Lucy, a major in the Gunners, became her only official fiancé. Theirs was the kind of conventional engagement of the period when house parties were the fashion and mothers were dedicated matchmakers.

When Reggie Lucy, a likable young man, returned to his regiment in Hong Kong with a picture of Agatha Miller in his pocket, our heroine settled down to wait the year or so before he would return.

What is interesting is that instead of sitting at home and sewing for her bottom drawer, like a newly engaged girl of the period usually did, Agatha continued to accept invitations out to dances and lead the normal heart-free life of a pretty young girl.

It was at one of these house dances, given by her friends the Cliffords at Chudleigh, that she met a man who was to change her life. When a friend Arthur Griffiths wrote to her that there was a fellow called Christie from his mess going to the dance and he had asked him to look out for her as he was a good dancer, Agatha Miller became interested. Quite early in the evening she met the dashing Lieutenant Archibald Christie, Regimental Number 61281 of the Royal Field Artillery. They danced the night away.

The Christie brothers—Archibald and Campbell—sons of Archibald Christie, a former judge in the Indian civil service, who retired to live in Bristol, were ravishingly handsome. They were the typical "flower of England" that Rupert Brooke was to immortalize in his poems a few years later.

Archibald entered the Royal Artillery and later transferred to the Royal Flying Corps where he was later awarded the C.M.G., D.S.O. His brother Campbell Manning Christie won the M.C. and ended his career as a distinguished major general.

Lord Balfour of Inchrye, who commanded the Squadron BE 2C, described Archibald Christie as "a good steady type, very popular, and one of the better types in a small elite corps."

Pictures of Captain Archibald Christie at that time show him as slender with curly golden hair parted in the center, intensely blue, if somewhat cold, eyes, a turned-up nose, a long pronounced upper lip, and wide sensuous mouth. He spoke with the clipped accent of a serving officer. There was not a woman who met him who did not think he was "madly handsome" and fall for his dissolute good looks. Besides he was an excellent dancer which was a considerable asset in those days of tea dances.

It is quite clear that from the moment she saw him Agatha Miller was swept off her feet. He had the kind of inborn arrogance found in the young "gods" of that pre-1914 period when a regular service background was the passport to all social doors.

There is no doubt too that Archie Christie was fascinated by the vivacious girl he had met. Within ten days he had not only ferreted out her address from his friend Arthur Griffiths but had arrived on his motorcycle from Exeter and introduced himself to Mrs. Miller. Agatha was out at the time but a hurried telephone call from her mother brought her home. Archie Christie was asked to stay for an impromptu supper and a new romance had begun in Agatha Miller's life.

The engagement, a tempestuous affair, lasted nearly two years before Agatha Miller married Archibald Christie by special license on Christmas Eve, 1914, at the parish church of Emmanuel, Clifton, a fashionable suburb of Bristol. The witnesses, William James Hemsley and Reginald Charles Fawdry, were friends of the Christie family. Mr. Hemsley was later to marry the widow of Archibald Christie, Sr.

There is no doubt from her autobiography that Agatha Miller would have preferred to wait. Could it have been a premonition that all was not well in their irrational relationship?

Despite a hysterical outburst from Christie's mother, and the knowledge that she was marrying without even the presence of her own mother, who was not told until the newlyweds arrived on her doorstep on Christmas Day, Agatha went ahead with the marriage. Instead of the wedding that Mrs. Miller had planned for her favorite daughter with a traditional white wedding dress and veil, Agatha was married in a coat and skirt and purple velvet hat and as she wrote, "I had not even time to wash my hands or face."

Why was the marriage not held in Torquay with a family party afterward at Ashfield? Could it have been that Mrs. Miller disapproved of the wedding and wanted her daughter to wait still longer? Or was it like so many marriages at the beginning of the 1914–18 war, an on-the-spot decision when Lieutenant Archibald Christie was suddenly posted abroad?

After her marriage the radiant bride moved back to Torquay to be near her mother and engage herself in war work. Now was the chance to fulfill a childhood ambition of being a nurse.

"The beginning of the 1914–18 war was the death knell of the glorious relaxed social life that had carried on in Torquay from Victorian days," Pickwickian Robert Rook, one of the city's most distinguished historians, commented. "Whatever category of social sphere in which a family found itself that war was fundamentally more disturbing in the domestic life of the nation's families than the more recent conflict of 1939–45.

"Agatha Christie found herself caught up in what was regarded as a novel and possibly dangerous experiment for a young lady to embark upon. She took up nursing. It must have been a very fundamental and violent change in her life as it was with everyone who came from her social strata."

Nurse Agatha Christie was assigned to the surgical ward of the Torbay Hospital and stayed there two years. The first casualties were coming back from the front in France and special trains were used to bring down the wounded soldiers and officers from London to Tor station where fleets of ambulances took them to the large villas which had been comandeered as convalescent homes.

The town hall, which had only been completed in 1913, had its large assembly hall turned into a ward which accommodated 110 beds while other rooms were transformed into operating theaters and dressing rooms.

Red Cross nurses and volunteers like Agatha Christie staffed the town hall and the Torbay Hospital, which was then known as White Cliff Hospital: Oldway, the Singer home, was also turned into a special hospital.

For two years Agatha Christie proved to be a most competent and efficient nurse and though she was at first shy of the pungent humor of the men she was a favorite with them. With her golden reddish hair piled up under her nursing cap she looked clean and wholesome, reminding them of their own young wives and sisters. She was also a good listener.

After a spell at nursing, punctuated by rapturous reunions with "Archie" when he came home on leave, she advanced to the dispensary, which she found "very rewarding, very enjoyable; you had a lot of responsibility."

During the years she was a dispenser she wrote one of her most engaging poems, which was published in *The Road of Dreams*. It is fascinating as it became clear why poisons were to remain an absorbing hobby forever after. Her accurate knowledge of them made it possible to "get rid of dozens of my victims in a clean and not a messy way."

In the archives of the Imperial War Museum in London lie half a dozen tape recordings made by distinguished people who served in various capacities in the 1914–18 war. One such tape was recorded by Dame Agatha a few years ago talking to the young American librarian from the sitting room of her house at Wallingford. There is nothing of great importance in the tape but merely her own amusing stories about incidents that happened in the hospitals where she served in Torquay.

Whereas every other person concerned has given full permission for his or her tapes to be heard at the discretion of the museum by serious-minded students, Agatha Christie left a proviso on hers. It can only only be heard with permission from her lawyers or family. And such is her posthumous power that even though the keeper of this department was more than willing for me to hear the tape, this was not possible, since Sir Max Mallowan would not give his consent to me nor as yet to anyone else. Even in these harmless wartime reminiscences Agatha Christie remained as secretive and abortive as she had done so many times in her life, though she relented a little in her autobiography.

In 1916 the war was at its height and the casualties were high. Agatha Christie had been working long hours at the hospital and had a short leave due to her. She and her sister had always argued a great deal about whether it was easy to write detective stories but the only ones they had ever read were Sherlock Holmes and a French novel called *Mystery of the Yellow Room*.

"I bet you can't write one in which I can't guess the ending," Madge taunted.

"Wait and see. I have an idea going round in my head about medicine," her sister replied.

"Why don't you go and stay on Dartmoor if you're going to write that book," Mrs. Miller interrupted.

So for three weeks Agatha Christie holed herself up in the Moorland Hotel at Hay Tor, on Dartmoor. This is one of the most beautiful areas in England with its 365 square miles of sweeping moorland, towering granite tors, sparkling streams, ancient stone circles, and quaint stone towns like Tavistock, where Drake was born.

All her life Dame Agatha was to claim that she had "stamina." It was more than that—she had a contained energy that she drew on whenever necessary and now it was being put to a literary test for the first time.

In two weeks she had almost finished her first detection novel, *The Mysterious Affair at Styles*. She drew her hero from her imagination and his name was M. Hercule Poirot, a beguiling character who was to stay with her for fifty-six years.

It was an inspired piece of timing to make Poirot a Belgian. Torquay at the time had opened its doors to an influx of Belgian refugees who had escaped from their country at the onset of war. Although she said later that in fact she never met any of the refugees, the idea of making her detective-hero a Belgian was undoubtedly inspired by this motley crowd. It never occurred to her to make him English.

"I could have made him American as my father was but somehow I didn't," she explained years later. "A Belgian came into my head. It was as simple as that."

Simple or not it was perceptive thinking. She could have made him come from any of the other Allied countries—France or Holland—but maybe subconsciously she realized that she could create a picturesque character with built-in charisma if she made him a Belgian.

"Poor, dear, brave little Belgium," was on everyone's lips in a euphoria of patriotism for its stand against "The Hun."

Agatha Christie described Poirot as that "extraordinary-looking little man." He was precisely five feet four inches tall; he carried himself with great dignity; his head was exactly the shape of an egg and he always had it perched a little to one side. And above all there was his mustache, very stiff and military and his pride and joy. There was the neatness of his attire, although it emerged only later that he always wore striped trousers, correct black jacket, bow tie, and patent leather shoes, and a muffler if the weather was less than hot.

Though she created Poirot on top of a bus, she did in fact see M. Hercule Poirot in person some years later. She told this story to Marshal of the Royal Air Force, Sir William Dixon, who repeated it to me:

"I was lunching at the British Embassy in Baghdad many years ago and was delighted to meet Sir Max Mallowan and his wife, Dame Agatha Christie. To my surprise I found myself sitting next to her at the table and found her a most charming and animated person to talk to. She was very amusing and in good form. It was then that she told me that she had seen Poirot in the flesh.

"'Can you imagine my surprise,' she said, 'when I was lunching in the grill room at the Savoy and as I looked up there sat Poirot just across at the next table, an exact replica in every way. I was so astonished that I sent for the head waiter and asked him for the man's name.

"'I do not know, Mrs. Christie,' he said. 'All I know is that he comes from Belgium.'"

Poirot is possibly the most loved of all the Agatha Christie characters though she herself tired of him and wished he had never been created. At the time of his death he would have been 117 years of age, having made his literary debut in 1920 when he was already retired from the Belgian police force.

The Mysterious Affair at Styles was based partly on Agatha Christie's own nursing experience and Styles was a replica of Torquay. The novel gave an illuminating picture of a Britain recovering from the "Great War" of 1914–18 and though she said that she disliked descriptive writing *Styles* proved her to have an accurate eye for recording social history.

The fact that she gave M. Poirot an assistant named Captain Hastings, an army officer who had recently been invalided home from the front, is reminiscent of Sherlock Holmes and his Watson. Hastings was as slow-witted and obvious as Poirot was mercurial-thinking and obscure.

The manuscript went the round of half a dozen publishers for four years before it was finally taken by John Lane of The Bodley Head. It had been in his office for eighteen months before he got around to contacting the author. John Lane, uncle of Sir Allen Lane, who was to play such a great part in Agatha Christie's career when his Penguin Books, Ltd., began publishing her in paperback, was not an easy man. He was kindly, with a small goatee beard and twinkling blue eyes, but professional enough to speak his mind.

Agatha Christie recounted years later how she first met him. He ushered her into a crowded office cluttered with manuscripts, chairs and tables, and oil paintings. Moving a canvas or two he then found room on a chair and dusted it before offering it to his newest author.

"About this manuscript of yours. It might have—I only say *might* have—possibilities. It would need a great deal of alteration."

Max Reinhardt, who now owns The Bodley Head, explains why there are no accurate details of the first two three-book contracts that Agatha Christie made with the publishing company.

"When the firm went bust in 1937 a lot of records were lost and most of the correspondence simply disappeared."

Through the courtesy and help of Dr. Michael Rhodes, archivist of the John Lane papers, which are kept at Westfield College, University of London, I tracked down thirty-four letters Agatha Christie wrote somewhat spasmodically to The Bodley Head during the period of 1920 to 1933. They are mostly written by hand and addressed to Allen Lane and Basil Willett. Any letters to John Lane himself seem to have been mislaid over the years.

What is clear through the correspondence with her publishers is that by October 1920 she was becoming very restive when there was no sign of the publication of *Styles*. Right from the beginning of her relationship with the firm her letters were businesslike and crisp. Here was no shy young author but a woman completely in charge of herself and her career.

In a sharp letter she wrote to Mr. Willett from Ashfield she asked, "What about my book?" She added that she was beginning to wonder if it was *ever* coming out as she had nearly finished a second one (*The Secret Adversary*). She was also interested to hear something about the cover.

When she did see the cover the following week she replied from her flat in Addison Mansions in London that she thought it would do very well as it was "quite artistic and mysterious." She wrote that she was very anxious to dedicate the book to her mother and wanted just the words "To My Mother." She also asked if Mr. Willett would note that in future her address would be Ashfield.

The only money that Agatha Christie made out of *The Mysterious Affair at Styles* was £26, part of the serialization rights. Her contract stipulated that she was to receive no royalties until the book had sold 2,500 copies and the actual sale fell short of this figure by 500 copies.

Styles was not published in America until ten years later but by the time Allen Lane launched Penguin Books in 1935 *Styles* was by then an accepted "must" for all detection book lists.

The Secret Adversary, which appeared in 1922, introduced two new sleuths—that naïve, but beguiling, couple Tuppence and Tommy Beresford. This book marked the beginning of a mammoth book-a-year record (often more in the thirties and forties), which by sheer volume and readability was to keep Agatha Christie on the best-seller list for the rest of her life. *Murder on the Links* (1923), the story of a millionaire who was murdered on his own golf links, was followed in 1924 by *The Man in the Brown Suit*, where the corpse is found electrocuted in a tube station in London.

Right from that first book Agatha Christie was to take more than an amateur interest in the covers of her books. When she did not like the proposed cover of *Murder on the Links* she arrived in person at The Bodley Head office and explained that it had no connection with the plot of her book. She described it as a "man in his pajamas having an epileptic fit on a golf links."

The cover was immediately altered and everybody knew that Mrs. Christie was no mere housewife-cum-author. She was professional to her finger tips, knew what she wanted and insisted on getting it.

Nor was she happy with the "wrapper" for *The Man in the Brown Suit*. She wrote that it looked like a highway robbery and murder in medieval times and nothing like a tube station. She said that she had in mind something clear, definite, and modern, and then suggested that as this appeared to be the artist's normal style she did not think that he would be able to alter it. Instead she asked that the cover should be given a background of white glossy tiles which everyone could identify as being a typical London underground station.

It was while she had called to protest about the cover of *Murder on the Links* that Agatha Christie met John Lane's nephew, Allen Lane.

Lane and Agatha Christie immediately became friends and she used to visit the flat which he shared with his two brothers. The Lane brothers were noted for their jolly literary parties where they gathered their favored authors and ate and talked long into the night, expounding their views on life.

Ethel Mannin, who now lives in Devon, remembers Agatha Christie as being very quiet and listening rather than talking. Rebecca West was another one of the Lanes' friends, though she and Agatha Christie were never to become close.

With his exuberance for living and gathering people around him Allen Lane and Agatha Christie were totally unlike yet there existed a friendship that lasted for life. Through the summers of the twenties he and his brothers used to holiday in their boat round the coast of Devon and always put in at the fishing port of Brixham so that they could all pile over to Ashfield "to see Agatha." They had a private arrangement whereby she lent him her Morris Minor for ten pounds a month whenever she was not using it during the holiday periods.

When Agatha Christie moved to Winterbrook House at Wallingford, Sir Allen used to send loads of manure regularly from his farm for her garden.

Publisher and author loved to go off on expeditions searching out the funny little antique shops round Torquay where bargains could be had for a snip or spending hours browsing round the local bookshops. No one seeing them together could have possibly known the identities of this oddly assorted couple.

All through this period Agatha Christie wrote constantly to

The Bodley Head, plotting and planning her career with infinite detail. There was the discussion about the title for a collection of short stories. It was originally called *The Curious Disappearance of the Opalsen Pearls,* then became *The Jewel Robbery at the Grand Metropolitan,* which she felt to be much better. When the publishers put up their suggestions, *The Gray Cells of Monsieur Poirot* or *Poirot Investigates,* for a collection of short stories, wishing to cash in on the Belgian detective's success, she chose the latter but insisted that the drawing by W. Smithson Broadhead, on commission from *The Sketch,* be used for the cover.

With an inborn sense of public relations she harassed The Bodley Head along to get the short stories published while the publicity obtained from an article that appeared in *The Sketch* and the syndication of *The Man in the Brown Suit* in the London *Evening News* was fresh.

Any alterations made by an editor in her script had all to be checked before the "copy" was set but she was also quick to appreciate if she had slipped up at all. When it was pointed out to her that she had made a mistake about the motor route from Charing Cross to Ascot she willingly agreed that "Miss Howse was quite right and you wouldn't go through Ealing and Hanwell."

She was not so accommodating when *Insurance* Company was altered to *Assurance* Company, which she thought "quite unnecessary."

Early in 1925 Agatha Christie had taken on an agent, Edmund Cork of Hughes Massie Ltd., who was to remain devotedly by her side for over fifty years. Today, aged eighty-three, he still keeps an eye on all of Agatha Christie's prolific literary interests.

One of his first jobs as her agent was to extricate her from her contract with The Bodley Head, which she found to be too binding.

"Edmund Cork told me the story only recently," Max Reinhardt of The Bodley Head recalls. "The Bodley Head already had six books of Agatha Christie's and he went to see John Lane to tell him that in future Mrs. Christie would only make a one-book contract each time. The terms offered were extremely reasonable. I think she was to get an advance of £250 a book. In any case John

Lane said he was not used to being talked to by an agent in this way and sent him away, whereupon Edmund Cork took Agatha Christie to Collins."

It is interesting to speculate that with Agatha Christie and the Bible, William Collins Sons & Co., Ltd., could not fail as publishers. Their entire financial future was assured. It also changed English publishing history because if Agatha Christie had stayed with The Bodley Head, which already owned world rights of the first six books, they would not have gone bankrupt and Max Reinhardt would probably not now be the firm's owner and managing director, a position he has held since 1957.

From the moment he took over The Bodley Head, Mr. Reinhardt reissued the six Christies that they had handled in a new format with what was then considered modern photographic jackets.

"The jackets were not jazzed up but they were very good," he remembers back today, "and were mostly photographs of members of our staff. We had a pretty good telephonist in those days who was an out-of-work actress. She figured on one of the jackets and then our publicity director appeared as the corpse on the cover of *Murder on the Links*."

The Bodley Head still has a profitable income from those first six Christies while Collins has the other eighty-odd detection books including the volume of short stories. The relationship between the two firms has always been amicable and whenever there is a complete edition sold abroad they work together as they have done with other authors they own jointly.

In 1919, after five years of marriage, Agatha Christie had her one and only child, a girl whom she called Rosalind after Shakespeare's heroine.

Though she was never a demonstrative woman in public, Rosalind added a great deal to Agatha Christie's personal happiness. Few mother and daughter relationships could have been closer as they shared with each other an inner sensitivity. This was made all the more poignant when Archibald Christie faded from their lives.

Colonel Christie had left the Royal Flying Corps in a blaze of glory. Clearly he was the right choice of war hero to be sent round

49

the world to promote the British Empire Exhibition that took place in 1922. At first Agatha Christie did not want to accompany her husband and felt that she should stay behind and look after Rosalind, whom they had nicknamed Teddy. Christie was adamant. Either his wife went or he would not go at all.

It was agreed that Madge, who had now become known as "Punkie" in the family circle, would look after Rosalind. Mrs. Miller was firmly on her son-in-law's side and explained to her daughter Agatha that a wife's duty was to go with her husband wherever he went.

Looking back on that round-the-world trip years later Agatha Christie said that it was one of the most exciting things that ever happened to her. The fact that she was hopelessly seasick all the time was totally eclipsed by the sight-seeing they managed to squeeze in between Archie Christie's business. The trip took in Madeira, where she wanted to leave the ship as she felt so ill, South Africa, Australia, Tasmania, New Zealand ("The most beautiful country I have ever seen"), Hawaii, Canada, and the United States.

On their arrival back the Christies had to face reality. All their slender savings were gone and the only money they had was £100 a year legacy which Agatha Christie's grandfather had left her. As yet her writing was not earning a great deal of money, although it was becoming more and more professional.

In 1932 Archibald Christie decided to go into business and joined Austral Trust Ltd., which is an offshot of Austral Development Ltd. Colonel Christie was immediately placed on the board of Austral Trust, where he remained until his death, at which time he was the chairman. He was a man of some importance in the city and was responsible for the share activities of Austral Trust apart from the Foreign and Colonial Investment Group. Exceptionally hard-working, he was popular with his associates although he was known to have a slightly abrupt manner. He could be curt and occasionally quick-tempered.

Colonel Christie's salary in the early twenties was around £3,000 per annum, which, added to Agatha Christie's own earnings, now placed the family in the comfortably-off bracket. [It was during the early twenties that the Christie marriage began imperceptibly to lose its glow. Christie was totally absorbed with his new business life in the city and the only social engagements which he wanted to attend were those concerned with furthering his career. To an ambitious wife, absorbed in her own career of writing, office parties must have been utterly boring. Outside her own family circle she was still painfully shy. Two associates of Austral Development remember her sitting glumly through a business dinner quite obviously hating every minute of it.

In 1923 Agatha Christie added another address to her collection of residences when the family moved to Scotswood at Sunningdale. They were to remain there for two years before buying another large house nearby, which they amusingly called Styles after her first book. She also retained a flat at 8 Addison Mansions in Kensington, where she did much of her business. By now Rosalind was four years of age, an alert, bouncy edition of her mother. She was idolized by her parents.

By 1926, well established in the fast-growing cult of detection writers, Agatha Christie created her masterpiece. *The Murder of Roger Ackroyd* is not only a classic but is the most discussed detective story ever to have been written. It was not only to place Agatha Christie at the top of her profession but wherever serious detection novel readers gather the question remains . . . did she break the sacred rules as set down by the Detection Club? Or did she not?

CHAPTER FIVE

How did agatha christie concoct those bewildering puzzles of hers? Many ideas came from her acute observation of everyday life. Not one single event was wasted and wherever she went those observant eyes were always storing up incidents in her memory bank for future use. Julian Symons, the current president of the Detection Club in London, writes about such a case in his extract "Mistress of Complication" in the book *Agatha Christie, First Lady of Crime* (edited by H. R. F. Keating and published in 1944 by Weidenfeld and Nicolson).

"At one of these [Detection Club] dinners I arrived late, and went straight into the dining room, just in time to see the end of my soup. My seat was opposite that of the president, Agatha Christie, and as we ate the next course I became aware of her mild unemphatic gaze which was often directed at . . . could it be my expanding but hardly visible waistline? Was there a mark on my tie? It took me a minute or two to realize that she was looking, in a speculative rather than censorious way, at my hands, and that they were rather grubby.

"As soon as I could easily do so I got up, washed my hands, and returned. There is no 'story' here, no comment was made, and I can offer nothing more than a personal conviction that Agatha Christie was viewing those grubby hands as a possible constituent element in some plot. *A man comes to the table—his hands are grubby—faintly marked with some kind of stain—yet half a dozen people are prepared to say that he spent the whole day in his office* . . . I feel sure that some such thoughts were passing through her mind."

Every journey in a train or bus, each visit to an antique shop, wherever something unusual caught her eye, was used in weaving her plots.

But at least one plot was given her. This was the inspiration for *The Murder of Roger Ackroyd*, the book that was not only to cause a furore in detection circles throughout the world, but to place Agatha Christie at the top of her profession . . . the undisputed Queen of Crime.

The idea was given to her by Lord Mountbatten fifty-four years ago.

When gathering photographs for this book I was intrigued to see a picture of the First Sea Lord wheeling Dame Agatha in her chair after a dinner at Claridges to celebrate the première of the film *Murder on the Orient Express*. I knew that Lord Brabourne, the producer of the film, was a son-in-law of Lord Mountbatten but I felt that there must have been another reason. Was it a friendship of many years which had prompted this gallant action? I wrote to Lord Mountbatten to inquire about that photograph and received the answer:

"I do have a story to tell you of how I gave her the plot for *The Murder of Roger Ackroyd*."

Here then was the answer. I arranged to visit Lord Mountbatten in his mews flat in Belgravia in London. The sitting room was comfortable with a deep pale sofa and soft carpet, low coffee table, and pieces of jade from the late Lady Mountbatten's collection, which she had inherited from her grandfather, Sir Ernest Cassells. Dominating the room was a massive desk set by the window. It was neatly arranged with pads, pens, paper, and all the paraphernalia of a constructive writer's life. Standing behind this in leather frames were photographs of members of his immediate family, for not only is Lord Mountbatten related to many of the royal families of Europe but he is also an involved family man. As the uncle of Prince Philip it was Lord Mountbatten more than anyone else who groomed the young Danish-Greek prince for his role as the future husband of the Queen of England.

"Yes it is true," Lord Mountbatten said as he came into the room. At seventy-eight years of age all the fabled charm still remains. He is devastatingly handsome. We settled down for a pleasant conversation about *The Murder of Roger Ackroyd*. Against the hum of the distant London traffic outside he spanned fifty-four years back to the days when he was a young lieutenant in the Royal Navy.

"I inherited from my mother [Princess Victoria of Battenberg] a great fondness for good detective fiction and I really devoured and read every book of Agatha Christie's when they came out. I did that all through my years in the Navy and even until after I married and had a family of my own. My two daughters Patricia [Lady Brabourne] and Pamela [wife of David Hicks the international interior decorator] acquired the same taste. In order to impress them one day in 1969 I said: 'You know her best book was *Roger Ackroyd* and I gave her the plot.' Which of course they did not believe.

"Pamela then said: 'If that is the case then you must prove it.' So I wrote to Agatha Christie: 'I wonder if you remember about 1924 that I wrote you a line giving you the idea of a plot for a story and saying that I had hoped to use it myself but that I had never got round to it.' I then told her that I wrote under a *nom de plume* occasionally. She immediately replied saying that she thought it was a very good idea and what was my *nom de plume*?

"It was in fact *NO* (Naval Officer) and I wrote three or four magazine stories of no consequence using it. I was rather shy about mentioning this so I didn't answer her letter. When *The Murder of Roger Ackroyd* came out, I read it and then realized that it was in fact my plot."

Forty-five years were to slip by before Lord Mountbatten was challenged by his daughter Pamela. With his customary punctiliousness he promptly wrote to Dame Agatha Christie once again. She was then seventy-nine years of age. Lord Mountbatten explained the whole story and why he wanted to know, as his honor was at stake with his children.

A letter, written by hand, came back from Agatha Christie chiding him that he had not answered her last letter and adding that more than once she had wanted to write to thank him and had never got around to it. She then went on to say that thank God he had written her as now she had a load off her conscience and she could acknowledge the origin of the plot.

She also told how she had once stood next to him at a cocktail party and that though she knew who he was, she was sure that he would not know her. She had wanted to say that she was Agatha Christie and did he remember the plot?

By next post Lord Mountbatten received a copy of the book *The Murder of Roger Ackroyd* with the following inscription: "To Lord Mountbatten in grateful remembrance of a letter he wrote to me forty-five years ago which contained the suggestion which I subsequently used in a book called *The Murder of Roger Ackroyd*. Here once more is my thanks. Christmas 1969 [signed Agatha Christie]."

At the time there were no hardback copies of the book on the market so Lord Mountbatten bought several paperbacks and pasted a photostat of Dame Agatha's letter on the inside front page. Here was proof enough and he gave each of his daughters a copy and one each to all his grandchildren. The original copy remains with his other personal books in his library at Broadlands in Romsey, Hampshire, which no doubt with his personal papers will one day be given to the library of a suitable university or naval college.

Of course I was enthralled and asked Lord Mountbatten to expand on his idea about the *Roger Ackroyd* theory.

"Basically my idea was a murder story based on the Sherlock Holmes-Watson relationship, which of course is Poirot and Hastings. The plot device was that the narrator of the story turned out to be the murderer, which had not been done before until I suggested it in 1924. I did not keep copies of my letters in those days but from memory I wanted her to use Hastings and said he'd have to keep the story going in the way that Watson does because he is keeping a running account of things which Poirot sees each day. He has to write it managing to include the incriminating phrases without Poirot noticing. I told her to test her skill, which of course she did.

"It has been said more than once that in taking my plot and working it out as she did Agatha Christie cheated but I don't think she did."

Dame Agatha and Lord Mountbatten were not to meet to discuss their joint effort until 1974 when they sat side by side at the gala dinner given after the première of *Murder on the Orient Express*. Though she was then eighty-four years old Dame Agatha kept up an animated conversation with Lord Mountbatten all during the dinner.

"I pulled her leg about *Roger Ackroyd* when we talked. I said, 'You really double-crossed me about the whole thing as I wanted Hastings not the locum doctor to be the murderer and she answered: 'I couldn't afford it. He had to go on.'"

I asked Lord Mountbatten if he had any more devastating detection tricks up his sleeve and whether in fact he would ever write one himself.

"To be quite honest I have. But I simply do not have the time. I get forty to fifty letters a day to answer and at seventy-eight I have never worked harder in my life before. But there it is. At least I gave her the idea for *Roger Ackroyd*."

The Murder of Roger Ackroyd was the first book to begin Agatha Christie's new deal with William Collins Sons & Co., Ltd. It became an overnight sensation but there were also howls of protest from the purists of detection writing.

"She has cheated . . . she has broken the Detection Club rules . . . she hasn't played fair" were the headlines.

"Tasteless, unforgivable let-down by a writer we had grown to admire," shrieked the *Daily Sketch*.

One vehement reader, a doctor, wrote to *The Times*: "Until now I have always been a great admirer of Agatha Christie but in the latest book I feel she has let the whole of the medical profession down and therefore propose in the future not to buy any more of her books." (Signed E.D.)

I traveled to Corfe Mullen in Devon to discuss the subject with Gladys Mitchell, a contemporary Christie member of the Detection Club, and herself author of over sixty detection novels.

Forthright and honest as she is, Gladys Mitchell exploded as we chatted in the sitting room of her sunny bungalow.

"I could have foamed at the mouth when I read *Roger Ackroyd*. I thought well of all the unfair things, and you know the only point it turned on was that there were ten minutes in the story unaccounted for. It comes very early on in the book when the narrator says:

> *The letter had been brought in at twenty minutes to nine. It was just on ten minutes to nine when I left him, the letter still unread. I hesitated with my hand on the door handle, looking back and wondering if there was anything I had left undone. I could think of nothing.*

Though Dorothy L. Sayers was to defend Agatha Christie in public by saying, "Fair! And Fooled you. . . . it's the reader's business to suspect everybody," it is generally thought by some of the senior members of the Detection Club that in private Dorothy L. Sayers felt that Agatha Christie had let the side down.

"I'm perfectly certain that Dorothy couldn't stand Agatha," Gladys Mitchell remembers, "but I have nothing to go on. I couldn't produce chapter and verse as it is only a feeling I have. Dorothy would not have approved of the technique of *The Murder of Roger Ackroyd*."

Another author on the Mitchell-Sayers side is Ernest Dudley, the BBC's well-known *Armchair Detective* of the fifties and creator of Dr. Morelle. He still gets "hot under the collar" when he remembers back.

"What she did was unethical. It's a damned awful cheat."

All through her life Agatha Christie never conceded that she had broken any rules. As she explained to Francis Wyndham:

"I have a certain amount of rules. No false words must be uttered by me. To write 'Mrs. Armstrong walked home wondering who had committed the murder' would be unfair if she had done it herself. But it's not unfair to leave things out. In *Roger Ackroyd* I made the narrator write: 'It was just on ten minutes to nine when I left him.' There's lack of explanation there, but no false statement. Whoever my villain is it has to be someone I feel *could* do the murder."

Though Lord Mountbatten may have been the instigator of

Roger Ackroyd Agatha Christie had earlier used a modified form of this kind of bluff in one of her most engaging novels *The Man in the Brown Suit*. It is true that here the story is only partially told by the villain but whereas it went totally unnoticed in 1924, when she was still struggling for recognition, why was there such an outcry just two years later?

The *Roger Ackroyd* story is a typical country house setting which no one does better. The rich squire is found murdered in his own study, stabbed in the throat. The red herrings thrown in for atmosphere are the usual butler, housekeeper, parlormaid, two housemaids, kitchen maid, and cook. All valid excuses for Mrs. Christie to have some fun shuffling her servants around and teasing her readers. Though she herself never indulged in such a luxury as a typical English butler only P. G. Wodehouse can surpass her in type casting this vanishing luxury of the English domestic scene.

By the introduction of the character Caroline, the doctor's sister, in *Roger Ackroyd* one suspects that had she chosen comic writing and not detection she would have equally made a name for herself as a storyteller. This portrait of a woolly-headed, well-meaning country gossiper is true even today and she can be found in every village in the Home Counties. They are as ubiquitous as mince pies for Christmas dinner.

Whatever the ethics of *The Murder of Roger Ackroyd* it received enough publicity to move Agatha Christie right to the forefront of detection writers. And for Collins it was the beginning of a glorious fruitful friendship that was to last the rest of her life.

It was one of the endearing qualities of Agatha Christie that she was loyal to her professional friends and rarely made any changes. Collins was to remain her publisher for over fifty years, Edmund Cork has been her agent for a similar period, and Peter Saunders has produced her plays for over thirty years. She has also retained the same solicitors, Hooper and Wollen of Torquay, who attended to all her mother's affairs.

With her career well established 1926 should have been an extremely happy year for Agatha Christie. She was young. She was clever. She was comfortably off and pleasing to look at. What went wrong?

CHAPTER SIX

O N FRIDAY, December 3, 1926, there occurred in Agatha Christie's life an event which was to color the whole of her future and turn a gay, fun-loving woman into a shy, intensely private one. The episode rankled throughout the rest of her life.

This news was broken to millions of her readers on the following Monday morning when she was headlined in all the national papers.

It was a day of surprising events. Mr. Winston Churchill was reported as going to the South of France to meet Signor Mussolini, the Italian premier. Lady Cynthia Mosley daughter of the late Marquis of Kedleston, said that in future she wished to be known as plain Mrs. Oswald Mosley (she was Mosley's first wife).

M. Claude Monet had died near his home at Giverny near Vernon and Lady Houston had won her legal fight to inherit £6,000,000 of the £7,000,000 estate of her late husband, shipping millionaire Sir Robert Houston.

Prince George, Duke of Kent, was on his way across Canada

and Charlie Chaplin said, "I'm going to fight to the last ditch—in every court in the land—for the custody of my children."

On that same day Professor Wegener of Austria expounded his theory that the continents of the world are not fixed into position but are slowly moving, and it was revealed that Consuelo Vanderbilt's consent to marry the Duke of Marlborough was in fact at the dictation of her mother Mrs. W. K. Vanderbilt. "Mother tore me from my sweetheart" was the headline.

Queen Marie of Rumania had arrived back in Bucharest from a visit to the United States and was met at the station by an ailing King Ferdinand and drove through the streets loudly cheered by the crowd.

Alongside these titillating headlines was the one in the *Daily Mail* "A Woman Novelist Vanishes" with the subtitle "Mrs. Agatha Christie, Clothes in Abandoned Motor Car."

Mrs. Christie's disappearance for ten days was as bizarre a story as any of her own detection novels and, despite the solution being partly resolved when she was found, the consequences of the whole affair were unpleasant.

"She was living out one of her own plots—only we shall never know the ending," says Lord Ritchie Calder, the eminent international scientific writer who was then a twenty-year-old junior reporting on his first crime assignment for the *Daily News*.

In order to follow the whole trend of this extraordinary story it is necessary to go back earlier in 1926.

It had been a traumatic year for Agatha Christie. Her mother had died after a severe illness, an event which affected her deeply. Theirs was an unusually close relationship as Agatha was so much younger than her sister Madge and brother Monty. When Mr. Miller died the whole responsibility of bringing up the family had fallen on Mrs. Miller. She and Agatha were inseparable.

In an interview with the *Daily Express* after his wife's disappearance Colonel Christie said that: "She is a very nervous case." He also told how they had earlier in the year spent a month in the South of France in order for his wife to recuperate from her mother's death and the stress of overwork.

What he did not reveal at the time was that the marriage had also deteriorated drastically. He had become infatuated with a young woman by the name of Miss Nancy Neele of Croxley Green, near Rickmansworth, who was also an acquaintance of his wife's.

This then was the background to the strange events which were to follow. To understand Mrs. Christie's future behavior one must realize that she was a highly imaginative and sensitive woman who had been betrayed by her husband in every possible way. The idyllic marriage set in a large country house, cemented by the birth of their child Rosalind, lay in pieces. Agatha Christie had been caught by surprise and was thrown totally off balance.

The police and Ritchie Calder firmly believed that in her great anguish she dealt with the situation on the level she understood. The world of mystery, deception, and revenge.

She planned her own disappearance with the same methodical care that she took in plotting one of her mysteries. It had all been carefully worked out to the last detail.

The week before her disappearance Agatha Christie had spent a couple of days in London. She went shopping with her sister-in-law in fashionable Albermarle Street, Mayfair, where she bought an elaborate white satin beauté nightgown trimmed with lace. She told the assistant who served her that she particularly wanted it "for the weekend."

Colonel Christie had already accepted an invitation to join a house party given by a Mr. and Mrs. F. James at Hurstmore Cottage, Godalming, where Miss Neele had also been invited. There were just the four of them and no other guests.

On Wednesday Mrs. Christie stayed at the Forum Club in London while Colonel Christie had a dinner engagement with his old R.F.C. squadron. She appeared to be of a perfectly rational mind and was only doing what she often did—having a couple of days in London.

The following day she went to see her agents, Hughes Massie Ltd., to discuss her novel *The Mystery of the Blue Train* (which she was later to claim was the worst book she had ever written). In her unhappy state of mind it was proving difficult and there were still two stories to be written to complete a set of six for publication in America.

When interviewed by the police a spokesman for her agent

said: "She appeared to be in the best of spirits, better indeed than for a long time. Her visit was connected entirely with her work and in no way did she suggest that she contemplated a journey."

Back at Sunningdale that night after dinner she went with her secretary, Miss Charlotte Fisher, to a dancing class at Ascot. She had recently taken up dancing lessons to learn some of the new steps as a therapeutic hobby to try and dispel her constant depression.

According to the parlormaid, on the morning of the disappearance Colonel and Mrs. Christie had an argument and bitter words were exchanged. Colonel Christie later denied this and said it was "absolutely untrue" but the fact is that he left the house just after breakfast to go to his office in London and then on to his weekend at Godalming.

Weekends away from his family appeared to have been a habit of Mrs. Christie's husband as he was later to tell a reporter of the *Daily News:* "It is a common practice of mine."

A close friend of Mrs. Christie's, Mrs. de Silva of Lindsay Lodge, Sunningdale, had telephoned her that morning to invite her over for a game of bridge, but she had said that she could not go as she had "an important appointment this afternoon."

Mrs. de Silva was also to tell the press that she and Agatha Christie were planning to go shortly on a holiday in Portugal and that almost all the arrangements for the trip had already been made.

One of the current rumors at the time was that a woman answering Mrs. Christie's description had been seen at the Sunningdale Hotel the previous week. She was said to have spoken to an elderly man, supposedly a peer, and during a pleasant conversation with him had been overheard to use the word "Switzerland."

On Friday, the day of her disappearance, Mrs. Christie lunched alone and then took her daughter Rosalind and dog for a visit to her mother-in-law, Mrs. Rosamund Hemsley, who had remarried after the death of her husband, Archibald Christie Sr., at her home Middle Lodge, Deepdene, Dorking.

In an interview with the *Daily Mail* Mrs. Hemsley later described the visit: "While waiting for the kettle to boil she sang a few songs and joked with Rosalind and I remarked to her that she seemed much better, 'Yes,' she replied, 'I do.' But a few minutes later she seemed to become depressed again."

As she continued: "In the middle of last year Agatha was commissioned to write a mystery novel around the famous Continental Blue Train and for this purpose she left with her sister and stayed in Corsica for some months to work out her plot and get the right 'atmosphere.'

"Returning home, she began her book and wrote rapidly. Her mother died a few weeks later and since then she has not written a word. She has talked a lot about her inability to complete *The Mystery of the Blue Train*. Before she left here she repeatedly muttered, 'These rotten plots. Oh, these rotten plots.'

"She had sent the manuscript to my younger son, Captain Campbell Christie, to see if he could help it along."

Agatha Christie was not wearing her wedding ring this day but only her engagement ring. Mrs. Hemsley recalled commenting on this fact to her: "She sat perfectly still for some time, gazing into space, and giving a hysterical laugh, turned away and patted Rosalind's head.

"I am inclined to think that my daughter-in-law planned her end and deliberately drove the car to where it was found. She knew the roads so well and even in the dark she would not lose her way. Although physically strong she could never crank up a car if it had stopped.

"She was devoted to her husband and child and would never willingly have left them. It is my opinion that in a fit of depression and not knowing where she was going or what she was doing, my daughter-in-law abandoned her car at Newlands Corner and wandered away over the Downs."

After tea Agatha Christie left in apparently high spirits about 5 P.M. She seemed a little brighter but sat deep in thought for a few seconds in her car before starting away.

Mrs. Christie dined alone and at 9:45 P.M. she told a member of her staff that she was going for a drive. She placed a letter on the side table addressed to Colonel Christie and also left one for her secretary, Miss Fisher, asking her to cancel weekend arrangements as she had planned to go to Yorkshire. She then went upstairs and kissed her sleeping child Rosalind, and after patting her dog Peter on the head, disappeared into her car and drove away.

What really happened on that Friday night is now conjecture over fifty years later. There are conflicting and confusing reports.

In the *New Statesman* in January 1976 in an article that appeared after Dame Agatha Christie's death, Lord Ritchie Calder, who is one of the few people alive to have been actively involved in reporting the case, wrote: "One thing that was established by press interrogation was that the secretary, whether at Mrs. Christie's suggestion or because she panicked, telephoned the country house at Godalming on the Friday night to warn Colonel Christie. A dinner party was in progress. This was more than an assignation; it was what the household described as an "engagement" party for Colonel Christie and Miss Neele. He was called from the table, took the call, made abrupt apologies and drove off in his car. The implication was that he was going to intercept her to avoid a confrontation at the house."

Another variation on this theme comes from Mr. James, who told the *Daily Mail* at the time: "Suggestions have been made that Colonel Christie was called up by his wife while he was here, or that he went and met his wife, or that she came here to meet him. Nothing of that kind happened. I believe that Mrs. Christie returned home and found that the colonel was spending the weekend with us and that she drove off in a fit of pique."

Was this in part true or a cover-up?

Today Lord Ritchie Calder is totally convinced that his version is correct.

The Berkshire police checked the times of both Colonel and Mrs. Christie's departures and there is every reason to believe that they could in fact have met at Newlands Corner.

Colonel Christie in an interview with the press claimed that he did not know of his wife's disappearance until the following day.

The cook employed by Mrs. James at the time said that a dinner party did take place. Next morning Colonel Christie came down to breakfast and was informed then by the police that his wife was missing. He had a talk with his hostess, Mrs. James, and then left the house.

The cook was told that Colonel Christie would not be in for luncheon "as his mother is ill."

Mrs. Christie did not return to her home that night or for many more nights. She had disappeared completely. Instead her car, a green bull-nosed Morris, was discovered by Jack Best, a fifteen-year-old gypsy, at Newlands Corner, Berkshire, as he was going to work as a beater at 8 A.M. on the following morning. The hood and side screens were up, the lights were still on and the bodywork was covered with hoarfrost.

He immediately reported his find to the local police station. Officers were soon on the spot and because the car was not damaged after it was pulled up on to the road, they were able to drive it away.

It was a curious fact that although the car must have run over the soft grass there were no tracks which showed the way it came over the high road. From the position the car was found in it was thought to have been deliberately allowed to run down from Newlands Corner with its brakes off.

On the seat of the car was a brown fur coat and a small dressing case which had burst open, scattering its contents of clothing. The suitcase contained two gray dresses, an evening dress, two pairs of shoes, an out-of-date driving license in the name of Mrs. Agatha Christie, and some papers. There could be no doubt at all about the identity of the owner.

It was all carefully established and the red herrings suitably distributed.

Everything pointed to foul play, an attempted suicide, or even murder.

With her seventh detection novel, *The Murder of Roger Ackroyd*, a current best seller, after serialization in the Lonon *Evening News*, Agatha Christie's disappearance caused a sensation.

When notified of her disappearance the Surrey Constabulary immediately issued the following statement which appeared in the Monday morning newspapers and thus the news was broken to the public:

> *Missing from her home, The Styles, Sunningdale, Berkshire, Mrs. Agatha Mary Clarissa Christie, age 35; height 5 feet 7 inches; hair, red, shingled part grey; complexion, fair, build slight; dressed in grey stockinette skirt, green*

jumper, grey and dark grey cardigan and small velour hat; wearing a platinum ring with one pearl; no wedding ring; black handbag with purse containing perhaps £5 or £10. Left home by car at 9:45 P.M. Friday leaving note saying that she was going for a drive.

Superintendent William Kenward, deputy chief constable of Surrey, was placed in charge of the search.

"I have handled many important cases during my career but this is the most baffling mystery ever set me for solution," he commented.

The center of the search was focused on the Silent Pool, a lake a quarter of a mile from Newlands Corner. Mrs. Christie had already used this famed beauty spot in a novel in which one of the characters is found drowned in the pool. The police thought that in her desperation she might have re-enacted the scene.

There was a legend concerning the pool which had become part of local folklore. It described how King John, while out hunting, had discovered a woodman's daughter bathing in it. When she realized that the monarch had seen her, she waded into the pool and drowned. In an effort to save this beautiful girl, her brother also waded into the dark broody waters. They were both never seen again and because of this local people believed the pool to be bottomless.

Special machinery was brought in to dredge the bottomless Silent Pool but the only thing that this confirmed was that the pool did have a bottom.

Light aircraft, packs of airdales and bloodhounds with their handlers, and police from four counties—Surrey, Essex, Berkshire, and Kent—were brought in and the press claimed that there were five hundred police as well as numbers of special constables and volunteers.

On Monday night Ernest Cross, a farmhand, came forward to the police with a strange story. He claimed to have tried to start Mrs. Christie's car for her at six-twenty on Saturday morning.

"I was going to work and I came upon a woman in a frenzied condition standing by a motor car near the top of Newlands Corner, a few yards from Newlands Corner Hotel.

"She was moaning and holding her hands to her head and her teeth were chattering with cold. She was wearing only a thin frock and a thin pair of shoes and I think she was without a hat. Her hair was covered with hoarfrost.

"The lights of her car were full on and I asked her if I could be of any assistance. She stumbled towards me and remarked that it was very late and said, 'Oh, do try and start it up for me.'

"As I approached the car she stumbled against me again and I wound up the engine, which was quite hot."

He claimed that she drove off toward Guildford but as this was in the opposite direction to where the car was found it would have meant that she had turned back again later.

The next two people to report having seen Mrs. Christie were Porter Fuett of Milford Station on the Southern Railway and Mr. T. Warner, a Milford carrier. They said that she looked as though she had been wandering about and her small white velour hat was covered with frost and in fact she had frost over most of her clothes. She asked for the road to Portsmouth. She then asked the way to Petersfield, which was also on the Portsmouth Road.

A cogent point is that the farmhand Cross reported that she had no hat and Fuett and Warner describe a white one. Did they in fact see Mrs. Christie at all—or had they let their imaginations loose, cashing in on the notoriety of the moment.

The men claimed that they watched her as she walked away in the direction of Hambledon. There was a milk train going through to Petersfield about the time but both witnesses were in fact sure that she did not travel on it.

On Tuesday the *Daily News* offered a £100 reward to anyone furnishing information which would lead to Mrs. Christie's recovery. When told of this Colonel Christie appeared to be very moved, but did not think it would do much good.

"I would be willing to give £500 if I could hear where my wife is or whether she is well," he said.

On Thursday morning when there was still no news Colonel Christie went to his office in London. During the week police had been on guard at his house and monitored his telephone calls.

When he called at his office on the sixth floor of the Rio Tinto Company in the City of London he rode up in the elevator with

Mr. Sebastian Earl, who had the office next door to him, and now lives in London.

"He was in a terribly nervous state and said that the police had followed him up Broad Street and all the way to the office and were now waiting outside.

"'They think I've murdered my wife,' he said. He then went into his office and though I saw him several times during the week when he looked progressively worse he never referred to it again—and of course I didn't either," Sebastian Earl recalled.

Lord Ritchie Calder remembers that Christie made a very poor impression with the police. On the following Thursday after he returned from London he did join with the police in searching, taking with him Mrs. Christie's dog Peter, who had been pining for her since the previous Friday. Peter sniffed through much of the undergrowth and though he "pointed" several times they were false alarms.

During the week Colonel Christie discussed with the police the theory that his wife had often mentioned the possibility of disappearing at will. He had heard her some weeks before telling her sister that she could disappear if she wished.

"That showed the possibility of engineering a disappearance had been running through her mind, probably for the purpose of her work," he said.

By the weekend following her disappearance, in answer to a police appeal, there were fifteen thousand voluntary searchers on the Downs. All roads leading to Newlands Corner were blocked as officials of the Royal Automobile Club and the Automobile Association directed the cars to various parking places and by Saturday afternoon no fewer than three thousand cars were parked on Merrow Downs.

As the volunteers gathered they were herded into parties of thirty or so and set off with a police officer in charge to beat various parts of the Downs. A party of horsemen carried instructions to the extreme flanks of the searching army. It was calm, orderly, efficient, and could have been taken straight from the pages of an Agatha Christie novel.

The *Daily Mail* claimed a newspaper scoop when they engaged

Edgar Wallace to expound his theory on Mrs. Christie's disappearance.

As he wrote in a long article on the subject: "The disappearance seems to be a typical case of 'mental reprisal' on somebody who has hurt her. To put it vulgarly her first intention seems to have been to 'spite' an unknown person who would be distressed by her disappearance.

"That she did not contemplate suicide seems evident from the fact that she deliberately created an atmosphere of suicide by abandonment of her car.

"Loss of memory, that is to say mental confusion, might easily have followed but a person so afflicted could not possibly escape notice."

He then summed up by writing: "If Agatha Christie is not dead of shock and exposure within a limited radius of the place where her car was found she must be alive and in full possession of her faculties, probably in London.

"It is impossible to lose your memory and find your way to a determined destination."

CHAPTER SEVEN

T HE DISCOVERY of Mrs. Agatha Christie was as whimsical as her disappearance. Once again every incident could have been a page from one of her own detection novels.

On Monday evening, the eleventh day after her disappearance, the Harrogate Police Station sent a message to Deputy Chief Constable Kenward of the Surrey police that they had every reason to believe that the missing woman had been living in that area since her disappearance.

What complicated matters was the apparent feud between the two police forces involved. Deputy Chief Constable Kenward of Surrey maintained all along that in his opinion she was dead and that her body would be found somewhere near Newlands Corner.

Superintendent Goddard of the Berkshire police had a different theory. He was convinced that Mrs. Christie was alive. After the first two days at Newlands Corner he switched his search to the West of England, Yorkshire, Lancashire, and North Wales. "When Mrs. Christie has worked out her problem she will return," he said.

Had not Mrs. Christie spoken for some time of going north for a rest? And clearly she had indicated the direction in her letter to her brother-in-law, which had been posted in London the Saturday after her disappearance.

Persisting in his belief that the body—dead or alive—would be found within forty miles of Newlands Corner, Kenward decided not to take any action on the Harrogate police's message and not to advise Colonel Christie. On the following morning the Harrogate police were again on the telephone and so insistent that their theory was right that Kenward decided to change his plans.

"The ridiculous thing," Lord Ritchie Calder remembers, "is that the Berkshire and Surrey police were hardly on speaking terms; the latter were complaining that the Wokingham police were keeping evidence from them, including the substance of the letters.

"The chief of the Berkshire police used to hint to us that these were incriminating letters and then we'd ask the Surrey police and they'd say, 'That's all we know about it.'

"The thing was that the Berkshire police were responsible for looking after Colonel Christie, who was under constant surveillance, and the Surrey police were in charge of the hunt. It was all very confusing."

Defending his actions later, Deputy Chief Constable Kenward said in his final report to the Home Office, which has been released fifty years later for the purpose of this book: "Acting on certain information which I received she might have been, as was strongly suggested to the police, the victim of a serious crime. I was convinced that she would probably be found dead from exposure or otherwise and felt it my duty to pursue the matter."

Mrs. Gladys Kenward Dobson, who acted as confidential secretary to her father in his position as deputy chief constable, remembers Mrs. Christie's disappearance vividly.

"The whole case broke my father's heart. He was criticized for continuing his search round Newlands Corner but he had to: he took his orders from the Home Office."

Deputy Chief Constable William Kenward never fully recovered from the worry of this case and died in his prime, aged only fifty-six years.

"When he retired my father ordered that all the personal correspondence about this case should be destroyed. I burned the copies of the letters, including the one Mrs. Christie left her secretary should she have died."

During the last war all the records at the Surrey Police Office were in fact destroyed and nothing remains at the Berkshire station.

Colonel Christie claimed to have burned his letter. The letter to his brother Campbell Christie was innocuous. Any suggestion of foul play may have been contained in the letter Mrs. Christie left her secretary, Miss Charlotte Fisher, who is now dead.

The scenario now switches to the Harrogate Hydropathic Hotel, one of the more flamboyant hotels in this elegant Edwardian spa. Once a famous coaching house, dating from 1700, the hotel had become a tourist center because of its accessibility to the Yorkshire moors and dales and the ancient cathedral city of York. Harrogate was a Mecca for rich Midlanders with its fine stores, some of the best antique shops in the world, and of course for the treatment for all kinds of illnesses.

With its 150 bedrooms, nostalgic palm lounge, impressive Edwardian dining room, the Hydro had a most agreeable, middle class atmosphere and was just the place for anyone seeking anonymity during a stressful period. At the time of Mrs. Christie's residence there were only fifty guests as it was almost Christmas.

In the evenings in the Palm Lounge the Harry Codd Hydro Dance Band—known to residents as the Happy Hydro Boys—played. Dressed in their neat dinner jackets, their hit tunes at the time were "Yes, We Have No Bananas" and "Don't Bring Lulu," suitable accompaniments for the Charleston, which was all the rage.

Bob Tappin, a greengrocer during the day, played the banjo at night and sang in the band. While he was singing his eyes had time to range over the guests and he became fascinated with the good-looking woman who sat alone in the corner of the lounge doing crossword puzzles or with her head immersed in the daily newspapers or detection books she borrowed from the hotel library. She was outstanding because of her shining golden-red hair, handsome but not necessarily beautiful countenance, clear skin, and calm blue eyes. A most attractive woman. To the guests in the hotel she was known as Mrs. Neele.

For several nights he kept his suspicions to himself and then confided them to his two chums in the band—Reg Schofield, the pianist, and Bob Leeming, the saxophonist.

Several people, including Mrs. Taylor, the manager's wife, were later to claim that they had recognized Mrs. Christie. During the week a guest from Birmingham showed Agatha Christie the photo of the missing novelist in the paper saying: "That is very like you, isn't it?"

Mrs. Christie replied nonchalantly: "Oh, is it?"

She openly discussed the disappearance with other guests and said: "It is extraordinary that a woman could disappear from the face of the earth without leaving any trace."

When one of the guests jestingly addressed her as Mrs. Christie she laughed and brushed it off.

It was Bob Tappin, however, who was so convinced he was right, that he went to the Harrogate police with his information. Had he in fact gone to the *Daily News* he would have been entitled to the £100 reward. He did not receive one single penny for his effort.

The Harrogate police, in conjunction with the manager of the hotel, decided to act. A detective was placed in the hotel for two days discreetly observing Mrs. Neele. Everyone on the staff was warned that in no way were they to arouse her suspicion. This is the story that the manager told the police about Mrs. Neele.

"She arrived by taxi on Saturday morning with only a small suitcase and asked for a bedroom on *en pension* terms and was given a good room [No. 105] on the first floor with hot and cold water.

"I did not see her myself but I believe that the price quoted to her was seven guineas a week. She accepted this without hesitation. Indeed from the first day she has been here she seems to have as much money as she wants. From the first her life in the Hydro has been exactly similar to that of our other guests. She takes her meals in the dining room and only once or twice has had breakfast in bed. She is a very agreeable guest."

Agatha Christie had signed the register in the name of Mrs.

Teresa Neele, a slight adaptation of the name of her husband's "paramour"—Nancy Neele. From the first day she was a charming, friendly woman and told fellow guests that she was on a visit from Cape Town.

When she arrived at the hotel on Saturday there was a dance that evening. Although she was wearing the short knitted dress that she disappeared in, which had been reported as covered with hoarfrost just twenty-four hours earlier, she mingled with the other guests in their evening clothes in the dance room. As Miss Corbett, the hotel pianist, said later: "She came into the dance room. I thought to myself, seeing she was not in evening dress, 'She won't dance.' But she did. She got up and did the Charleston when the band struck up 'Yes, We Have No Bananas.'"

On Monday she apparently went shopping because from then on she appeared in different clothes every day. "She was constantly buying herself clothes," Miss Corbett told the police.

During the following week Mrs. Christie went to church, took tea in a local tea shop, and went for long walks. When the guests collected their newspapers on the hall stand in the mornings and evenings she took hers without any hesitation. There was no attempt at disguise in any way.

In the evening she was persuaded to play billiards and on several occasions accompanied herself on the piano and sang in a sweet, soprano voice. Only once did she portray any emotion when she partially broke down singing a sentimental song. Even that was totally acceptable to the other guests who had been given to understand by her that she was on a trip from South Africa to recover from the loss of her baby.

At all other times she was charming, perfectly normal—"There was no trace of any self-consciousness in any of her movements and if she had been trying to disguise her identity she surely would sometime or other have been taken off her guard," one guest recalled. "But she never was."

During one of her shopping expeditions Mrs. Christie bought the music of "Angels Ever Guard Thee" for one of her fellow guests and autographed it "Teresa Neele."

On the morning of Saturday, December 11, there had appeared

in the personal column of *The Times* an announcement: "Friends and relatives of Teresa Neele, late of South Africa, please communicate—Write Box R 702, *The Times*, E.C. 4."

On Sunday morning Mrs. Neele asked Miss Corbett whether it would be possible to get a copy of Monday morning's edition of *The Times*.

"She appeared to be most anxious about it," Miss Corbett later reported.

The police were later to check the entry and found that it had been posted personally to *The Times* by Mrs. Christie.

Later when Mrs. Christie's deception was exposed, her husband, always gallant in public, even had an explanation for this strange behavior on the part of his wife:

"She thought the relatives and family must know where she was although she could not remember who they were. At last hearing nothing of them she became worried and advertised asking them to communicate with her."

In those days there existed between the police and the press a closer relationship than today. Often when the police could not break through an alibi the newspapermen would go interviewing suspects individually and try to find the flaw. They could not print anything but this enabled the police to follow through.

When it was leaked to the press on the Monday that Mrs. Neele was under observation by the police, the local reporters immediately telephoned their news desks in London.

The *Daily Mail*, which had led all the way in the search, sent a special train from King's Cross to Harrogate containing a team of their top reporters and photographers. Young Ritchie Calder was among the first to arrive for the *Daily News* in his role as feed reporter to Sidney Campion, one of their top reporters, who in his later career was to be a barrister, leading civil servant, and internationally known sculptor.

The police had thrown a special cordon around the hotel. All the staff had been warned to carry on their duties normally and they were not to speculate about the matter in case the suspicion was not justified.

Ritchie Calder, with superb panache or ignorant of the fact

that he might have upset the police's master plan, walked into the hotel and up to Mrs. Neele, who was in the lounge, and addressed her as Mrs. Christie.

"There was no melodrama. She was not flustered. When I asked how she got there she said that she did not know and she was suffering from amnesia.

"I feel that the fact she used the word 'amnesia' was much too clinical a word for someone supposedly surprised into conversation, and if, as her doctor later suggested, she had an 'identity crisis,' well by golly there was no 'Teresa Neele' lurking in the self-possessed woman I met."

Before Calder could ask any more of his penetrating questions Mrs. Christie quickly turned around and went up in the elevator to her room where she remained for the rest of the afternoon.

It was just after 9 A.M. on Tuesday, December 14, that Deputy Chief Constable Kenward tried to telephone Colonel Christie at his home, Styles, and was told that the colonel had just left for his office in London.

When the superintendent asked Miss Fisher if she would accompany him to Harrogate to identify Mrs. Christie and save time, she refused. She explained that she felt her place was to stay with Mrs. Christie's small daughter Rosalind, who did not know of her mother's disappearance. Rosalind had been told that her mother was away writing a book, a state of affairs with which she was familiar and accepted.

Christie was eventually contacted at his office and left by the first available train for Harrogate.

First with the news that Mrs. Christie was likely to be found at Harrogate was the London *Evening Standard*, which printed the story in their 2:30 P.M. edition. This London evening paper had the scoop of the week for two whole editions ahead of any other newspaper.

Colonel Christie arrived at Harrogate at 6:45 P.M. and was met by Superintendent McDowell of the Harrogate police force. Within a few minutes they had driven to the Hydro where a crowd of people had gathered outside the cordon and the two men were whisked into the privacy of the manager's office.

The situation was obviously delicate and difficult for two

reasons. In the first place the suspected woman might not after all be Mrs. Agatha Christie, and secondly, if she was, and was genuinely suffering from loss of memory, the sudden shock of seeing her husband again might have some disturbing and serious consequences.

By some illogical reasoning it was decided, therefore, that the lady would not be approached in her room and that it would be preferable for the police and Colonel Christie to wait downstairs. Neither Colonel Christie nor the police knew that in fact "Mrs. Neele" had admitted to Ritchie Calder earlier in the day that she was Mrs. Christie.

It was known that Mrs. Christie was in the habit of passing through the lounge every evening just before dinner to pick up her evening papers on the side table by the office. A ruse was planned. Colonel Christie was to hide behind a newspaper in an obscure corner of the lounge and nod to the superintendent if he recognized his wife.

Just after 7 P.M., wearing an orchid pink dinner dress, Mrs. Christie came down in the elevator. Colonel Christie nodded the affirmative to McDowell, and as she appeared completely composed, went up to her. There was no scene, no embarrassment. Turning to her fellow guests she said: "Fancy, my brother has just arrived."

According to another guest, Mr. Pettleston, who watched the reunion: "They sat down in front of the fire with several chairs between them as if they had had a quarrel."

After a few minutes Colonel and Mrs. Christie got up and went in to dinner together as if it was a perfectly normal occurrence. The guests, who were already seated at their tables, were by now totally aware that the handsome man at "Mrs. Neele's" side was in fact her husband, Colonel Christie, and that she was indeed the missing writer whom they had been talking about all week.

Earlier on Saturday morning Mrs. Christie had confirmed that she would join the hotel party that was going to a neighboring hotel where a dance was being held. During dinner she turned to some of the guests and said, quite casually: "I am sorry that I will not be able to go to the dance with you as my brother has arrived."

After dinner husband and wife retired to a suite of rooms Colonel Christie had taken and left orders that they were not to be disturbed.

By now all the press was clamoring downstairs for a statement for their newspapers and naturally they all wanted their own exclusive interview. Archie Kenyon, the Yorkshire *Post*'s resident staff man in Harrogate, was chosen as the spokesman for the press and his interview with Colonel Christie was "pooled" to all the other reporters. There was no question of the free-for-all mass interview that would happen today.

Colonel Christie was calm and composed as later that night he gave out his statement: "There is no question about the identity. It is my wife. She has suffered from the most complete loss of memory and I do not think she knows who she is.

"She does not know me and she does not know where she is.

"I am hoping that the rest and quiet will restore her. I am hoping to take her to London tomorrow to see a doctor and specialists."

He then, through the press, expressed his thanks to the police for their splendid co-operation in finding his wife. According to *The Times*, Colonel Christie continued: "Some papers had made a stunt of it."

The Christies' departure from the hotel on the following morning was in keeping with every other aspect in this mystery story. Just after 9 A.M. the hotel coach drew up outside the Hydro and a man and woman decoy were seen to get into it and were much photographed by the press. It is odd that Mrs. Christie willingly accompanied her husband, whom she "does not know."

Meanwhile at the side entrance of the hotel Colonel and Mrs. Christie slipped out into a waiting limousine. Mrs. Christie kept her head well down and did not look at the porter holding the door but otherwise appeared to be composed. As she was leaving the hotel several people said, "Good-by, Mrs. Christie." She looked surprised and said, "Am I Mrs. Christie?"

The *Daily Mail* had thought of every contingency and had placed one lone photographer just in case the Christies did use this entrance. He got his picture, admirably.

It shows Mrs. Christie looking elegant in an expensive cloth coat banded with fur on the collar, cuffs, and hemline. It is the picture of a serene woman facing up to what must have been a terrible ordeal for her.

Mrs. Christie's sister, Madge, and her husband, Mr. W. Watts, had arrived at the hotel from their home near Stockport to travel back there with the Christies.

At the station to greet the party was a contingent of reporters. The man from the *Daily Express* wrote: "She walked with apparent composure down the long platform, hanging on her sister's arm, and glanced round half wonderingly and half amusedly.

"I tried to speak to her but her companion whispered hurriedly, 'This is not Mrs. Christie.' It was she, however. She turned her head, smiled, and appeared about to speak when her companion said, 'Do come along. You will be upset.'

"At that moment Colonel Christie rushed forward and said, 'You must not go near that lady. She is not well and must not be interfered with. It is a case of loss of memory.'

Colonel Christie then apparently cleverly maneuvered himself between his wife and the reporters, photographers, and fast-gathering crowd. A couple of pictures were "snatched" which appeared in the papers next day and that was all.

The blinds of the first class compartment in which they traveled from Harrogate to Leeds were drawn and the compartment was labeled "Mr. Parker's Party"—Parker being the name of the stationmaster.

Just before the train left Harrogate Colonel Christie appeared on the step of the carriage. To a press inquiry he replied:

"My wife does not remember leaving her house or anything before it. She only knows that she arrived here by train and took a taxicab to the hotel. I believe she is beginning to have a faint recollection of who she is."

At Leeds, Colonel Christie and his wife and the Wattses left the train and walked to another platform where they entered the Manchester train. Mrs. Christie walked ahead, chattering cheerfully to her sister, and Colonel Christie, carrying two suitcases, followed with Mr. Watts. One was probably the suitcase that

Mrs. Christie began her wanderings with and the other may well have been supplied by the Wattses to accommodate the additional clothing she had bought in Harrogate.

On arrival at Manchester, Colonel Christie took over and with military precision escorted the party into a waiting chauffeur-driven limousine. A trail of press cars quickly juggled into position behind it forming a cavalcade as they set off for Abney Hall, the home of the Watts family at Cheadle. As the Wattses' motor car swung through the iron gates a gardener jumped out from the lodge and clanged them together, securing them firmly with a padlock and chain.

Abney Hall completely fitted into the Christie mystery story. Built in the early 1800s for the Watts family, who were prominent in the Manchester clothing trade, it stood in twenty acres of mellow parklands with adjacent farm lands. The people at Cheadle had never been nosy folk and did not trouble themselves much at what went on at the hall. It was the perfect hideaway.

On Mrs. Christie's arrival there was a severe warning posted on the gates that anyone found trying to scale the walls would be prosecuted. All telephone calls to Abney Hall were balked. The receiver had simply been taken off the hook.

In the afternoon of the Christies' arrival at Abney Hall, the *Daily News* sent an urgent telegram to Mrs. Christie. It read: "In view wide spread criticisms your disappearance strongly urge desirability authentic explanation from yourself to thousands of the public who joined in costly search and shared anxiety and who cannot understand loss of memory theory in view of reports your normal life at Harrogate and assumption name of real person named Neele."

A reply came back from Colonel Christie, acting on his wife's behalf.

"Wife suffering from loss of memory and probably concussion. She has no recollection of events on Friday or Saturday before arrival Harrogate. Has only recollected true identity today. Remaining quietly here under doctor's orders."

That, in fact, was the first time the words "probably concussion" had been used.

Later that same day two esteemed doctors called at Abney Hall

Empire Day as celebrated at Torquay in 1905. Agatha Christie was then fifteen years old and undoubtedly took part in the festivities. Note the fashions of the little girls with their middy dresses and sailor hats.

A view from the pier at Torquay at the time when Agatha Miller was born. Fishing fleets and trawlers operated from this harbor and many others all along the south coast, giving the town a lively fishing industry.

Bathing sheds at Anstey's Cove, Torquay, where Mrs. Miller used to take her daughter Agatha bathing. It was not until the end of the nineteenth century that mixed bathing was allowed.

As a young girl, Agatha Miller frequently took part in amateur theatricals at Cockington Court, Torquay. She is pictured third from right in the front row in a burlesque of Bluebeard and his wives.

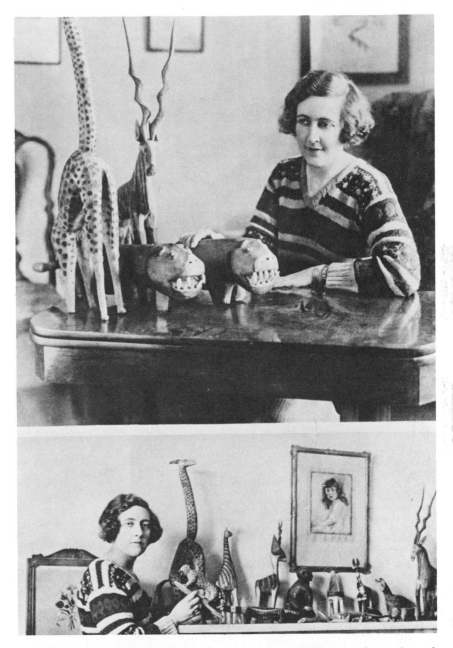

Agatha Christie poses for photographs in 1924 with her collection of carved wooden "beasties," which she brought back from a trip to Rhodesia with her husband, Archibald Christie. All her life, Agatha Christie collected various objects which at one time spilled over into the eight houses that she owned. (Photo credit: Raymond Mander and Joe Mitchenson Theatre Collection)

Agatha Christie poses for her first publicity pictures after the publication of *The Mysterious Affair at Styles*. The page appeared in March 1923 in *The Sketch* magazine.

(Left) One of the first publicity photos issued of Mrs. Agatha Christie at the time of the publication of *The Murder of Roger Ackroyd*.

A photo published in the national press of Agatha Christie, taken a short time before her disappearance.

Lieutenant Colonel Archibald Christie, C.M.G., D.S.O., Royal Flying Corps: the dashing officer Agatha Christie fell in love with and married.

A portrait taken in Australia of Mrs. Agatha Christie and her daughter Rosalind the year before her disappearance. This picture was issued to the national press for identification during her disappearance in 1926.

A photo spread from the London *Daily Mail* at the time of Mrs. Agatha Christie's disappearance. (Photo credit: *Daily Mail*)

Mrs. Agatha Christie, who claimed to be suffering from amnesia, leaves the Harrogate Hydropathic Hotel in some of the new clothes she bought during her "disappearance." This was the only photograph taken as she left the Harrogate Hydro. (Photo credit: *Daily Mail*)

Right) An article that appeared in the *Daily Express* announcing a bulletin which had been issued by two doctors certifying that Mrs. Agatha Christie was suffering from an "unquestionable loss of memory."

BULLETIN
ON
MRS. CHRISTIE

LOSS OF MEMORY CERTIFIED BY DOCTORS.

"UNQUESTIONABLE."

HUSBAND'S LETTER TO THE 'DAILY EXPRESS.'

" Daily Express " Special Correspondent.

MANCHESTER, Thursday.

LATE this afternoon two doctors held a consultation over Mrs. Christie, and in the evening Colonel Christie, who is staying with his wife at Abney Hall,

MRS. CHRISTIE AND HER DAUGHTER.

Cheadle, handed to me the following bulletin :—

"After a careful examination of Mrs. Agatha Christie this afternoon, we have formed the opinion that she is suffering from an unquestionable loss of memory, and that for her future welfare she should be spared all anxiety and excitement.

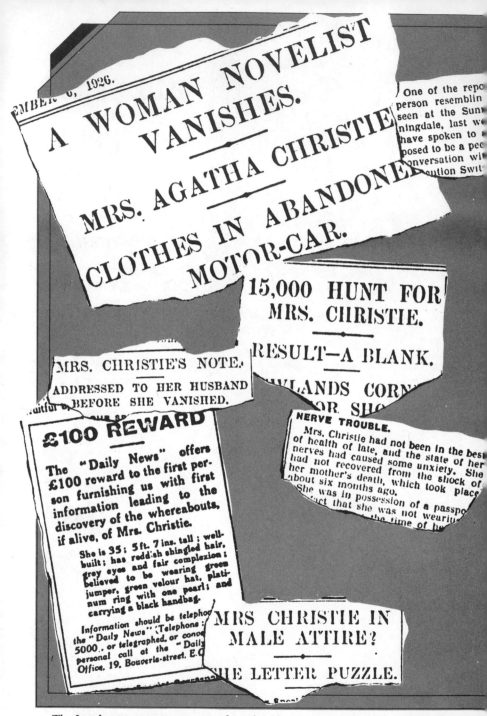

The London newspaper coverage of Agatha Christie's disappearance in December 1926.

The Harrogate Hydro—now called the Old Swan Hotel—where Mrs. Christie fled at the time of her disappearance in 1926. It was one of the most respectable and prominent hotels in the north of England. (Photo credit: Walter Scott)

Deputy Chief Constable William Kenward (arms outstretched) directs a party of searchers. It was to this police officer that Agatha Christie sent the mysterious fourth letter which indicated that she might have been the victim of foul play.

Some of the 15,000 volunteers who turned out in answer to the police and newspaper requests. They are pictured here searching the Silent Pool near Guilford, where it was thought that Mrs. Christie's body might be found.

The Harry Codd Hydro Dance Band—the Happy Hydro Boys, as they were known to residents. Bob Tappin, third from left, was the first person to link "Mrs. Teresa Neele," the good-looking guest, with the name of Mrs. Agatha Christie, the missing crime writer. He went to the police with their suspicions. All were later to receive a silver pencil from Colonel Christie in reward for their efforts.

Agatha Christie as she appeared in 1932, during her most productive period, with such successes as *Peril at End House, Why Didn't They Ask Evans?*, and *Murder on the Orient Express*. (Photo credit: Bassano)

This portrait of Agatha Christie was also taken in 1933 at the beginning of her creative success. By this time, she had been married for three years to Professor Max Mallowan, who remained by her side until she died. (Photo credit: Raymond Mander and Joe Mitchenson Theatre Collection)

Agatha Christie at her dispensing desk at University College Hospital, London, during the 1939–45 war. She qualified as a dispenser by gaining the Society of Apothecaries certificate. (Photo credit: Raymond Mander and Joe Mitchenson Theatre Collection)

In her own houses (and at one time she owned eight), Agatha Christie was always known to the staff as "Lady M." Although her work left little time for actual housework, she sometimes did the cooking and claimed that she was "a very good cook." However busy she was, she always found time to do the flowers, which were a feature of her many houses. This picture was taken at Winterbrook House, her Wallingford home in Berkshire, where she lived during the spring and autumn. (Photo credit: Popperfoto)

In her approach to work, Agatha Christie was totally professional. She took her portable typewriter into whatever room she fancied at the moment and got on with her three-finger typing. Much of the plotting of her books was done in the garden or on country walks. (Photo credit: Popperfoto)

Agatha Christie and her husband, Sir Max Mallowan, on one of the brisk walks which became a feature of their married life. (Photo credit: UPI)

Dame Agatha Christie, pictured in 1946, sits with her husband, Sir Max Mallowan, on a gun rampart dating from Napoleonic times, on their estate, Greenway, in Devonshire. (Photo credit: Popperfoto)

The boathouse and bathing place at Greenway, home of Agatha Christie and her husband, Sir Max Mallowan. (Photo credit: Popperfoto)

and held a consultation over Mrs. Christie's health. Later that evening they issued the following cautious statement: "After careful examination of Mrs. Agatha Christie this afternoon we have formed the opinion that she is suffering from an unquestionable loss of memory and that for her future welfare she should be spared all anxiety and excitement." It was signed Donald Core, MD., Henry Wilson, M.R.C.S

Dr. Core was a lecturer in neurology at Manchester University, an assistant honorary physician to Manchester Royal Infirmary, and author of several works on nervous disorders. Dr. Wilson was a Cheadle general practitioner.

Despite Colonel Christie's report and the medical diagnosis, many members of the public, as well as the press, found their explanations unacceptable. There were simply too many anomalies.

At no time during her stay at the Harrogate Hydro did the vivacious Mrs. Christie give the appearance of a woman suffering from loss of memory or ill health.

The choice for a pseudonym of the name "Neele" was hardly consistent with loss of memory.

Colonel Christie was later to give his explanation to reporters: "My wife has been to South Africa and she does know people by the name of Neele. There is also a Teresa in her family. In her confusion she must have chosen these names to fit in with her new identity."

A woman who has allegedly lost her identity and was reported to have only between £5 and £10 on her is not likely to have been able to buy the new clothes that she did. Her two bank accounts had been stopped by the police and there were no credit cards then, therefore she must have had a considerable amount of money on her.

There was also the odd incident that during the week in London previous to her disappearance, when she had clearly been Mrs. Agatha Christie, she had lost a diamond ring at Harrods. When she realized this she wrote to the store from Harrogate describing the ring and asking that it be forwarded to Mrs. Teresa Neele, giving the address of the hotel at Harrogate. And the store did.

Discussing the case with Dr. Anthony Storr, clinical lecturer in psychiatry at Oxford University, some fifty years later, he explained the possibility of the veracity of Mrs. Christie's suffering from amnesia.

"Your description of her going away and taking on another identity is something which psychiatrists are familiar with although it is not now terribly common. It is called a hysterical fugue, the fugue meaning 'flight from,' and there have been well-authenticated instances of people who disappear and perhaps are found a year or two later or a month or two later in some completely different place having assumed a different identity, having taken on a job, and apparently remembering nothing of what went on before or how they got there.

"It is a well-recognized condition in people under great strain or tension. It is escaping from the mental as well as the physical pain of a situation if things have become too intolerable.

"I think the fact that she took on the identity of the mistress is interesting. Here is a hated person—a person she must have resented passionately—and yet she puts herself in her shoes. In her disturbed state she may well have thought, 'How can I be like her to get my husband's affection back. How can I put myself in her shoes?' Something of that kind must have been going on in her mind.

"You remember the play *Black Chiffon* when a lady stole a black nightdress and there was a great defense about it. This is rather the same sort of thing."

The medical profession recognizes three types of fugues. In *Modern Clinical Psychiatry*, Alfred Noise wrote: "In fugues of short duration the patient usually wanders aimlessly, is highly emotional and when found is agitated and confused."

Almost all the people vitally concerned in this case are now dead: Agatha Christie, Colonel Christie, his wife, the former Nancy Neele, and Deputy Chief Constable Kenward.

I was only able to track down four who are still alive. Lord Ritchie Calder, who lives in Edinburgh, Mrs. Gladys Kenward Dobson, daughter of Deputy Chief Constable William Kenward, Tom Roberts, now retired, who as a young police recruit took part in the hunt, and W. K. ("Bill") Hoenes, retired editor-in-chief of the Middlesex County *Press*, who had just been recruited to the staff of the Harrogate *Herald*.

The press's suggestions that the whole escapade was a publicity stunt are preposterous. Mrs. Christie neither sought nor needed publicity. She was already a best-selling author and a woman of substantial means. She had always considered publicity to be vulgar.

Writing to Christianna Brand, a fellow member of the Detection Club, just a few years before her death, Agatha Christie said that the press had always made it out to be a publicity stunt but she preferred this to airing her private life in public. As she said, anyone who knew her well at all would realize how publicity had always embarrassed her horribly.

She also explained that it was the result of having had too many troubles all at once—the death of her mother after a harrowing illness, earache, toothache, gastritis, lapses of memory, sleepwalking, and buckets of tears.

The doctors gave their opinion, the family had its story, but as a woman of many years' experience and having researched the entire episode for many months, I am of the opinion that Mrs. Agatha Christie knew exactly what she was doing.

Mentally distraught, filled with revenge, and in the degradation of her misery, she just did what many other women would have also done. She decided to teach her husband a lesson.

In her modesty she could not possibly have foreseen that once the powerful press got hold of such a story, an incident that should have remained private would be fanned up into a sensation. She had only one recourse and that was to sit tight until she was found and stick to her story of amnesia.

Was she role-playing or testing a theory from the fantastic world of crime that she had created. She had once dedicated a book to "all those who lead monotonous lives, in the hope that they may experience at second hand the delights and dangers of adventure." Had her own life, estranged emotionally from her husband, become unbearably lonely, driving her to seek new excitements?

In one of her short stories, "The Disappearance of Mr. Davenheim," Agatha Christie had a discussion between two of her detectives about the possibility of being able to disappear. About the three categories relating to disappearance: the most common was the voluntary disappearance; second, the much abused "loss of memory" case—rare, but occasionally genuine; and third, the muder, and a more or less successful disposal of the body.

Today, fifty years later, Lord Ritchie Calder sticks to his theory:

"If she had intended suicide and if her body had been found in the Silent Pool, I have no doubt from what I knew of the police attitude, that Colonel Christie would have been held, on circumstantial evidence.

"Instead she found out that she did not have to go to the trouble of committing suicide, she just had to disappear and the police would be after him and make his life impossible, which they did. And there she was, sitting in Harrogate, reading the papers every day, and enjoying it."

All through my research on this period of Agatha Christie's life I felt that there was something missing. Something that would tie the whole miserable story together and make it understandable.

By now I had spoken to a great many people, spent a long time in the British Museum library reading old newspapers and documents of fifty years ago, and the Home Office had also opened its files for me.

The newspaper coverage was not conclusive. The press wrote of three letters—three vital clues in the mystery. The letters were addressed to Colonel Christie, her brother-in-law, Captain Campbell Christie, and her secretary, Miss Charlotte Fisher. Lord Ritchie Calder called them "Agatha's paper chase."

At last in a lonely farm cottage in the West Country of England I tracked down Gladys Kenward Dobson, whose father, Deputy Chief Constable William Kenward of the Surrey Constabulary, had taken such a stand in his continued searching at Newlands Corner.

As I drove up in the pouring rain she was waiting at the gate to meet me. Her gray, curly hair tossed about her head in the wind. She was standing with the help of a walking stick, since she is now partially disabled, but the eyes were clear and the voice authoritative. Her brain was crisp and her memory astonishing for a seventy-five-year-old. Many years of active service in the police force as her father's confidential secretary had seen to that.

Gladys Kenward Dobson still has strong affiliations with the Surrey Constabulary and each year she is the only woman guest at the reunion dinner to which she donates a trophy of a magnum of champagne. She is part of "the old days"; the men love her and every year there is a get-together photograph taken with this diminutive woman seated in the front row flanked by grinning retired police officers.

We had spoken on the telephone several times at great length but she would not relent and see me personally. Now eyeball to eyeball she put me through three grilling hours. Only after I had described her father's elegant flowing signature on his secret Home Office report, which I had seen, would she expand.

"Yes, there was a fourth letter. It was addressed to my father and marked "private and confidential," posted on the Friday night that she went missing. He received it in the 10 A.M. mail on Saturday and brought it to our home nearby to show me before going over immediately to inform the Sunningdale Police Station and begin investigations."

The letter was from a woman who told how she feared for her life and that she was frightened what might happen to her. She was appealing for help.

The signature on that letter was Agatha Christie.

CHAPTER EIGHT

WHATEVER UNITED FRONT the Christie family and relatives had shown in public was not to be reinforced in private. It would have been appropriate if husband and wife could have been reconciled after the distress of the past ten days but they were not. For both Agatha Christie and Colonel Christie the recriminations on both sides from family, close friends, and the press had become unbearable. There was no way back.

On December 17, Colonel Christie left Abney Hall and returned to London but his wife remained there recuperating until January 15. Whatever the cause of her total physical and mental collapse it was obvious to everyone concerned that the gay, fun-loving woman who had danced the Charleston at the Harrogate Hydro was now in the depths of a dark and disturbing *crise de nerfs*.

In an effort to comfort her, Rosalind, her small daughter, was brought up from Sunningdale by her nurse and remained with her mother until after Christmas. According to a statement given out by Colonel Christie to the *Daily Express* before he left for London: "She remembers nothing for two or three years and does not even remember her child."

In the excitement of the moment Colonel Christie apparently exaggerated, as until now the "amnesia" theory had only been a question of days.

The cost of the whole case had been overestimated by the press and some reports were as high as £2,000 to £3,000. Nothing could have been further from the truth. The number of police quoted as being engaged in the search was totally wrong and questions were asked in the House of Commons concerning this.

According to Deputy Chief Constable Kenward's report to the Home Office on the first two days of the search only thirty to thirty-eight regular police were involved. Many officers voluntarily gave up their Sunday to join the large army of volunteer special constables and the public.

The airplane and special dredging equipment had all been given voluntarily and this also included the various packs of bloodhounds and other hunting dogs.

Deputy Chief Constable Kenward placed the police cost of the whole operation at something like £25, which was used in the hire of conveyances and refreshments for his officers. Colonel Christie paid the £6 bill for the printing of special posters.

In a statement to the press Colonel Christie said: "I am not prepared to pay a penny for other costs. I pay rates and taxes and the police are there for the benefit of the public. I did not call them in. They were engineered into this by the agitation of the press. If I am to believe the press today the only expense that was incurred was that of providing tea and buns for some special constables."

The public, who had taken immense interest in the story from its first days, were generous to help. Deputy Chief Constable Kenward's office was flooded with letters every day, all enclosing money to defray expenses.

"The public have sent so many contributions toward the cost of the police services that the total would be sufficient to build a house," he reported to the *Daily Mail*.

The letters came from all classes of the public and one man wrote that as soon as the full cost of the search had been estimated he wished to be told as he would send a check to cover all expenses. All the unsolicited contributions were acknowledged by a busy police secretarial staff and returned to the donors.

Typical of the angry letters to the press concerning the expense of the case was one dated December 14 and written to the editor of the *Daily Mail.*

> Sir, May I ask without any disrespect to Mrs. Christie, what is the principle which guides the police in cases of this kind. Hundreds of police have been hunting, a number of high officials have presumably dropped their normal activities to engage in the search, thousands of pounds have been spent, and today it has been decided to employ divers at considerable further expense.
>
> I do not object to these remarkable and almost unparalleled efforts. I merely ask would they be made if I disappeared, and if not, why?
>
> Signed: An Ordinary Woman.

The three members of the band who were responsible for recognizing Agatha Christie and informing the police each received a silver pencil engraved "A. Christie." The A stood for Archibald not Agatha and was accompanied by a letter of gratitude. All three are dead today but Mrs. Schofield, widow of Reg Schofield, told me that her husband used his pencil all through his life and lost it only a few months before he died a couple of years ago.

The newspapers' relentless pursuing of the Agatha Christie disappearance story was not entirely just to be sensational. They belonged to the middle class, which earlier in the year had made news during the General Strike when sympathy for the miners and the discipline of the Trade Union Council had brought the whole country to a standstill. It was the middle classes who kept the country running.

As the *Illustrated London News* wrote: "We feel that the heart of England must be sound when we read . . . that Mr. C. E. Pitman, the Oxford stroke, is driving a train on the Great Western Railways from Bristol to Gloucester . . . The Headmaster of Eton [Dr. Arlington] and about fifty of his assistant masters have enrolled as special constables . . . Lord Chesham is driving a train. The Hon. Lionel Tennyson is a 'special.' Mr. Roger Wethered, the golfer, was yesterday working on a food convoy from the docks . . . But perhaps the most encouraging fact of all was that at Plymouth, on May 8, the police played a football match with the strikers, and the wife of the Chief Constable kicked off."

Colonel Archibald Christie and his wife Agatha Christie were very much a part of the spirit of England in the twenties—he as a glamorous ex-war hero and she as a successful writer—so that anything they did would have made news headlines.

Mrs. Christie's recovery could not have been hastened by the reviews of her new novel, *The Big Four*, which was published by Collins at the end of January. It was a fanciful collection of four stories in which a Chinese mandarin, American millionaire, French woman scientist, and English actor form a cartel and plot the downfall of civilization. Hercule Poirot, and the Belgian's short-lived brother Achille, are called in to solve the problems. As the *Daily Mail* was to write:

"We are glutted with murders and thrills. Those who come to expect subtlety as well as sensation in Mrs. Christie's writing will be disappointed."

Early in 1927 Agatha Christie returned south to make the painful decision of putting Styles plus all its contents on the market for £5,500. It was withdrawn when it did not reach the reserve price but she never lived there again and wanted to shed all past associations of her fourteen-year marriage to Colonel Christie.

Like thousands of other young people in Britain, the failure of the Christie marriage may well have been the result of the war years they spent apart. Separated for long periods, they had each developed their own interests and own independence. Another cause could have been that Archie Christie had become a golfing fanatic, leaving his wife for the golf links every weekend.

Though Agatha Christie has written fully in her autobiography of the collapse of her marriage, it is fascinating that she completely omits any reference to her disappearance, the one facet of her life that her readers want to know about. Was the subject too painful or just too embarrassing?

Sebastian Earl, who knew Colonel Christie in his first jobs after the war, is one of the few people alive who knew them both during this period.

"Well, I disliked her strongly. I just didn't like her. We were to meet at various dinner parties. I used to rack my head to know what to say to her during our conversations. He, on the other hand, was a delightful chap, handsome, intelligent, and a great charmer.

"I was also to know his second wife only slightly. She was not particularly pretty but much easier to talk to."

With the added incentive that she was now on her own, Agatha Christie was determined to recapture the reputation she had achieved with *The Murder of Roger Ackroyd*. Money would not necessarily have been her first consideration: it is much more likely to have been a consuming desire to bury her head back in the world of her own fanciful creation and to prove to herself that she could write another best seller.

As she explained: "I used to write poetry. That was in my age of innocence before crime attracted me. When once you adopt crime it's difficult to give it up. I know I could never do so. Crime is like drugs."

In 1928 *The Mystery of the Blue Train*, which had given her so many problems, was finally published. She had used a setting that she was familiar with, the luxury boat train from London to the Riviera on which she had last traveled with her husband in 1926. Considering how she disliked the book, because of its associations during her unhappy marriage period, it is to her immense credit that she was able to finish it at all.

All through that amazing career, Agatha Christie was extremely tough with herself—and always totally professional.

In the 1920s England was still decidedly backward in the way it handled divorce and the obtaining of a divorce was distasteful and difficult. It was not until long after the war that in fact there was no stigma attached and the breaking down of a marriage was at last socially accepted. The last social drawbridge was when the royal enclosure at Ascot admitted divorced people.

In April 1928, Mrs. Christie was granted a divorce from her husband. The grounds were adultery with an unknown woman in a London hotel and Miss Nancy Neele was in no way involved.

There was no defense and Richard Edward Huskisson, a solicitor's clerk, and Albert Clarke, a waiter at the Grosvenor Hotel in London, were called as witnesses. Both Colonel and Mrs. Christie wished to have a quick divorce and this unsavory way was the only course open to them.

The president of the court, Lord Merrivale, in his judgment said that Mrs. Christie had made out her case.

"It is difficult to believe that a gallant gentleman like Colonel Christie would resort to a hotel on various occasions with some unknown woman in order to rid himself of a marriage which had become distasteful to him. But it has happened in this case and therefore the court grants a decree nisi with costs and custody of the one child of the marriage to Mrs. Christie."

Colonel Christie and Miss Neele were to marry as soon as the decree nisi was made absolute and lived happily ever after until their deaths over thirty years later. Mrs. Nancy Christie was to die of cancer in 1958 and Mr. Christie, who suffered with asthma for many years, died four years later. Their son, Archibald Christie III, entered into an associated company of his father's and is still alive today.

Unpalatable as it must have been for Agatha Christie to retain her former husband's name, her publisher advised her to do so as by now she had built up her own established reading public. Her readers would have been confused if she suddenly called herself by a man's name as she suggested.

Now that her life had sorted itself out and she was once again writing fluently, in 1930 Agatha Christie decided to take a long holiday and chose the West Indies. She had bought her tickets and everything had been booked when suddenly she changed her mind and decided instead to go to Baghdad. It was totally unlike her normal behavior and she was never able to explain the reason afterward except that fate had always played a hand in her life. "You don't write your own fate, your fate comes to you" was one of her favorite axioms.

Antiques, archaeology, anything old and mysterious interested Agatha Christie. During her visit to Baghdad she met Leonard Woolley, a distant acquaintance of her family, and was invited to visit the site where he was in charge of the joint British Museum and Museum of the University of Pennsylvania Expedition to Ur of the Chaldees.

She quickly became friendly with Mrs. Woolley and was encouraged to remain with the digging team. She proved to be such a congenial companion and was so adept at piecing small fragments of broken treasures together that she was asked to return the following year, which she did.

This again was coincidence simply because as yet she had not caught "the digging bug" to the same degree as she did the following year. On her return the next winter one of the digging team was a shy graduate of New College, Oxford, who up till now was known more for his passion for Assyrian ivory figures than for women.

Max Mallowan, a classical scholar, had turned to archaeology by accident more than intent when it was first suggested to him at Oxford that he join Leonard Woolley's team. He had in fact been part of it the year before when Agatha Christie had visited Ur but an operation for appendicitis had prevented him from being at the site when she was there.

What was the intriguing chemistry that brought a shy, unworldly young man together with a popular writer who was divorced and fourteen years older than he was? Their love of detection was at least part of it.

While Agatha Christie spent her time investigating the lives of people surrounding her and the motives behind their behavior pattern, Max Mallowan set his sights on a civilization that had vanished 6,000 years before. The results in either case were not too dissimilar.

Sir Max, knighted in 1968, became one of Britain's most distinguished archaeologists and the author of several books on the subject, including the definitive work on excavation at the biblical Calah, *Nimrud and Its Remains*. He is a Fellow of All Souls, the most elite of the Oxford colleges, a professor emeritus of western Asiatic archaeology in the University of London, and a trustee of the British Museum. For many years he was editorial adviser to Penguin Books archaeological list and was responsible for persuading many distinguished scholars to write for it. His own autobiography, *Mallowan's Memoirs* (Collins), published in September 1977, was completed during the last months of his wife's life.

During the archaeological season in the Middle East which stretched from October to March, Katherine Woolley, who later became Dame Kathleen Kenyon, designated the young Mallowan to show her distinguished guest Baghdad and the desert. Dame Kathleen was a forceful woman and did not take no for an answer. Dutifully Max Mallowan undertook the task. It was during one of these trips when the car bogged down in the sand that he noticed Agatha Christie's reaction. She accepted the calamity with merry complacency. He knew at once that here indeed was a most unusual woman.

Love entered the friendship when Mrs. Woolley suggested that Max Mallowan should be Mrs. Christie's traveling companion on a trip back to England. They were passengers on the Orient Express and this was to be the first of many trips together on that gloriously romantic train.

What better place for romance to bloom than in the mahogany and cut-glass ambiance of the restaurant car with its soft-shaded silk lamp shades and superb food. "A little caviar, Madame? . . . "I can recommend the Château Mouton" . . . "Our bombe glacée is flavored with orange water and studded with crystallized violets" . . . "Would Madame prefer Indian, Ceylon, or China tea, with milk or lemon."

And outside each day a different panorama, picture postcards floating by, the mountains of Switzerland, descending into the plains of Italy dotted with cypress trees, along the wild coastline from Trieste into Yugoslavia, on to Turkey, the gateway to the Middle East; the shining pale glow of Istanbul in the early morning, crossing the Bosporus to the Asian coast. Into a waiting train at Haidar Packa for the final step to Aleppo and Beirut.

During those five days on the Orient Express people fell in and out of love. Lives were changed. Destinies were plotted.

The Orient Express was in fact to become part of the very fabric of Agatha Christie's life. Not only was she to travel on it almost every year with her husband but it was the setting for one of her most successful novels. It was also to be the film made from one of her books which she enjoyed the most. Inexplicably the première of *Murder on the Orient Express* in 1974 was to be the last time Dame Agatha was seen in public.

On September 11, 1930, Mrs. Agatha Christie and Professor Max Mallowan were married quietly in Edinburgh to avoid the sensation that it would have caused in the London press. The ceremony took place at St. Cuthbert's Church in the district of St. Giles with her daughter and two secretaries, Charlotte and Mary Fisher, as witnesses. In order to avoid publicity and to conform to the Scottish marriage laws Agatha Christie had lived for fifteen days in a hotel on the Isle of Skye.

On the marriage certificate the maiden name of the bride's mother had been Anglicized from Beochmer to Beamer and her father's occupation was given as a produce broker.

Another irregularity of the marriage license was how the newlyweds overcame for posterity the fourteen-year difference in their ages. Agatha Christie gave her age as thirty-seven, whereas it should have been forty, and Max Mallowan wrote his as thirty-one, whereas in reality he was only twenty-six years old. They made sure that at least on paper the difference did not look so harsh.

Undoubtedly Agatha Christie belonged to an age when women enjoyed their privacy and went to any lengths to preserve it. It was also a custom that all family secrets should be kept well away from probing public eyes. A little doctoring of documents was considered perfectly acceptable and even logical and it probably never entered her head that she was in fact distorting the truth.

Was it some inborn feminine wile that made this intelligent, highly successful woman fall prey to such vanity? Or was it all part of the mysterious world of Agatha Christie's own books where deception and truth went hand in hand.

The Mallowans had bought a house at 22 Cresswell Place in London, which Agatha Christie had decorated from top to bottom herself. It was a charming house with a music room at the top where she intended to play the piano and do her writing.

Almost immediately after the wedding Professor and Mrs. Mallowan set off on a honeymoon which took them on their first trip abroad together.

"We will go to Venice and then wander through Greece," she

told Allen Lane. In confiding in him about her marriage, Agatha Christie said that she had been quite determined never to marry again and "did not know how it happened."

She explained that Max Mallowan was a great deal younger than herself and that it was "very unsuitable." Allen Lane had in fact met Max Mallowan but as Agatha Christie was quick to point out that Lane would not remember him because he never spoke. She added that she could not think how she could be such a fool—but safety at all costs was really a repulsive creed.

People who saw Agatha Christie at that time were captivated by her happiness. As she was to tell her publisher: "Oh, Allen, 1930 is a marvellous year."

Max Mallowan of the impeccable manners and scholarly charm could not have been more different from extrovert Archie Christie.

The marriage lasted forty-six years and was to be an indelible influence on Agatha Christie, who divided her life with uncommon dexterity between her own writing and assisting her husband in photographing, restoring, and cataloguing his archaeological finds.

It was to be a marriage of great companionship and enjoyment. In an interview with the late Godfrey Winn many years later she said:

"Well, I don't think mutual tastes matter in the least. Those of my husband are academic and intellectual while mine could be described as frivolous and fictional. However, we seem to manage splendidly. Now mutual respect, that is important. Equally so in all lasting friendships."

If there were any inner scars left from her nervous breakdown and "amnesia" period, after her marriage to Max Mallowan they were not apparent and she had now entered into an extremely contented period of her life.

Agatha Christie had always traveled a great deal—Australia, New Zealand, the United States of America, South Africa, the Middle East, as well as the more conventional trips to Europe, and now after her marriage were to come several months wandering round the idyllic countryside of Greece and Iraq with her new husband.

During the periods she was away, daughter Rosalind was sent

95

first to a local school in Torquay and then to boarding school at Bexhill-on-Sea and there was always Agatha Christie's sister Madge to look after her during the shorter holidays.

They were halcyon days at Ashfield during the summer holidays of the early thirties. Agatha Christie herself did not do any housework and employed a cook-housekeeper, Mrs. Potter, who looked after the house while her husband worked in the Torquay General Post Office. Their son Fred, a playmate for tomboyish Rosalind, is now a refrigeration engineer in Torquay.

Agatha Christie liked to amuse herself painting the garden furniture and personally always kept the house filled with vases of flowers.

Most of all she enjoyed escaping with Peter her wire-haired terrier into the small wild and wooded part of the garden where coltsfoot, brambles, and shrubs were allowed to grow naturally. Here was the summer house where she went when she wanted to be alone, and half hidden in the shrubbery was a marble statue which was particularly effective on moonlight nights.

The small walled garden, which had once been an orchard, was now covered over and laid with wooden parquet flooring; it had been turned into an indoor games room where quoits and other hand games were played. There was much laughter at Ashfield in those days.

The interior of the house was cozy, comfortable, and surprisingly colorful. Every year there was a great painting program and even if Mrs. Christie had chosen the paint herself and workmen had completed it, on her return next holidays, if she did not like it, the whole thing had to be done again: this is in fact exactly what happened to the drawing room.

Professor Mallowan's bedroom was given a royal blue and red treatment and an amusing touch to his bathroom were transfers on the walls reminiscent of his various archaeological trips. A favorite guest bedroom had walls and ceiling covered with wallpaper with oranges and green leaves as its design. It looked like an orangery transported from fairyland.

Through the early years various rooms had been added to the white stone house; a whole new section contained a dining room, two bedrooms, and the schoolroom on top.

The schoolroom had been left with cupboards of toys just as it was when she was a child and it is here at an old bureau that Agatha Christie worked during those summer holidays. Although she did very little actual writing at Ashfield she spent some period of each day there alone planning and plotting books, making notes, or proofreading future books.

The whole atmosphere of the house was congenial. With Mrs. Christie's beautiful manners, she put children, staff, and tradespeople at ease. There was a house rule that all workmen should be treated with the utmost courtesy. Special mugs had been bought for their morning coffee and afternoon tea and, should they work late into the evening, Agatha Christie always requested Mrs. Potter to cook a meal for them.

With her enjoyment and knowledge of good food the meals at Ashfield were English cooking at its most delicious. Mrs. Potter, a splendidly capable woman, was always busy in the kitchen and did all her cooking on an old black lead stove which was coal-fired. It was her pride and joy and she kept it in immaculate condition with frequent coatings of black lead and lots of elbow grease.

Agatha Christie was always trying to persuade her to try the new appliances coming on to the market but she stuck to her stove until it literally began to fall to pieces and was replaced with an Aga solid-fuel-burning one.

All the cooking was wholesome but had a refinement seldom found in the family life of the middle class. There was always cream, bowls of thick Devonshire cream, and one of Mrs. Potter's specialities was chicken fried in butter with fresh cream poured over just before it was served bubbling hot.

Banana cream was another favorite of the family, and apple hedgehog with sliced almonds stuck all over to make the quills. Coffee *gâteau* and creamy fruit fools made from raspberries, red currants, and strawberries were treats everyone enjoyed.

Agatha Christie's own favorite drink was a concoction of half milk and half cream.

In the larder was an old icebox and every other day men from the ice factory would deliver huge slabs of ice, carrying them in with metal tongs. Lobsters were delivered regularly as deviled lobster was a favorite of the Mallowan family.

Nothing was ostentatious or vulgar although it was a house of plenty. In the larder hanging from hooks during the game season there would always be a brace of pheasants, partridge, snipe, and quail. The cellar was well stocked with shelves of bottles of wine which, judging by the sediment, had probably been laid down during Mrs. Miller's lifetime.

Bathing and picnics were always a high spot of the summer holidays. Agatha Christie used to scoop up all the children and her house guests, which invariably included the two Fisher sisters, Mary and Charlotte. Two of the most enjoyable picnic places were Labrador Bay, which is halfway between Torquay and Shaldon, and Teignmouth.

The food, which was always delicious and packed in a large basket hamper, was comprised of sandwiches made of turkey and chicken, Mrs. Potter's homemade pheasant paste, and various salads.

Agatha Christie was a strong swimmer and regularly went swimming in the sea well into her old age.

Rosalind Christie and Fred Potter enjoyed playing in the garden when Hawkins the gardener was around. On one occasion Fred found a wasps' nest and became fascinated watching the wasps come out of the hole at one end. As all wasps' nests were usually destroyed by Hawkins, Fred thought he would do the job for him. He placed a large stone over the entrance but the wasps promptly found another exit. Not to be outsmarted, the boy then rammed a hollow tube down this end. Within a minute twenty or thirty furious wasps came belting up through the tubing and made straight for the back of his neck.

As fast as he ran to the house he was followed by the whole swarm of wasps in an angry stream. The child was crying furiously as Mrs. Potter got to work with the "blue bag," every household's remedy in those days.

Agatha Christie was working in the schoolroom but on hearing all the fuss came downstairs to see what it was all about. This small domestic incident gave her an idea for a Poirot short story, "Wasps' Nest," and she also used the wasp theme in one of her full-length novels, *Death in the Clouds*, where a wasp flying round in a luxury air liner gave the murderer the perfect excuse to kill his victim with a blowpipe dart covered with arrow poison.

Time and time again Agatha Christie stored such trivialities in her memory bank to be brought out and used in her books at a future date. She never wasted one small experience.

Though she was never known to pay high wages, there existed between Agatha Christie and her employees a great deal of friendship and respect.

Fred Potter still cherishes the autographed copy of *Dumb Witness*, whose American title is *Poirot Loses a Client*, which Agatha Christie gave to Mrs. Potter because she was fond of the family dog, Peter, who inspired that book.

Easters were always spent at Ashfield with a large party of friends, relatives, and children. An annual event was the Easter egg hunt in which everyone took part, including the staff and their families. The eggs, each with a name on, were hidden in various parts of the garden. Everyone was told how many eggs he or she had to find and if they found someone else's egg the player had to replace it secretly.

Agatha Christie had always enjoyed the company of young people, and her own happy childhood was never far away in her mind. As opposed to Rosalind, other children were slightly in awe of Mrs. Christie. With her reserved nature she tended to hold them at a distance and did not involve herself too closely.

Between mother and daughter there was a strong devotion which was to endure until Agatha Christie's death. During the last years of her mother's life at Greenway, Rosalind, then a middle-aged woman, took delight in finding the first violets of spring and always placed a small posy on the table by her four-poster bed.

Agatha Christie always said that Rosalind was her sternest critic and she alone was able to guess the ending when she read her mother's books.

Charles Hawkins was the gardener at Ashfield for many years, and as a child Rosalind and young Fred Potter took great delight in tormenting him, which somehow he managed to accept with good grace. He was a plain, even-tempered man.

There is the family story of the day that Hawkins put up a hammock for Agatha Christie between two trees. On completing the task she asked him: "Is it safe . . . is it completely safe?"

"Yes'm," he replied, touching his cap. "I am an expert on knots and ropes."

Agatha Christie, who was certainly well built at that time, climbed in. She just had time to become comfortably settled before the "expert" knots came undone and dumped her fair and square on the ground.

Hawkins was not renowned for his tact and "fell about laughing" only to receive a verbal lashing from an irate employer. Hawkins had to check his own knots in future.

At the end of every summer when the holidays came to an end it was a heart-rending time for everyone leaving Ashfield. Rooms were closed up, furniture put under dust sheets, and the old house went to sleep until it was opened up again a few months later. The Potters stayed on as Mrs. Potter always found plenty to do keeping the house maintained.

It is doubtful that Agatha Christie would ever have liked to live in Devon permanently. She was a restless woman who enjoyed moving and a change of scenery as so much of her life was led within the confines of her own study, sitting writing. At one time she is said to have owned eight houses, some of which she let when she no longer needed them. She claimed that her passion for houses stemmed from childhood and the hours spent playing with her doll house.

With her ever increasing passion for privacy and to escape from readers who came to Torquay hoping to catch a glimpse of the now famous author, in 1939 Agatha Christie bought a secluded Georgian mansion called Greenway House on the upper reaches of the river Dart above Dartmouth. It was once the home of Sir Walter Raleigh, half brother of Sir Humphrey Gilbert, of Compton Castle. The Mallowans bought it from the family of the late Charles Williams, who was Member of Parliament for Torquay.

During the war years the Admiralty occupied Greenway, as the family called the house, and the story goes that an American serviceman stationed there painted a colorful frieze round one of the reception rooms with various scenes of naval life, which he was unable to complete. When Agatha Christie moved back to the house after the war she tried through many channels to find the

American as she wanted him to come back and finish his work of art. She had grown inordinately fond of it.

Greenway became the family holiday home and is now occupied by Mrs. Rosalind Hicks and her husband, Anthony. Grandchildren still arrive over the summer holidays and the house has acquired much of the happy family atmosphere of Ashfield.

Agatha Christie had hoped that the Potter family would have moved with her to Greenway but instead Mrs. Potter decided to open her own boardinghouse and transferring to Dartmouth would also have meant that Mr. Potter would have had to give up his senior job in the Torquay post office. For years after she had moved to Greenway, Mrs. Mallowan used to call on Mrs. Potter during her summer holidays and they would talk over old times together.

All during the thirties Agatha Christie continued to turn out one major book a year as well as short stories. She had not yet begun writing her own stage plays but saw several of her novels adapted and produced in London. Many critics think that these years were vintage Christie, with such best sellers as *Murder at the Vicarage* (1930), which introduced Miss Marple for the first time, in novel form, *Peril at End House* (1932), *Why Didn't They Ask Evans?* (1934) (called *The Boomerang Clue* in America), *Murder on the Orient Express* (1934) (tamely renamed *Murder in the Calais Coach* for America), *Death in the Clouds* (1935) (entitled *Death in the Air* for America), *The A.B.C. Murders* (1935) and *Death on the Nile* (1937).

CHAPTER NINE

IN THE LATE TWENTIES in London a unique and select club was formed among twenty-eight people which remains as mysterious today as it did then. The idea was dreamed up by Dorothy L. Sayers and Anthony Berkeley, who named it the Detection Club. Basically a dining club it has remarkably strict rules as to who is eligible and who is not.

The club is still selective, fastidious, and snobbish. Today its fifty members consider themselves the elite of the detection writers since they must be sponsored before acceptance by the committee. Once they have been elected there is a kind of unwritten law—a sort of understanding—that authors never mention to anyone that they have in fact become members. They just arrive at the next meeting as though by an act of God. An even stricter rule is that no member of the press is ever invited to any club activity.

Everything about the Detection Club is shrouded in mumbo-jumbo secrecy from that first moment when a sponsor lays on the committee table a couple of books written by the proposed member, to the hilarious quasi-comic highlight when he or she is actually initiated into the club. Masonry has nothing on the Detection Club for secrecy and ceremony.

The first president was G. K. Chesterton, the inventor of Father Brown, and original members included such established writers as Freeman Wills Crofts—kind, essentially modest, but very much a best seller—Anthony Berkeley, E. C. Bentley of *Trent's Last Case*, Hugh Walpole, Baroness Orczy, Dorothy L. Sayers, then at her most self-assertive, A. A. Milne, Clemence Dane, on whom Noel Coward is said to have modeled Madame Arcati, A. E. W. Mason, Helen Simpson, Gladys Mitchell, and surprisingly, Agatha Christie, who by nature was not a club person.

I write surprisingly since, with her shyness toward people she did not know, it is a wonder that Agatha Christie could ever face the initiation ceremony let alone share the presidency with Lord Gorell from 1958 till her death in 1976. But she did and quite obviously enjoyed every minute of it.

The club originally had seedy rooms in Gerrard Street, a colorful area in the middle of Soho which had an oyster bar at one end and ladies of the night at the other. Many of the upstairs rooms above the shops were places of residence for the prostitutes who worked in that area. Whatever it lacked in style Gerrard Street certainly had character. There was nothing posh about the normal meetings where members sat around drinking tea or beer and listening to Dorothy L. Sayers expound her view on life in general and detection writing in particular. Dorothy was a great one for talk.

In those days the twice yearly dining meetings, for which about fourteen members would turn up, were held at a restaurant called L'Escargot Bientu in Greek Street, round the corner from Gerrard Street. Though she was not president Dorothy L. Sayers always insisted on sitting at the head of the table. It was not until many years later that the dinner transferred to the Café Royal, by which time the membership had more than doubled. At these dinners the men wore dinner jackets and the women wore dinner dresses. For many years Dorothy L. Sayers appeared in her inevitable Chinese brocade jacket worn over a long black skirt and Agatha Christie would be in something like vieux rose Georgette or pale mauve cloque and tong-crimped hair. Most of the other women members wore a little black dress. The women members also all wore red carnations to signify that they were a member of the club until Christianna Brand begged and beseeched the other members that there should be a choice of red or white.

"I was always wearing mauve or some other color that shrieked with red," she recalls. Christianna was one of the youngest members and going through "my dressing-up time."

"I was thrilled to the marrow to be in this thing and I made up my mind that I would never have the same dress or my hair done the same way twice. I used to swirl myself in tulle and dress myself up like dog's muck—just for the fun of it."

The dinners had something of the air of a children's party about them and everyone was out to enjoy himself or herself. It was here that the strange initiation rituals took place and still do.

Imagine G. K. Chesterton in all his flamboyance and hugeness wrapped up like a parcel in robes of black and scarlet with a little cap topping his lionlike head. There he sat in the dark until the moment when the doors were opened and in came a procession of members who could have stepped straight from a Dennis Wheatley novel. Heading the column was the skull bearer. He or she carried a purple cushion on which rested a skull called Eric—no one today knows why—which had a lighted flashlight inside. Originally there was a candle but with the march of progress a flashlight was eventually substituted. In between the semiannual ceremonies I am told today that Eric lies ignominiously in a cupboard at the Café Royal. Behind the skull bearer trailed the other members, all carrying lighted candles and props relating to the detection writers' craft of murder—half a brick, phial of poison, a club or dagger, and so on.

In the days of Chesterton it must have been an occasion of colorful splendor as his voice boomed out the opening words of the ceremony: "What mean these lights . . . these candles, these symbols of death . . ." And thus on to the sonorous reading of the rules of the club which all members solemnly promise to obey.

Some of them are embarrassingly naïve, such as "not to eat peas off a knife" or "not to put your feet on the dinner table" and "not to put two mysterious Chinamen into one book" . . . and so on. Others are more serious—to promise to write the Queen's English at all times, not to use poisons unknown to science, not to use other writers' plots whether they are given under the influence of drink or not, and not to use a secret passage in order to assist the solution. If there is a passage it has to be mentioned earlier in the book so that the reader is aware of it.

One of the most serious rules, thought to have been instigated by Dorothy L. Sayers, is that members must put all their clues on the table so that if the reader is surprised at the end of the book, which every author hopes will happen, that he or she can then go back through the book and be able to say: "Oh yes, I didn't spot that." In recent years H. R. F. Keating (creator of Inspector Ghote) has transposed all the rules into verse, which makes them all much easier to remember.

In G. K. Chesterton the club had not only its most picturesque president but one of the most brilliant after-dinner speakers that England has produced in this century. His only rival was the Queen's Counsel Sir Patrick Hastings.

Chesterton was a witty speaker and always made fun of his size in the most delightful way. His anecdotes were delivered with verve and good humor, and his audience was spellbound.

In those early days half a dozen of the members decided to get together and write a book, the proceeds of which were to be paid into the club funds. Agatha Christie was asked to join in but when she was told that she would receive no money she changed her mind and said, "But surely we write for ourselves?"

In retelling the story to me Gladys Mitchell said that she had been amused and amazed as at the time Mrs. Christie was considered to be a financially successful writer whereas she was living on a teacher's salary and only made something like £50 out of each book she wrote.

"For me to sacrifice £14 was one thing and several of us felt that Agatha could have done that too. But she would not join in at all."

Nor does Gladys Mitchell ever remember Agatha Christie taking part in the small beer parties back in the club rooms in Gerrard Street after the official dinners. This was simply not her scene.

One of the most vivid memories of Agatha Christie during these early Detection Club days comes from Christianna Brand.

"Dorothy was very bossy and self-opinionated but I can't believe that Agatha Christie and Dorothy Sayers would ever have had a personal set-to in their lives, even if they had wanted to, as there would always have been eight or ten other people round them. There was never to my knowledge even the faintest bit of ill-feeling between them. Agatha was a very large-minded person. I don't think she could ever have been mean or bitchy. I am sure that there was nothing but niceness and kindness in her and after all both she and Dorothy were violently anti-publicity."

Both these authors had an absolute horror about giving interviews and rarely broke it.

Christianna Brand continued:

"We are not going to make a 'raree' show of ourselves," Dorothy would say. 'Raree' was one of her 'olden' words that she liked to punctuate her speech with.

"After the war we moved to rooms in Kingly Street behind Regent Street. Agatha would arrive in some kind of old fur coat she had in those days and slip quietly in at the back of the room. Dorothy would be sitting holding forth with her legs wide apart showing yards of blue Bloomers.

"I remember one time hearing her going on about what to do with Mac's ashes and how they had been trailed up and down the country. Agatha just sat there. You could almost hear her listening as she hung on every word."

When Dorothy L. Sayers' husband, Oswald Atherton Fleming, whom she called Mac, died, he left an express wish that his ashes should be scattered in a church in Lanarkshire, where most of his family were buried. The ashes lay around as Dorothy could not find the time nor inclination to dispose of them in the way her late husband wanted. Finally a doctor friend arrived at her house and promised to relieve her of all that remained of Mac—a small casket of ashes which had stood on the mantel shelf. Placing it in the boot of his car, he set off on holiday and when passing through Lanarkshire visited the churchyard and completed the job. Dorothy L. Sayers enjoyed recounting the story whenever she had a captive audience.

Dorothy L. Sayers' inauguration as president in 1949 was nearly a disaster. Just as everything was being prepared at the Café Royal some part of the regalia was found to be missing. It had been left in the club rooms at Gerrard Street. At Dorothy's instructions a party of five members piled into a taxi, accompanied by Norman Kendall, the assistant commissioner for crime at Scotland Yard. He went with them simply because although they all had keys to the club room on the third floor no one had a key to the main door, which was kept firmly locked.

It was with some apprehension that Kendall picked the lock while the others stood guard in case a policeman came along and caught him in the act.

Not everyone was delighted when it was suggested that Agatha Christie should be elected to the presidency in 1958. Several members stayed away and refrained from voting on the grounds that it was time that the co-founder of the club, Anthony Berkeley, should at last be given the honor which he had desperately longed for.

In addition to this Agatha Christie had made it quite clear when her name was suggested that she did not want the presidency at any price. It says much for Agatha Christie's personal prestige in the fifties that the majority of members wanted to have her because of the cachet her name would bring to the club.

"I cannot make a speech to save my life and I would be absolutely no good at it," Agatha Christie insisted at a preliminary meeting. But her objection was overruled when Lord Gorell, an ambitious man, jumped up and said that he would help Mrs. Christie out if he was made co-president.

Despite any nervousness that she might have felt on the night of her initiation Agatha Christie was splendid. As Harry Keating explained to me: "If you are going to do something absurd like that it is necessary to act while you do it. If you are terribly conscious about how silly it all is then it simply becomes something rather embarrassing. It's just an amusing thing that people do—like playing cricket."

Agatha Christie filled the Chesterton robes with aplomb, spoke up in a good clear voice, and did not giggle. She did it very well, onlookers remember.

As Keating says: "I remember saying to myself, 'Ah yes, you know, that's the little spark of whatever it was that she had. Here she was perfectly capable of hamming this up in just about the right way.'"

Dame Agatha remained in office until her death, as have all the other presidents, although she was not able to attend any of the dinners the last year of her life. True to her word, she did not make a single speech during her eighteen years of office.

Of the many members of the Detection Club with whom I talked only Michael Underwood can throw any light on her normality and ordinariness. Other members have no recollection at all of anything special about her.

During one dinner he was sitting close to Dame Agatha at the top table where, among the special guests that had been invited, were Kingsley Amis and his wife, Elizabeth Jane Howard. Michael Underwood was saying how he liked to "toddle around the kitchen." Agatha Christie then kept everyone spellbound as she told him the best way to make meringues and éclairs, with Elizabeth Jane Howard chiming in with her views.

As Michael Underwood told me: "I remember thinking what a charming picture it was. These two eminent lady writers giving tips to a bachelor on cooking."

Elizabeth Jane Howard only faintly remembers the conversation but what does stay in her mind is "Dame Agatha's beautiful manners and that she behaved neither like somebody who was very famous nor somebody who was very old."

During her term as president Agatha Christie delighted in turning these dinner occasions into a family party and would arrive not only with Sir Max Mallowan, her daughter, son-in-law, and grandson, but with several younger friends of his.

Sir Max was extremely popular among members and at one of the smaller dinners which was held at the Garrick Club, Michael Underwood remembers him going up to somebody and saying: "I don't think we have ever met before. I'm Agatha's husband." "I thought, well there he is a man famous in his own right, introducing himself to someone like this."

Agatha Christie was always interested in other crime writers and what they were doing. She was totally void of jealousy and went out of her way to be generous.

When writer Nigel Moorland was editing the *Edgar Wallace Mystery Magazine* he was in touch with Agatha Christie about reprinting certain stories. She immediately gave permission and did not want any money as she thought the magazine was "a hopeful renaissance for the crime story, which is done so *very* well in England." When the magazine died after five years, simply because the magazine habit has diminished in England, she told Nigel Moorland: "Why do people neglect *real* entertainment? Never mind, you did a *splendid* job."

Her interest in Edgar Wallace was touching. Could it have been that in contrast to herself he was flamboyant and an extrovert, so much a part of the world which she was not?

One day in the thirties when they were both shopping at the same time in Harrods, Edgar Wallace left the store and was standing on the pavement waiting for his Rolls-Royce and chauffeur to appear. As it always happened, when Edgar Wallace appeared in public, he was instantly recognized and a small crowd gathered round.

"Good old Edgar . . . Hullo, Mr. Wallace . . . Edgar, I love your books . . . What is the next one, guv?"

Edgar Wallace acknowledged his fans with a suitable regal wave and nod. No one took any notice of the motherly housewife just a few yards behind him watching it all.

In recounting the story to Nigel Moorland, Agatha Christie said she would have "passed away" if such a thing had happened to her. She disliked being recognized even by her fans in the street. Caught unawares, she suffered almost a paranoiac shyness.

Whenever she met anyone who knew Wallace, Agatha Christie always wanted to hear "another story" about him. This one kept her chuckling for a long time.

Edgar Wallace thought that he was putting on weight and it was suggested to him by Nigel Moorland's mother that he should do some walking. Mrs. Moorland and his brother Jim Wallace went with him to Harrods as he wanted to be correctly equipped for this new pastime. He bought a thornproof knickerbocker walking suit, cap, stockings, heavy shoes, and a walking stick. "Feeny," his chauffeur, was ordered to be outside his house in Portland

Place at 8 A.M. the following morning. When the hour came Edgar Wallace emerged from the house in his walking gear with the rest of the household on the step to watch.

He strode manfully along the pavement, "Feeny" pacing him in the Rolls-Royce. The procession continued for two- to three-hundred yards. A few minutes later the automobile came back and out climbed Edgar Wallace. He had decided that he did not like walking just for its own sake and would not do anything like that again.

Agatha Christie never tired of hearing this story and always commented: "It was so original and typical of him."

Nigel Moorland, who knew Agatha Christie over a number of years as a "fringe friend," had this to say to me about her.

"She was a very kind, very modest, and genuinely original woman in as much as she was not aware of what a charmer she really was. She was never 'clever' or superior but very sweet—I always thought there was a great deal of the real Agatha Christie in Miss Marple."

Like many other people I have talked to, on hindsight Nigel Moorland does not think that she had a real sense of humor. Sense of mischief yes, but not humor. She could find things amusing but somehow she did not have the taste for subtle humor.

"Once or twice I did mention people like James Thurber, Alex Woollcott, and one or two others of the satiric, biting, or 'black' humor worlds; they never really registered with Agatha Christie but Wodehouse she did admire."

On another occasion he was invited to play whist at his mother's house in a woman's party which included Agatha Christie. He did not know the game nor her moods well enough to recognize the gleam in her eye as he leaned to her and asked something like "Can I play this card?"

"Yes, if you can get away with it," she replied.

He played the card and the other ladies literally screamed with horror at what he had done. Agatha Christie laughed so much that she nearly tumbled off her chair.

As he remembers: "I think I 'fell' for her that moment, and always admired and adored her because she was such an utterly nice woman, if I can use the word in its unprissy sense."

CHAPTER TEN

T HE WAR BROUGHT another change of address for Agatha Christie. Her husband, Professor Mallowan, joined the Royal Air Force Voluntary Reserve with the rank of wing commander. With his intimate knowledge of the Middle East, through his digging expeditions, he was immediately posted to the Allied Headquarters as adviser on Arab affairs. He was later promoted to secretary of Arab affairs at Tripoli and finally deputy chief secretary for western Libya.

Like so many other Englishwomen, for the second time in her life Agatha Christie was to be separated from her husband for long periods. The Devon home, Greenway, had been taken over by the Services, but instead of burying herself in the safety of the countryside she preferred to live in London. This time she moved to Lawn Road, Hampstead, a block of avant-garde flats which had been commissioned by Jack Pritchard, a leading furniture maker, with Wells Coats as the architect.

The flats were completed in the early thirties and even today have stood the test of time so well that they are considered among the more notable blocks in London. Clean-lined, functional, it was built in one-bedroom units with small kitchen, dressing room, and bathroom. Downstairs there was a restaurant and bar and the ambiance was more like that of a club than an apartment building. The residents were interesting too in that they were artists, designers, architects, writers. Walter Gropius and Marcel Breuer were among Pritchard's friends and the evenings spent in the restaurant were more like intellectual seminars than the landlord and his tenants.

Everyone was involved in some way in connection with war work whether it was intelligence, fire watching, camouflage, or whatever. The sprit of Lawn Road, like all London, was alive, creative, and forceful. Agatha Christie's next-door neighbor was architect Stefan Buzas, who told me about these days.

"I don't remember ever seeing her downstairs in the bar or joining the rest of us, though she possibly used the restaurant. While we other tenants did things together she never joined in. I used to pass her in the corridor, a cuddly-looking, comfortable lady who one felt was much more likely to grow roses in her back garden than write detective novels."

What Agatha Christie was in fact doing during the days when she left in the morning and came home at night was voluntary dispensing in the University College Hospital. As soon as the war began she contacted her old friend Mrs. Margaret Lunt, chief pharmacist at the Torbay Hospital, and asked her whether she could find her similar work in London. It was arranged that she would take up an appointment at University College Hospital in the summer of 1941. *Martindale's Extra Pharmacopoeia* had always figured prominently in her library and all through the years from the 1914–18 war she had kept herself up to date with her knowledge of poisons.

Three times a week Agatha Christie left Lawn Road early in the morning and took herself across smoking London to University College Hospital, which is near the British Museum. Once there she put on a white coat and became the efficient dispenser, clear of head and sure of hand.

Toward the end of what was called "the phony war" of 1940 many London evacuees, impatient with country life and desperately missing London, simply took the law into their own hands and returned to their homes. The result was that many did not get enough sleep because of the bombing and the out-patient department in the various London hospitals were jammed with people all suffering from minor accidents or nervous illnesses.

The dispensing department was an extremely busy and important one at all the London hospitals. At University College Hospital no one could possibly have realized that the cozy lady behind the pigeonhole door, who always had a kind word to say, was "The Duchess of Death" herself. She was efficient, co-operative, and endlessly untiring. She never grumbled and never complained. It was as though she enjoyed every minute among her beloved poisons.

When the intensive bombing began on London, one of the first people on the telephone to the hospital every day was Mrs. Mallowan, as she was known to the staff, asking whether any of the dispensers were unable to get in. If they were, because of home or travel difficulties, she would set off from Hampstead and do an extra day's work filling in.

In the evenings when she returned to her one-room world she sat down to write after a long, tiring day. It could not have been easy. The novels included *Ten Little Niggers*, 1939 (titled in America *Ten Little Indians* or *And Then There Were None*), *One, Two, Buckle My Shoe*, 1940 (American title, *The Patriotic Murders*), *Evil Under the Sun*, 1941, and *Sparkling Cyanide*, 1945 (in America *Remembered Death*). They were all vintage Christie at her most decisive and compelling reading. Three plays also come from that period; *Peril at End House*, 1940, was adapted by Arnold Ridley, but Agatha Christie herself adapted from the novels of the same name *Ten Little Niggers*, 1943, and *Appointment with Death*, 1945.

The solitude of those long, dark, wartime nights, with nothing but memories for companionship, produced the third of the romantic novels which she wrote under the name of Mary Westmacott. Was it nostalgia for the Middle East that made her set *Absent in the Spring* (another title from Shakespeare) in the desert where a young wife finds herself marooned between buses at one of those forsaken stations set amid miles of nothing but sand?

Again one feels this is a truthful dip into her own conscience and the experiences of her early life when she describes the agony of the wife Joan, who finds that her husband has accepted the love of a younger woman, Leslie. The parallel is to be found right back in 1926 when Archibald Christie confessed his love for Nancy Neele.

All those hours of lonely soliloquy in the desert as Joan dips hurtfully into her own subsconscious are surely Agatha Christie baring her innermost thoughts as she sat cooped up typing long into the night. Was it a purging of the soul or the necessity to transfer her thoughts to a time and place where, away from the stresses of detection writing, she had discovered an inner tranquility and the presence she felt of a life-force guiding her destiny? The writing is pure and personal and infinitely pleasurable.

As the Westmacott novels at that time made no commercial impact, or even enhanced her reputation, one wonders why she bothered at all to have them published. Was it a kind of masochistic exposé—a literary shorthand—to tell her faithful readers that underneath her crisp detective books was a deeper woman who had suffered all the pangs of living just as they had? In that case why not use her own name and not a pseudonym? Or was it simply that Christie did not believe in wasting one word she wrote? The creation of these novels she said gave her great pleasure and having written them it seemed pointless to waste them. Even in those days each word she wrote was probably worth £1.

It is an amusing thought that while the intellectuals at Lawn Road were downstairs nightly thrashing out the problems of a war-torn world, upstairs Agatha Christie sat solving her own personal problems on her portable typewriter and using her three-finger technique.

When the new sterile laboratories in a much enlarged pharmaceutical department at the University College Hospital were opened in 1956 Professor and Mrs. Mallowan were both among the guests. It was the hospital's very personal way of saying "thank you" for all she had done during those wars years and it was to be the last time that she stepped foot inside that London hospital.

During those war years, in between writing her detection

novels, Agatha Christie picked up again a book that she had begun in the early days of her marriage . . . the story of her involvement in the digging expeditions in the Middle East that she took part in with her husband, Professor Mallowan. Few marriages were more companionable, more rewarding, than that of the Mallowans. During those nights of the doodle bugs and the sirens it is feasible that in writing about the times they spent together that wife and husband were joined in spirit.

The result was a book called *Come, Tell Me How You Live* (Collins), which was published in 1946 under the name Agatha Christie Mallowan when Professor Mallowan had returned from the war and they had moved back to their house in Cresswell Place. It is a joyous book and one sees an uninhibited Agatha Christie as she leaves Victoria Station and notices the small knot of family, including her daughter Rosalind, fading in the distance as the train pulls out. One feels the anguish which she assured us lasted precisely forty-five seconds before the sheer exultation sprang up again at the thought of setting off once more by train across Europe to her beloved desert.

Here are Agatha and Max Mallowan as they really were together—tough, realistic, humane people. The story of Constipation Day is hilarious when they dosed an Arab with horse medicine after every known aperient had been administered without success. Professor Mallowan offered a large bakshish should the patient's insides move before sunset. The whole camp was anxious as they watched the wretched man being walked up and down the encampment with no apparent success until a quarter of an hour before the limit was up they heard loud cheers—"the floodgates have opened."

The Mallowans had an aura of grandeur around them in archaeological circles and to be invited to visit their sites at Chagar Bazar was considered a great honor.

A London archaeologist who visited the Mallowans' camp at Chagar Bazar in Iraq describes a transformed Agatha Christie: "It was quite a different Agatha Christie from anyone I had known in England. There was no shy psychological hang-up. Here was a woman in a man's world who knew that she was being accepted at face value. She worked like a beaver, sometimes in heats as high as 120° F., photographing and mending the finds as they were catalogued at the end of the day. No professional could have done it better and the conditions under which she worked were far from easy. Whereas the men could sometimes be tetchy when things went wrong she always saw the funny side and was mainly responsible for the good humor that prevailed on all the 'digs' organized by her husband.

"I had never met Max's wife before but she was pretty impressive in her way, with a large jolly face and an air of authority about her as she organized the comforts of the camp site. Margaret Rutherford could not have played the role better."

We get glimpses of this in *Come, Tell Me How You Live* as she pokes fun at herself when she is forced to put on her Empire Builder wife's shantung coat and skirt as her cotton frocks had not come back from the laundry.

Professor Mallowan was aghast when he saw his wife wearing the outfit for the first time: he described it as frightful and that she looked like the most offensive kind of mem-sahib—straight from Poonah.

One can hear her girlish laugh and mock anger as she chides her husband for describing the pattern on a frock as the Tell Halaf running lozenge pattern. She explained that she wished he would not use pottery terms for describing her clothes lime-green and like "a running lozenge" which was a disgusting term—like something half sucked and left by a child on a village shop counter.

There are glimpses right through this book of the human side of the woman as she described one night waking up and finding, after putting out the lamp, that small mice were running "all over one's face and tweaking your hair."

She confessed to becoming hysterical and declaring that in the morning "I am going into Kamichlie to wait for the train and I am going straight back to Alep. And from Alep I shall go straight back to England. I cannot stand this life. I will not stand it. I am going home."

There is not a woman in the world who could not feel for Agatha Christie Mallowan at that moment.

What is amazing about the book is her apparent total recall at conversations some years before. In the course of his work and his future writings about it Sir Max Mallowan always kept a diary, which was completed every night, but it is more than likely that this is what Agatha Christie Mallowan did too with a thought that perhaps one day even these experiences would make a book.

Come, Tell Me How You Live was first published in 1946 and then revised and reprinted in a new format by Collins in 1975. Seen against the present oil boom in the Middle East, and the influx of the Western way of living, it is as nostalgic as it is charming. Her foreword is a modest one but so typical of the lasting influence that the desert had on her thinking. She described it as a very little book—small beer.

Whenever the Mallowans returned from the Middle East their friends were delighted to hear any new stories. One of Dame Agatha's most amusing ones was how she was invited to attend a hanging. As her host said: "Surely you would not want to miss the hanging of a woman who has poisoned three husbands." This was however something that she did want to miss.

It is clear through this book how much she enjoyed those days "on the dig" with her husband and among people she felt at ease with and whose company she enjoyed.

"I retreat into myself with my fiction and I emerge from myself in my husband's work," she said.

The book is inscribed "To My Husband, Max Mallowan; to the Colonel, Bumps, Mac and Guilford, this meandering chronicle is affectionately dedicated."

During the war years there was a boom in light reading like romantic novels or thrillers because libraries regularly serviced the underground shelters where thousands of people spent the nights. They found that Christie books were the best antidote against blackout and shelter depression. Just before dark, like colonies of ants and armed with sandwiches, Thermos flasks, paperbacks, and bedding, thousands of Londoners disappeared below ground while searchlights combed the skies above. Agatha Christie's country houses, which were staffed with servants, their easy reading and harmless puzzles were just the thing to soothe frayed nerves.

It was during this period at University College Hospital that she began another one of her collecting hobbies. As medicine bot-

117

tles were in short supply a charity called Crusade of Rescue organized a bottle rescue operation. They had a highly efficient collecting service for bottles of all sizes which were then washed and resold to the hospital for fifty pence a gross. Agatha Mallowan used to go first thing in the morning and take a look at the bottles. If there were any odd shapes that could not possibly be used for medicine she was allowed to take them home. They were then filled with eosin, copper sulphate, acriflavine, gentian violet, and so on, and formed a fantasy décor in her spartan little flat.

In a memoir which he wrote for *The Pharmaceutical Journal* after the death of Dame Agatha Christie Mallowan, Dr. Harold Davis, C.B.E., recalled:

"She came into University College Hospital, but being somewhat shy, and never seeking publicity, few people in the hospital were aware that we had such a famous person dispensing in the out-patients department. She loved to exchange pleasantries with the patients whose appearances were restricted to the pigeonhole apertures so typical of the dispensaries in the London voluntary hospitals at that time. I was often amused to conjecture at what those patients would have thought had they known their medicines had been compounded and presented to them by none other than Agatha Christie. She loved the work and was to stay with us several years."

One patient however did recognize the dispenser. During the blackout Lord Ritchie Calder was found unconscious in Euston Square and was taken on a passing army weapon carrier to University College Hospital. He was suffering from a subforachnoid brain hemorrhage and when he regained consciousness he was startled to see a figure in a white coat by his bed pouring a liquid into a medicine glass. Though befuddled in the head the recognition was instant and mutual. They had last met in the lounge of the Harrogate Hydro on December 14, 1926.

Dr. Davis, who was later chief pharmacist at the Ministry of Health, became a close friend of the Mallowans during those war years. He tells how once Mrs. Mallowan offered to give his little daughter, who was blind, a puppy called Pepper as the child was just recovering from chicken pox and was thus unable to go away on a family holiday. Virginia had a small album with a tartan cover and shyly asked the famous author for her autograph. Without a moment's hesitation Agatha Christie wrote:

> Little Virginia was going away
> Little Virginia came out one day
> With sundry spots in sundry places
> So Virginia made the most AWFUL faces.
> Love, Agatha Christie Mallowan.

The album along with several autographed books has been cherished by Virginia Davis all through the last thirty years.

He also tells of another amusing incident illustrating Agatha Christie's sense of fun. *Ten Little Niggers* had been adapted into a play and was opening at the Harrow Coliseum. She knew that the Davis family lived nearby in Harrow Weald and sent them tickets for the first night.

The curtain rose on a typical Christie country house interior with two or three characters present. From the wings a police officer entered announcing, "Davis is the name—Davis."

"Our reaction can be imagined," Dr. Davis said. "When we met Mrs. Mallowan a few days later she said with an intriguing smile, 'I am so glad you enjoyed the play.' No further comment was made but how we laughed."

CHAPTER ELEVEN

In the 1920s sophisticated London had become orientated to "thrillers" as they were called at the time. The detective story was considered intellectually acceptable whereas the crime and adventure story was not.

Edmund Cork, Agatha Christie's agent, had been approached by Michael Morton for permission to turn her successful detection novel *The Murder of Roger Ackroyd* into a play. It was a Hercule Poirot story that had created a sensation because of the unorthodox plot which had been suggested to Agatha Christie by Lord Mountbatten.

One of the most successful impresarios in London at the time was Bertie Meyer. When he agreed to produce *Alibi*, as the play was to be called in 1928, this gave him four successful plays running in the West End at the same time. Apart from *Alibi* there was *Her Cardboard Lover* with Tallulah Bankhead, *Lucky Girl* with Jean Gerard and Clifford Morrison, and Edgar Wallace's *The Terror*, starring Denis Neilsen and Mary Glynn.

Bertie Meyer was elegant, fastidious, likable, and one of the best-dressed men in London. He was part of the very structure of theater land as he was the man responsible for the building of the Cambridge Theatre and the St. Martin's. He worked until he was ninety, walking every day from his flat nearby and climbing the stairs up into his small office in the St. Martin's Theatre.

It was Bertie Meyer's daughter Frances who suggested to her father that a young man called Charles Laughton, who had received good notices in A Man with Red Hair, should be given the part of Poirot. Henry Daniell, later to play with Laughton in the film version of Witness for the Prosecution, was cast as the icy faced butler in the production.

Alibi opened at the Prince of Wales Theatre to a glittering first night. The memory of the ugly days of the General Strike of 1926 had receded for the Bright Young Things and London's night life was thriving more than ever before or since. The first night of any play in those days was a glamorous event. Every man in the stalls wore a white tie and in the dress circle black tie was de rigueur.

After the theater everyone went on to such places as the Hotel Metropole for the Midnight Follies, the Piccadilly Hotel for Piccadilly Revels, or the Savoy, Trocadero, or Princes, where Charles B. Cochran and André Charlot presented such effervescent stars as Beatrice Lillie, Sophie Tucker, and Alice Delysia. Debutantes, with their newly shingled heads and daring short evening dresses, piled into Kate Meyrick's "43" Club: the mood was for frothy escapism at any price.

If Agatha Christie was disappointed with her leading man Laughton as Poirot, the rest of London was not. She in fact was "totally shocked" at the idea of transforming her dapper Belgian detective with his "egg head and little gray cells" into a young lover. The play however was a commercial success and ran for 250 performances. Whatever Mrs. Christie thought, the public loved Charles Laughton with his picturesque appearance, flawless Belgian accent, and the electrifying moment at the end of the play when with bravura he denounced the villain.

"You have no idea of the agony of having your characters taken and made to say things they never would have said and do things they never would have done and if you protest all they say is that it is good theater," she said in later years.

Nor did even such a fine actor as Laughton find it easy to cope with Christie dialogue. In his biography of Charles Laughton (published by W. H. Allen), in 1976, Charles Higham writes: "Given the difficult challenge of making a real human being out of Miss Christie's pasteboard figure of Poirot, Charles gave an excitingly detailed performance."

A possible reason for the difficulty most actors have with Agatha Christie dialogue is that her talent is essentially a cerebral construction for solving an equation within a given space. The characters are two-dimensional simply because if they were three-dimensional they would give themselves away. In the confines of a theater stage the psychological aspect becomes much more important. On these grounds her most successful play of all was *Witness for the Prosecution* where the main scene is set in a replica of the Old Bailey court in London and the action of the play is a battle of wits.

One of the most attractive short stories Agatha Christie ever wrote was called "Philomel Cottage" and was from the *Listerdale Mystery* collection. In 1936, helped by Frank Vosper, she adapted this into a play called *Love from a Stranger*, which ran for 149 performances at the New Theatre. London audiences loved every minute of it.

A three-act play called *Akhnaton*, written by Agatha Christie in 1937, has as yet never been performed as it requires many sets and extras and is not considered a viable proposition. It is only interesting to recall in that it shows how Agatha Christie's interest in the Middle East quickened after her marriage to Professor Max Mallowan and her painstaking research into life in ancient Egypt.

A few years later Arnold Ridley again adapted her novel *Peril at End House*, which opened at the Vaudeville Theatre on January 1, 1940, starring Francis L. Sullivan once more.

Although she had given her consent for these adaptations Agatha Christie was never completely satisfied with the productions and felt that the only way for her was to persevere and write her own stage plays. She was determined to master the craft and be in charge of her own characters. Her audacious choice was *Ten Little Niggers*, directed by Irene Hentschel, which opened at the St. James's Theatre in 1943 and played for 260 performances.

Agatha Christie took her titles from nursery rhymes in many of her most successful stories as they permitted her readers to follow the plots logically. What they seldom guessed, and this is where her particular brilliance lay, was just how the murderer would operate to make his crime fit the rhyme.

It is interesting that in the novel Agatha Christie used the original ending of the nursery rhyme, which was composed in America by Septimus Winner and later adapted in England in 1868 by Frank Green—"One Little Nigger Boy left all alone, He went and hanged himself, and then there were none." When she came to adapt the story for the stage she preferred the more harmonious ending which she had learned as a child "he got married and then there were none."

When the book was published by Dodd, Mead in America the word "Indians" was substituted for "niggers" as the latter was considered offensive in the light of racial discrimination.

In America the novel had no less than three titles—*And Then There were None*, which was changed to *Ten Little Indians* and finally *The Nursery Rhyme Murders*.

In the English stage production the ten little figures molded in rubber were taken from an Ethiopian statue while in the American version small Indian dolls were used, each dressed with a different colored blanket.

Ten Little Niggers has remained one of Agatha Christie's most successful plays. The way in which she disposed of every character in full view of the audience in the one stage set titillated her public and people returned time and time again to see Christie ingenuity at its best. She, too, enjoyed it as at last she had proved to her critics that she could write her own stage plays unaided and make them work.

Two film versions were made, one with Barry Fitzgerald and Walter Huston under the title *And Then There Were None* and later Wilfrid Hyde White and Stanley Holloway in *Ten Little Indians*.

An interesting aspect is that whereas the title *Ten Little Niggers* had been perfectly acceptable in England in 1939, by 1966 the climate of public opinion concerning race relations had so changed that when the play was revived in Birmingham more than twenty members of the Co-ordinating Committee Against Racial Discrimination picketed the front of the theater. On one placard was the Oxford Dictionary definition of the word "nigger" —"A contemptuous reference to colored people." Agatha Christie was consulted and agreed to the title being changed to the original American one.

All through her career it was quite ordinary observations that captured Agatha Christie's imagination to turn into plots. Francis L. Sullivan told this story how *The Hollow* came to be written first as a novel in 1946 and later transformed into a play, which was performed at the Fortune Theatre in London and ran for 376 performances.

Although Francis L. Sullivan had met Agatha Christie at rehearsals for *Black Coffee*, which opened at the Embassy in London in 1930, he did not get to know her really intimately until later when he approached her to write another play for him.

"I was living at Hazelmere in Surrey at the time and Agatha came to stay with us for several weekends while discussing what the play should be. On one of her weekend visits I had an excellent chance to observe the outward manifestations of this creative phase of her work.

"At the back of the house my wife, in a moment of insane optimism of the English weather, had caused a swimming pool to be made with half a dozens paths leading down to it through the chestnut wood. One fine Sunday morning I discovered Agatha wandering up and down these paths with an expression of intense concentration."

" 'Larry' Sullivan asked her what she was doing but as she did not answer he left her and dived into the pool. The sequel came about a year later when a copy of *The Hollow* appeared in their post with a printed dedication to "Larry and Danae with apologies for using their pool as the scene of a murder."

Francis L. Sullivan's conception of the Belgian detective, Hercule Poirot, was the nearest thing to perfection in the eyes of Agatha Christie. All previous and subsequent portrayals did not come up to his and even Albert Finney, thought by many to be the epitome of Poirot in the film *Murder on the Orient Express*, did not eclipse Sullivan in her opinion.

There are two known versions as to why Bertie Meyer did not produce *The Hollow* in London in 1946 after his initial success with *Alibi*. One is that in a perverse mood Agatha Christie did not want him to have it as he already had the option on one of her plays and she was not going to offer him another until he had produced it. The other version, which Bertie Meyer's daughter Mrs. Frances Carver believes to be correct, is that not only did her father not like the play but felt he could not cast it.

Looking around the London scene for a likely producer, Agatha Christie's agent, Edmund Cork, telephoned Peter Saunders, a recent newcomer to the London scene. He suggested lunch and came to the point immediately. They met at lunch and Cork asked Saunders if he would like to read Mrs. Christie's latest play, *The Hollow*.

Saunders read the play the same afternoon and telephoned Cork. Of course he wanted to do it, and was almost incoherent over the phone in his attempt to appear nonchalant.

Peter Saunders then chose as a possible director Hubert Gregg, who had successfully done a few shows for the Sunday Societies but was yet untried on a major production. Both men went off to luncheon at the Carlton Grill to meet Mrs. Christie, extremely nervous because they knew that, though she had all the appearance of a county lady up for a day's shopping in London, they would be under stringent observation. If she did not like them nothing would make her change her mind. Already she had the reputation in the theater of being a woman with decided opinions.

What they could not envisage of course was that Mrs. Christie turned up flanked by her family . . . her husband, Professor Max Mallowan, daughter Rosalind, who had grown into a large lady, and son-in-law Anthony Hicks, who was a barrister. The luncheon began on a social note with polite talk over the lobster thermidor and canapé Diane and did not become serious until the coffee when the plot was discussed at some length. The ambiance was agreeable and once again Agatha Christie did not mince words and stated quite firmly her views of the characters.

Peter Saunders offered to escort Mrs. Christie up Regent Street into Piccadilly. She declined.

"You just want to make sure that I don't get run over," she

said, and then with one of her toothy smiles and twinkles she melted into the passing crowd.

The Hollow proved as difficult to cast as Bertie Meyer had predicted. When the late Dorothy Mather of Film Rights Agency, as outspoken as she was shrewd, saw the script she telephoned Peter Saunders and said: "I have read the script and beg you, dear Peter, not to put this play on. It really is awful."

Even Hugh ("Binkie") Beaumont of H. M. Tennent Limited, the most prolific and prestigious producer in London, turned it down on the grounds that while the name of Agatha Christie might be a box office draw *The Hollow* was just another one of her plays filled with cardboard characters. Had Binkie Beaumont had a different opinion he might well have joined forces with Peter Saunders and so ultimately have had a share in *The Mousetrap*.

More in despair than conviction Jeanne de Casalis was offered the feminine lead in the play and although she was not keen on this piece of casting Agatha Christie left the final decision to Peter Saunders and Hubert Gregg, the director. *The Hollow* played for 376 performances at the Fortune Theatre proving once again that whatever the hierarchy of the theatrical world thought about those early Agatha Christie plays, and they mostly denigrated them, the public had different views. They entertained. Nothing more, nothing less. Her plays did just what she set out to do.

Peter Saunders was undeniably the key figure in Agatha Christie's theatrical career. It is problematical if without him she would ever have attained the success she has in this field or for that matter would Saunders have done so well without Christie?

Behind her twinkling-eyed façade, Agatha Christie could be awkward, obstinate, august. She and Peter Saunders not only understood each other, and respected each other's judgment, but the genuine friendship between them and his tactful good manners made it possible for him to give her advice that she would never have accepted from anyone else.

He not only produced two of her early theatrical successes—*The Hollow* and *Spider's Web*—but is the main reason why *The Mousetrap* has reached its twenty-fifth year. It is his effort, his ingenuity, and his persistent and inventive public relations that have produced a packed audience for this mediocre play year after year.

Peter Saunders was born in London of comfortably off parents, though his father was subsequently to lose his money in a business venture. He began his working life as an assistant cameraman in the British film industry and worked on the American production of *Diamond Cut Diamond* starring Adolphe Menjou and Benita Hume. He was also involved in a British film in which Herbert Wilcox directed Anna Neagle, whom Wilcox later married.

When it became patently clear that the film industry was not overwhelmed by Saunders' talents he switched to journalism, free-lancing in Glasgow for the *Daily Express*. Again journalism did not prove to be his niche so he moved on to public relations, ending up as band leader Harry Roy's press representative.

Then came the war and a spell as 7688259 Private Saunders, in the Corps of the Military Police, which was part of the Intelligence Corps at that time. He served in France, gained a commission, and became a civilian again in 1946 after six years in the Army.

With only his immense charm, abounding optimism, and a meager capital, he decided to go into the theatrical business. For £50 he bought the rights of *Fly Away Peter*, which had been written by an old army chum, Sergeant A. P. Dearsley. In this way began his career as a theatrical impresario, which has given him lasting satisfaction ever since.

Although Agatha Christie's name has been in lights in the West End of London for more than forty years it is Peter Saunders who has kept it twinkling nightly for the last twenty-five years.

CHAPTER TWELVE

Wᴇɴ ǫᴜᴇᴇɴ ᴍᴀʀʏ was approaching her eightieth birthday in 1947 she was asked by the Director General of the British Broadcasting Corporation how she would like them to celebrate this event. The BBC was in fact prepared to put on anything from grand opera to Shakespeare in honor of this much loved queen.

But such is the precocity of the BBC and the invitation couched with such mystery and secrecy that Agatha Christie was later to say that at first she really did not realize who she was supposed to be writing a play for. All she knew was that it was of great importance.

Some weeks therefore went by before the BBC received a letter from Major John Wickham, private secretary to Queen Mary, saying that she would like to celebrate with an Agatha Christie play. For many years Queen Mary had been an enthusiastic fan of Mrs. Christie's and had enjoyed her crime novels as much for their clever characterizations of the minor characters as for their detection plots. She had a standing order with her bookseller for every new Christie published and kept a special bookshelf for them.

Whenever Queen Mary and Princess Victoria of Battenberg, Lord Mountbatten's mother, met, the conversation invariably turned to the latest Agatha Christie, each enjoying comparing notes as to whether it was as good as the last one. Queen Elizabeth, the Queen Mother, Princess Margaret, and to a lesser extent Queen Elizabeth II, who galloped through them as a teenager, are all Agatha Christie fans.

The thirty-minute play for the BBC, which was called *Three Blind Mice*, took Mrs. Christie a week to write. Queen Mary and a few friends listened to the broadcast in the sitting room of Marlborough House where she was celebrating her birthday. It proved a very satisfactory present and her Majesty was simply delighted.

After this the play remained in the archives of the BBC and the original copy was locked away in a drawer at Mrs. Christie's home. It stayed there for five years until one day she decided to extend it into a three-act play.

It was a technique that Agatha Christie used all through her career—turning short stories into novels, novels into plays. Not only did it save creating other plots but it gave her great satisfaction to see one plot operating successfully in several fields. It was the kind of mental economy that she enjoyed.

When the play was completed she showed it to her agent, Edmund Cork, whose advice she valued. It was his suggestion that it should be first offered to Peter Saunders, who had already proved that he liked producing the Christie type of thriller entertainment. Though a sparse production in every way, *The Hollow*, which he had put on, ran for several months.

It was just after Christmas in 1951 that Mrs. Christie telephoned Peter Saunders and invited him to lunch. They chatted away in her cozy fashion about various events happening in her family circle and the theater world. It was not until the end of coffee that she in fact revealed the reason for the luncheon. With a superb piece of timing she fixed him with her small, mischievous eyes and slipped into his hand a brown paper parcel tied with pink ribbon.

"I have a little present for you," she said. "Don't unwrap it until you get back to the office. I hope it makes some money for you."

Peter Saunders returned to his office and opened the parcel to find a manuscript stained with coffee cup circles, but on reading it he knew immediately that within this typical country setting, in this case a guest house, was a pleasing family play with the added piquancy of a spectacular surprise ending that the Christie public had come to expect from her.

What he could not possibly have guessed is that it would run for a quarter of a century and beat the world record of the Los Angeles production of *The Drunkard*, which lasted for twenty years and three months and was later revived as a musical. That it would span the dissolution of a great part of the British Empire until the pink on the map had shrunk to a quarter its size and the communist red had doubled its area. That America would have produced five presidents and Britain seven prime ministers. That it would survive in the postwar revolution between the sexes and classes and remain as nostalgically titillating since the night it opened in Nottingham on Monday, October 6, 1952. Sir Winston Churchill was then Prime Minister of England, Mr. Harry S Truman was President of the United States of America, and Joesph Stalin headed the mighty U.S.S.R.

The play still retained its original title, *Three Blind Mice*, which in characteristic fashion Mrs. Christie had taken from a nursery rhyme. The difficulty about this particular title was that impresario Emile Littler had used the same words in a play he had produced some years before and took exception to anyone else using them. It was then that Mrs. Christie's son-in-law, Anthony Hicks, produced an alternative, *The Mousetrap*, from a quotation from *Hamlet*, Act III, Scene Two.

King Claudius: "What do you call the play?"
Hamlet: "The Mousetrap . . . 'Tis a knavish piece of work; but what of that?"

As usual the casting of *The Mousetrap* had many problems as Agatha Christie plays have never been popular among leading actors and actresses.

130

Having created her characters, her one concern was to further the plot and not to further the characterization. In addition to this, part of the resourceful Saunders technique when launching her plays was to make Agatha Christie the star, with top billing outside the theather. The actors took second place. It was a ruse that worked and is certainly one of the ingredients which made *Mousetrap* history and open up a whole new field of readers for Mrs. Christie.

Peter Saunders' first choice for the role of Detective Sergeant Trotter was Richard Attenborough, who with his boyish looks not only looked the part of the sturdy "police officer" but was one of the most likable actors on the British stage. With his integrity and enthusiasm, whatever role he undertook instinctively came to life. At the time he was appearing at the Garrick Theatre in the long run of *To Dorothy a Son* and after a luncheon with Mr. Saunders agreed to read the script. Quite apart from all this there was one important hindrance and that was whether in fact he could fit the role into an already crowded acting schedule.

As added bait Peter Saunders said that there was also a nice little part for his peaches and cream actress wife, Sheila Sim, daughter of the incomparable actor Alastair Sim. Few husband and wife actors can resist a guaranteed run in the same show and this was to become the major factor that clinched the deal. Richard Attenborough finally agreed to go into rehearsal seven months hence.

Agatha Christie always vetted her leading players and was to meet Sir Richard and Lady Attenborough, as they are known today, at a luncheon party arranged by Peter Saunders. Though she was sure that Sheila Sim, at that time co-starring with Joan Miller and Hartley Power in Peter Cotes's production of *Come Back, Little Sheba,* was right for the role of the pretty young wife, Mollie Ralston, oddly enough she was not so certain about Richard Attenborough. The whole credibility of the play rests on the character of Detective Sergeant Trotter; she may have felt that Attenborough was too small in stature for the part.

Remembering back to that momentous lunch in a BBC interview Sir Richard Attenborough says: "One felt right from the start that she knew her own mind. But to look at her she resembled everyone's favorite aunt and the last person in the world to have anything to do with crime or violence. She was the calmest, gentlest character I have ever met and as we got to know her over the years we found her frankly incredible."

It was in fact "Dickie" Attenborough who was to suggest Peter Cotes as director for *The Mousetrap*. Peter Cotes had years earlier had an outstanding success as the director of *Pick-up Girl*, the controversial play about juvenile delinquency, which, although banned for public performance, Queen Mary had insisted on seeing for herself at the club theater Cotes owned at the time, the New Lindsey. Later—in 1946—this "private" production was seen by the general public when it was transferred for West End runs at both the *Prince of Wales* and *Casino* theaters.

Peter Cotes was a highly experienced and successful director with a number of murder plays already to his credit. He also had a knowledgeable interest in criminology and finally with some reluctance accepted the engagement to direct *The Mousetrap*. His West End productions of *A Pin to See the Peepshow*, *The Father*, and *The Biggest Thief in Town* had all recently been acclaimed by the critics before the offer for him to direct *The Mousetrap*.

As with most Agatha Christie plays there was some rejiggling done before *The Mousetrap* went into rehearsal. Before they met personally Peter Cotes wrote to Agatha Christie outlining seven major points that he felt could be incorporated to give the play more credibility and strengthen the plot. Within four days she wrote back apologizing for the delay and adding that there were twelve guests in the house and she never seemed to get a moment to concentrate.

One of the most interesting views in this letter concerns the murderer's lust for killing. As she explained, the murderer—and there is no cheating in this book—wanted an excuse for a third murder "and why not? There were three little blind mice. One for each."

Another major decision by Cotes was to cut an entire nine pages of the author's original Scene 1, Act 1. He felt that the dialogue there between characters called, Bill, Alf, and Mrs. Casey was tedious and holding up the action of the play. Instead he suggested to Mrs. Christie, and she fully agreed, that the play should open with a prologue of mime played in the dark with whistles, footsteps, shouts, and so on. This remains in today's production and sets an enigmatical scene for an evening of enjoyable murder. There were many occasions after this when author and director met or chatted over meals while the play was being licked into shape at rehearsals and the written word transformed into theatrical shadow that finally became substance.

Peter Cotes remembers the last days before the opening night in Nottingham on October 6, 1952.

"Most of us were staying at the same hotel. Agatha Christie came to the dress rehearsals on both the Sunday evening and the Monday before the opening. She sat well back in the stalls, sometimes alone, occasionally with me. She was always quiet and unobtrusive at rehearsals and never spoke directly to the actors if she had anything to say but always to me. At the final rehearsal she was very quiet, making few comments, but doubtless as excited as we all were."

Before the first night there was more than the routine "chummy" telegrams everyone sends everyone in the theatrical business. Peter Cotes has kept to this day his mementos of an epic occasion that became theatrical history. "Just to say thank you," Agatha Christie's read. "Very best of luck and my grateful thanks for your untiring work," was placed on record by a "sincere" Peter Saunders, and from the appreciative Attenboroughs an endearing, "Darling gnome bless you for all your unbelievable help and guidance we are both so grateful fondest love Sheila and Dickie."

Agatha Christie's first night gift to Peter Cotes was a copy of her book *Towards Zero*, inscribed "With love from Agatha."

"After the first night curtain fell, and the cast called for rehearsal the next day, we all went to supper," he recalls. "There was Agatha Christie and I seem to recall her daughter was there, too, as well as Dickie, Sheila, and Peter Saunders. We all sat around making our own predictions."

Whatever she felt privately about the success of the play, and Agatha Christie did have innermost doubts that she may have fallen between two stools—that of a comedy and a detection thriller—Mrs. Christie kept to herself.

"Cheer up," she was to tell the cast. "It's not a bad little play."

Later on, with supper and conference ended, and most of the others abed, Peter Cotes found Mrs. Christie sitting in one of those paneled ingle nooks which tourist hotels in England delight in. She asked him: "How long, Peter, do you think we have got?"

He replied that it was anyone's guess but judging from the applause and the fact that the "tricks" had worked, by the time it had run a few months, touring the larger towns in the provinces, it should arrive in London "well run-in," greased, and highly polished.

After the first-night tryout in Nottingham, according to Peter Saunders, he suggested to Agatha Christie that if he could remove half a dozen laughs in the places where there was tension, the play would work better. There were still plenty of laughs left to keep the play alive. This she agreed to do.

Agatha Christie did not trail around the various big cities (Nottingham, Manchester, Leeds, Birmingham, Glasgow, Oxford, Edinburgh, and others). However, Peter Cotes, who was subsequently to produce another thriller in the provinces called *The Man,* which with Joan Miller and Bernard Braden transferred successfully to Her Majesty's theater in the West End, used to cross the country from one city to another to keep an eye on the production and hold rehearsals whenever they were needed.

"A director who is conscientious will never leave his production if there are things to be done. However, if a director is very busy, as I was at that particular time, and a production is running smoothly on its tryouts in properly ordered and professional theaters, you leave the routine rehearsals to your stage manager. It is his job to see one's production is carried out and adhered to. The captain on the bridge commands; his lieutenants supervise the ship's smooth running."

The Mousetrap finally opened in London at the Ambassadors Theatre on November 25 to, on the whole, a very good press indeed. "Peter Cotes proved as a producer that he is as much at home with Agatha as Ibsen," wrote Beverley Baxter in the *Sunday Express.* "Even more thrilling than the plot is the atmosphere of shuddering suspense," wrote John Barber in the *Daily Express.* "No one brews it better than Agatha Christie."

"What a wily mistress of criminal ceremonies Agatha Christie is. She is like a perfect hostess serving hemlock at a cocktail party," was the *Evening Standard*'s comments. "There is none of this hiding of vital facts in Mrs. Christie . . . it is this honesty of procedure that pits her so high in the ranks of police novel writers."

"Mr. Peter Cotes's production is taut and exciting," commented Harold Hobson in *The Sunday Times*.

"There remain alarming silences, which are perhaps the true test of such a piece on the stage. That we feel them to be alarming can only be thanks to the director, Mr. Peter Cotes," wrote Anthony Cookman in *The Times*.

"The play is produced for every ounce of its tension by Mr. Peter Cotes," T. C. Worsley commented in the *New Statesman*.

There is always a mystery surrounding anything to do with Agatha Christie so it is not surprising that Peter Saunders and Peter Cotes, who had worked so closely together in complete harmony, should fall out a couple of weeks after the play's opening night in London.

What then could possibly have gone wrong between producer and director? With his production running smoothly, and having recouped its production cost even before it reached the West End, Peter Cotes absented himself—a customary procedure among busy theater directors when necessary—for what was to be a few weeks in New York where he was to direct the Broadway production of his London success *A Pin to See the Peepshow*, starring Joan Miller. This fact had been publicized and was known to both cast and management well in advance of Peter Cotes's departure for America.

It was on his journey that a cable was received that he would no longer be welcome at the Ambassadors upon his return to London. Despite an offer to be "bought out," Peter Cotes held on, and found no reason to relinquish his position as director.

The miserable offshoot of this *contretemps* is that when the play has celebrated its various landmark birthdays the man who brought it to life so brilliantly at its initial inception has not been invited to join the celebrations. On its sixth year in the West End, Agatha Christie did in fact send Peter Cotes the published edition of the play containing the *original* production and taken from the prompt script of the first production. It was formally signed "To Peter Cotes on our sixth Birthday from Agatha Christie." Was there a streak of ruthlessness in Agatha Christie that made her waste no time on unessentials? Peter Cotes had served his purpose.

Today Peter Cotes, more in sorrow than in anger, looks back over the twenty-five years since *The Mousetrap* opened.

"It's history that I am the director of the first highly successful production of the longest running play in the world, in the same way that Peter Saunders is the producer and Agatha Christie the author. I am the *original* director; subsequent productions since that time have been based upon my production, however differently may have been the final results."

And though today his name no longer appears on the program, due to his notable contribution, plus a watertight contract, Peter Cotes still inherits royalties from a "structure" upon which he worked as one of its leading architects.

What is the secret of *The Mousetrap*'s success? It is certainly not the dialogue as Mary Law, who first played in *The Mousetrap* in 1957 and then again in 1976, explains:

"Her dialogue does not bear any resemblance to what one says in normal life. She always seems to have a great deal of repetition. You have to say 'horrible, horrible, horrible' three times or 'he's dead, dead, dead.' It's very strange but in fact she was absolutely right when she refused to let us cut it down to one. It's much better in a funny way when you say it three times. Whether it is because the foreigners in the audience only get it on the third round I am not sure, but for the actors making these repetitions sound viable it is very difficult. I reckon if you can act in an Agatha Christie play you can play in anything.

"It's rather like a lesson. I think that everyone at drama school should be made to do an Agatha Christie. If they can make it real and make it sincere then it works 100 per cent, let's face it, but if they can't, it is better to give it up. It is a real test for everyone."

The Mousetrap has a typical Christie setting. Monkswell Manor, a sprawling country house, has been taken over by an engaging young couple, Mollie and Giles Ralston, and turned into a

136

guest house. All the action takes place over a period of a couple of days when five disparate house guests and a detective sergeant are marooned there due to a snowstorm. Amid this a murder is introduced and the red herring trails begin to appear with tantalizing dexterity.

The production of *The Mousetrap* has undoubtedly over the years meandered away from Peter Cotes's initially realized taut conception. For instance in 1952 post-war rationing still existed. This and many other topical references to the period have now been updated in the script. The weekly charge at the guest house then was eighteen dollars. Dame Agatha had to approve all script changes but she was agreeable in recent years when an "absconded bank clerk" was neatly phased into a "drug pusher."

A great deal of the success of *The Mousetrap* lies in its surprise ending and it says much for the majority of British theater critics that they remained loyal to Agatha Christie and kept the secret. In fact during the last twenty-five years it has become the most guarded secret in the theater and few of the millions of people who have seen it are such blackguards as to give it away.

I have heard of only one case and this is probably apocryphal. It concerns a disgruntled London taxi driver who felt he had not been tipped sufficiently by a Scottish tourist. As he pulled his cab away from his passenger on the curb of the St. Martin's Theatre, to where the play had moved in 1974, he called out:

"And so and so did it, you stingy bastard."

Most of the royal family has seen *The Mousetrap*, including Queen Mary, who as usual had her special seat sent from Marlborough House. When Sir Winston Churchill saw it in the early years Peter Saunders set up an impromptu bar on the stage during the interval so that the elderly statesman would not have to climb the stairs and join the crush in the normal bars. Sir Winston guessed the killer during the interval much to Lady Churchill's skepticism.

All throughout *The Mousetrap* publicity Peter Saunders has been consistent in never using the word "murderer." Instead he always refers to "the killer." It is his contention that the word murderer has the connotation of a man as distinct from murderess. It is a pernickety point but an example of the painstaking and conscientious care he has taken over twenty-five years in every publicity detail concerning this profitable production.

No one really knows why *The Mousetrap* became such a phenomenon. It is a theatrical conundrum that will be debated in reference books for years to come.

There are the basic obvious reasons. As Agatha Christie once said: "I've thought about it a lot. Of course it is a small play in a small theater, which helps. It hasn't got terrific running costs or overheads. But I think it really is the sort of play you can take anyone to. It's not really frightening. It is not really horrible. It is not really a farce. But it has got a little bit of all those things. After about the eighteenth time I had seen it I decided it was a well-constructed play. The interest keeps up and that's difficult."

Whenever word reached backstage that "the duchess," as they called her, was sitting out front the cast was understandably nervous and it was with some trepidation that they learned the contents of the little notes she used to send backstage. They were always polite and to the point but it was clearly understood that no actor or actress could ignore them. She had definitive ideas about her characters and wished them to remain just as she created them. Any actor who attempted to stray from the original conception was quickly put in his place with a note or reminder.

"In those early days when I played in it she reminded me tremendously of Queen Mary," Mary Law remembers. "She wore toque hats and lovely soft mauves, beige and pink. She had a large bosom and always had lots of beads hanging around it and a big brooch. She looked enormous to me but you know how when you are much younger things do seem bigger and I think because I was very much in awe of her she was probably blown up to an enormous size in my mind."

When the play looked like it would be a marathon box office winner Peter Saunders decided early on to change the cast every year so that the actors-actresses would not become stale. Several of the early cast have returned after a break of a few years and resumed their original parts.

Whenever the cast was changed and Agatha Christie was in the country she was always invited to be present at the auditioning. The role of Mollie Ralston depends greatly on the actress's ability to scream—one long piercing scream soon after the curtain rises which has become almost the play's signature tune.

In an interview in the *Daily Mail* with that ubiquitous English journalist the late Godfrey Winn, to commemorate her eightieth birthday, Agatha Christie said:

"I really think I must go and see *The Mousetrap* again. I feel that would be only appropriate since I wrote the original story, *Three Blind Mice*, to commemorate Queen Mary's own eightieth birthday.

"No, it isn't my favorite. That's *Crooked House*. Do you know they change the cast of *The Mousetrap* every year to prevent staleness? But there is one character they have never succeeded yet in casting exactly right."

When Godfrey Winn asked, "Which part is that?" she replied archly: "Oh, it wouldn't be fair to say. It would be cheating."

Agatha Christie's opinions changed from time to time as she has also mentioned four other novels as being her favorites, *The Murder of Roger Ackroyd* (1926), *The Pale Horse* (1961), *Moving Finger* (1943), and *Endless Night* (1967).

Playing any long run becomes a hazard for actors and actresses but Agatha Christie is more difficult than others simply because of the suspense angle. As Geoffrey Colville, a *Mousetrap* veteran, explains:

"When somebody dries up that is difficult if you have been in a play for a long time. We had this during the 1976 run when somebody dried up for about four minutes and we literally didn't know why. We all had to make up the context, which was very difficult because firstly, we weren't really on the ball thinking and secondly, we couldn't give away the plot. You had to suddenly think terribly quickly when really you had been going along not thinking at all. This is the only time I have ever known anyone to ad-lib in a Christie play."

During the times that he played Christopher Wren in *The Mousetrap* Geoffrey Colville only remembers Mrs. Christie going backstage once to meet the players. He was one of several players who returned to the cast after a break of some years.

"I never could quite believe that she was as shy as everyone said. Perhaps she just didn't want to be bothered. I mean no one is really so shy that they can't come and say 'hello' or 'thank you' when you've been in a play as long as some of us had. I just thought that she ought to have come backstage every time she came to the theater."

In an interview with the BBC to commemorate the first ten years of *The Mousetrap* Mrs. Christie said that she had in fact seen the play about forty or fifty times. The last time she saw *The Mousetrap* was in 1971 when she was eighty years of age.

Once when the cast were having a party for somebody's birthday in the wardrobe department, Peter Saunders excused himself because he could not be there, saying, "I've got to look after Mrs. Christie downstairs."

Mary Law asked him: "Why isn't she coming to our party?"

"You know she never comes up, Mary," Mr. Saunders replied. "You go and ask her yourself but you had better be careful as she won't want to come."

"I did a thoroughly good job," Mary Law remembers.

"You are going to come, aren't you?" Mary Law asked.

"You don't want me," she replied.

"You only wrote the thing so I don't see why you shouldn't come to our party," Mary challenged.

"Do you think I'd be in the way?" Agatha Christie replied.

"Not at all. Of course we all want you," Mary Law replied.

"I don't like parties," Agatha Christie remonstrated.

"It doesn't matter. I don't like them either," Mary replied stubbornly. "We'll have a drink together and discuss the weather, your family, or whether I should get married."

Agatha Christie, who was keenly interested in music, was intrigued to know that the man in Mary Law's life was in fact the conductor Kenneth Alwyn and she followed this romance with interest right up to the altar a few months later.

Mary did persuade Mrs. Christie to go to the party, but although she smiled a lot and allowed herself to be photographed with some of the cast, she never looked entirely at ease and was obviously relieved when she could make her escape.

All through the years Mathew Prichard, Dame Agatha's grandson to whom she gave *The Mousetrap* as a gift when he was a boy of eight years of age, has consistently refused to discuss the fortune he has made out of the play. What he has said in various newspaper interviews is that it made little difference to the kind of life he would have had anyway.

He lives in an eighteenth-century manor house in Glamorgan in Wales set in three hundred acres of some of the most beautiful countryside there. He also holds the position of high sheriff of Glamorgan. In Derbyshire he has also an estate of three thousand acres where he spends much of his time improving the sheep and dairy herd. He is an energetic man in his mid-thirties, which must have pleased his grandmother, who once said that because of *The Mousetrap*'s success she feared that he would never have to work.

CHAPTER THIRTEEN

IN THOSE EARLY YEARS of *The Mousetrap* there were periods when the theater was certainly far from full. Holidays and Christmas played to packed houses but during the summer, before it had become the tourist attraction it is today, business was not always so good.

Although he had done considerable research to see what effect there would be when Richard Attenborough finally left the cast after two years, eighteen months longer than he had originally intended to stay, Peter Saunders could not forecast what in fact actually did happen. His absence was not missed for six months and then quite drastically business suddenly began to drop and Peter Saunders was advised by Herbert Malden, the manager of the theater, who ran it for the lessee, ex-Windmill girl Edna Chalker, to announce a closing date as he wished to make new arrangements for letting it.

Peter Saunders was doubly keen to keep open the next three months as by then he would have reached one thousand performances, which had only been obtained by fourteen plays in the history of the British theater. It was then that he made a momentous decision and personally took over the remaining three and a half years of Edna Chalker's lease. From that day on business began to pick up with everyone geared up to celebrate the thousandth performance.

On the thousandth performance every member of the audience received a white silk program. There were press and radio interviews when the one millionth visitor turned up and won herself a night out in London with armfuls of presents. The Saunders' publicity machine went into full action, and as usual was effectual.

When the play had run for five and a half years it became the longest running play in the history of the British theater beating the five-year-run of *Chu Chin Chow*. Other long runners in more recent years have been *Oliver, Salad Days, My Fair Lady, Sound of Music, Black and White Minstrel Show,* and *No Sex Please We're British.* To celebrate, Peter Saunders planned a spectacular *Mousetrap* party to which one thousand guests were invited. Just as he had hoped, the press called it "Night of a Thousand Stars" as almost every popular actor or actress could not resist the chance to see and be seen. Though hardly of the Royal Shakespearean Company they represented a great cross section of English talent and included such husband and wife teams as Richard Attenborough and Sheila Sim, Cicely Courtneidge and Jack Hulbert, Bebe Daniels and Ben Lyon, Bernard Braden and Barbara Kelly, Evelyn Laye and Frank Lawton, Dulcie Gray and Michael Denison, Doris and Robertson Hare, Anna Neagle and Herbert Wilcox.

The guest of honor nearly missed the party. When Agatha Christie arrived at the Savoy she found that she had left her invitation at home. The doorman, not recognizing this cozy middle-aged woman as she wanded among the crowd in the foyer, was reluctant to let her in until someone rescued her.

Recalling the incident later, she said: "I know many people don't know me but authors are shy people—we prefer to stay home. But they *did* let me in."

Peter Saunders and seven hundred bottles of champagne succeeded in giving this mammoth party a great feeling of informality as he and Agatha Christie stood for the first hour and personally greeted each guest on his arrival. If she was shy or uneasy Mrs. Christie did not show it as she stood there looking like everybody's favorite aunt giving each early arrival a toothy smile and limp handshake. It was a great family party and this she knew how to enjoy.

It was a night of speeches too, with everyone in sparkling form. Playwright Sir Alan Herbert, one of London's most witty after-dinner speakers, told an enthralled audience that while the critics never revealed the murderers in Agatha Christie plays they always gave away the adulterers in his. Cicely Courtneidge spoke on behalf of the theater, John Mills represented the film industry, and Philip Hope Wallace the critics.

All her inherent shyness returned when Agatha Christie rose to give her reply. Shyly, almost coyly, she said in that strangely girlish, fluted voice:

"I'm not good at speeches. I would rather write ten plays than make one speech," and everyone present knew that she really meant it as she sat down.

John Mills presented Agatha Christie with a gold program of the record-breaking performance, and too shy to give it herself, she asked him to present Peter Saunders with a specially made golden mousetrap, complete with mouse, which to this day stands in the foyer of the Ambassadors Theatre. The inscription reads: "Presented to the Ambassadors Theatre by Agatha Christie in grateful commemoration of the run of *The Mousetrap*, 25th November 1952–   ." The final date will be filled in when the play has its last performance.

Though there were many *Mousetrap* parties to follow this was the one that Agatha Christie treasured most all her life. It was not only her recognition as a playwright of importance on the London scene but a token of the affection and esteem with which she was held in the world of show business.

Another landmark in *The Mousetrap* saga that particularly pleased her was when the Morality Council lifted their ten-year ban on *The Mousetrap* as being unsuitable for children. The fact that there had been an interdict at all had astonished the author, a woman of high moral principles, who saw her plays only as entertainment and had conveniently overlooked any aspersions cast on the law in *The Mousetrap*.

All through the next five years, until another celebration party was held, it was Peter Saunders alone who kept *The Mousetrap* euphoria going in the strong belief that "publicity was still a vital factor in achieving the longevity that almost becomes perpetual motion." *Mousetrap* actors and actresses found themselves leaving the church under an archway of mousetraps—all carefully organized by the management for the national press. When the company gave a performance of the play at Wormwood Scrubs, the notorious London jail, not even Peter Saunders could foresee the extent of the publicity this would provoke. Two prisoners used the occasion as an excuse to escape and so *The Mousetrap* became front page news the next day.

Because of Agatha Christie's audacious and foresighted business acumen *The Mousetrap* is not permitted to be produced professionally on either Broadway or in Australia until six months after the end of the West End run. The film rights were sold some years ago to Romulus Films and have now passed to director Victor Saville. Though Peter Saunders has twice asked if he could buy back the rights, Mr. Saville refuses to sell and is prepared to sit and wait. As he says, "I have a gold mine here."

To date, apart from Britain, America, and Australia, the play has been produced in forty-one countries and been translated into twenty-two languages. It is the favorite of all Agatha Christie plays for amateur dramatics. The Sidenham Players, an amateur company in Wallingford, Oxfordshire, of which Agatha Christie was president for twenty-five years, have consistently asked to be allowed to be the first amateur company in England to produce the play but as yet they have been denied this due to the embargo that Peter Saunders and the owner of the copyright, Mathew Prichard, have imposed.

By the end of the fifties tourists had discovered *The Mousetrap*. Though way down the list somewhere between Madame Tussaud's and Harrods, visitors to London were beginning to place their reservations before leaving their home countries. New York theater and travel agencies especially reported steady business. *The Mousetrap* had become an international name.

For the tenth anniversary when one thousand guests again had been invited, Peter Saunders had engaged Shirley Bassey to give the cabaret. Again Agatha Christie was delighted to attend simply because at large parties little was personally expected from her and she could sit and observe as opposed to smaller parties where she was expected to play an active part. One chore she happily took part in was cutting the half-ton birthday cake made like a mousetrap which the chefs of the Savoy had cunningly created. As the ovens of the Savoy were too small, individual cakes had to be made and then stuck together with icing to form one glorious whole before the icing and tiny sugar mice were set into position.

Of the many people I have talked to at that party no one can remember the exact words that Agatha Christie greeted them with.

"One remembers her as being pleasant and her face all smiles and she looked very elegant in a dress of silk brocade. She so obviously enjoyed these parties," Mary Law remembers; "but whereas in the theater at rehearsals she had very definite opinions, at parties she seemed to withdraw into herself and found it difficult to communicate."

Speeches this year were cut down to three. Quite the most succinct speech was made by Dame Sybil Thorndike, a next-door neighbor of Agatha Christie's in Swan Court, a block of flats in Chelsea. Though not intimate friends they had known each other for many years. "I have been chosen to make this speech I think because *The Mousetrap* is the oldest run in the theater, and I am one of the oldest girls in show business."

In handing Agatha Christie the original Lord Chamberlain's script, bound in gold, she said: "Gold is nice to have in your room, because it only wants a handkerchief and a bit of spit to keep clean."

She also confessed that she had never seen *The Mousetrap*.

In 1972 when the play had been running for twenty years Peter Saunders gave another one of his thousand star parties; this time it was a luncheon. There were grave doubts as to whether Dame Agatha Christie would be able to be present as her broken hip still gave her great pain. People who had not seen her for some time had a shock as a frail-looking old lady came in wearing carpet slippers. She had shrunk to almost half her former size and had become rather like a dormouse. When she arrived at the door she suddenly turned to Peter Saunders, who was there to receive her, and said: "I can't go in. I've left my teeth at home."

There was no time to send a car to collect them so a compromise was made and it was agreed that no one would be permitted to speak to her, unless it was an intimate friend, as she did not want to open her mouth. However, the sparkling atmosphere was too much for Dame Agatha and she chuckled her way through the amusing incidents of the luncheon.

All through the party her eyes, now hooded with age, searched the room. When they found a friendly face they lingered for a while and she smiled before passing on. It is more than probable that she, too, realized, along with many of the guests there, that this would be her last *Mousetrap* party.

That year the cast had been allowed to bring their husbands, wives, or lovers and everyone sat down to a splendid luncheon of smoked salmon filled with *mousse de truite,* which was followed by steak and then a most admirable ice cream with black cherries. Dame Agatha, now eighty-one years old, played with her food and at times seemed far away.

No one, not even Agatha Christie, with her genius for timing, could have foreseen that *The Mousetrap*'s twenty-fifth birthday would fall in the Queen's silver jubilee year. Months before the event on November 25 Peter Saunders had booked the Savoy. All the same faces were there once again except the astonishing Dame Agatha. The Prime Minister, the Right Honorable James Callaghan, was guest of honor.

Statistics are cold and unemotional and rarely give a truthful picture, but in the case of *The Mousetrap* they make amusing reading. In November 1977 the play completed twenty-five years. More than 4 million people have seen it and in the process consumed over a million ice creams and drunk over half a million glasses of squash. During the play's run the shirts worn by the male members of the cast have been ironed to a total length of forty-six miles. The curtain has risen and fallen 121,250 times. The cast, which is changed every year, has to date had 134 players in it. The various *Mr. Parvicini's* have smoked 10,344 cigars, and 160 tons of programs have been sold.

During the first four and a half years of the play's run, electrician Alf Woolfe, sitting backstage, solved 1,998 crossword puzzles and never saw a performance during that time.

One or two props remain from the opening night—a leather armchair and a mantelpiece clock. Peter Saunders has retained this clock for a special reason. The hands of a clock going round can prove highly distracting, but this particular French clock is a design which prevents the hands from being seen from the auditorium.

In June 1965, Peter Saunders formed *The Mousetrap Club* and presented special ties to 98 "Male Mice" who had been connected with the production in some form or another since the beginning. The tie has a dark blue background with a motif of a little red mouse and a white "T," which stands for trap. The membership of the club is now up to 195.

On March 23, 1974, *The Mousetrap* finished its twenty-one-year run at the Ambassadors Theatre and transferred the following Monday next door to the larger St. Martin's Theatre without a break in the continuity of the run.

Pam Burford probably holds the record for the number of times she has seen the play—over 140 times and all during the two-year period that Richard Attenborough was acting in it. After he left the cast she did not see it again. When Peter Saunders saw her outside the stage door of another play in which Dickie Attenborough was appearing he asked her how many times she had seen that play.

"Only once," she replied. "I don't like the play."

Today *The Mousetrap* has become a kind of theatrical freak, and people like seeing freaks. As Peter Saunders explains: "It is a puzzle with all the ingredients of the best of all quiz programs. It has comedy. It has drama. It's a guessing game and the whole family can see it. I don't think this is the answer as to why it has run so long but this is why people like it and they tell their friends and the friends see it and so it goes on."

Unlike many London productions *The Mousetrap* does not have to rely on chartered coach parties from the provinces. It has a built-in audience among the millions of tourists who flock to London every year and can keep going comfortably on 150,000 people a year, which gives a gross £500 each performance.

Looking round the audience on my visit it was easy to spot the Americans in their warm, casual clothes and well-coiffured heads. The Germans are the most boisterous at the bar during the interval, while there is always a fair sprinkling of Japanese businessmen.

I was unable to buy a ticket as the house was sold out but just as I was turning away a man with twenty or so American teenagers approached the ticket box and asked if he could get a refund on one ticket as one of the children was sick and could not come. I immediately asked if I could buy the ticket from him and he replied: "Sure, but I hope you don't mind sitting with the kids."

This was a party of school children from New York middle-class families who were making an eight-day trip to England, taking in sight-seeing by day and theaters by night. Their school looked after the cultural bookings while the children were allowed to choose their own show on their one free night. *The Mousetrap* gained the most votes.

They were quiet well-behaved young people as we filed into our seats. The teacher took half of them on one side of the dress circle and I sat with my lot on the other side. It was the first time I had seen the production so we were all keyed up. After the first quarter of an hour the girl on my left fell asleep and the boy on my right began to fidget. In the interval I asked them why, if they were not enjoying it, had they decided to come at all.

"My mom, she picked it for me," the girl, Debbie, answered. "My mom and dad saw it when they came to England on their honeymoon in 1959."

This simple explanation might well be the unknown secret of *The Mousetrap*'s success. Agatha Christie wrote not only a play but a nostalgic snowball.

CHAPTER FOURTEEN

T HE FIFTIES were the golden years in the theater for Agatha Christie. *The Hollow* ran for eleven months and with it began a fantastic four-year period of success in the West End of London.

By now she was as completely at ease writing for the theater as in her novels.

"I find that writing plays is much more fun than writing books. For one thing you need not worry about those long descriptions of places and people. And you must write quickly if only to keep the mood while it lasts and to keep the dialogue flowing naturally. I didn't care much for what occurred when other people tried to turn my books into plays so in the end I felt I had to do it myself."

When 1955 began Agatha Christie was in lights outside three of London's most famous theaters. The productions were *Spider's Web*, *Witness for the Prosecution*, and *The Mousetrap*. *Witness for the Prosecution* had also crossed the Atlantic and was an astonishing success on Broadway.

In addition to her theatrical orientation Agatha Christie was continuing to produce two books a year as well as a crop of neatly turned short stories. It was an incredible feat for a woman who said:

"Perhaps one day they will find me out and realize that I can't really write at all."

In 1953 Peter Saunders was once more to prove his brilliant timing in knowing just what the public wanted. While staying with Agatha Christie at her home in Devon, during one of the lazy afternoon talks on the lawn, watching the river Dart go by, he mentioned that he had read a short story of Mrs. Christie's called *Witness for the Prosecution*, which he felt could be turned into a play.

Mrs. Christie was adamant. Whether in fact it was her shrewd assessment of her own limitations and concern at handling a large court scene "live" or whether she truly did not think the story was theater material is not known.

"It just won't work," she said.

With his persuasive way, all through the next few months, whenever they met Peter Saunders brought up the subject of *Witness for the Prosecution*, until finally Agatha Christie said:

"If you think there is a play in it write it yourself."

And this is exactly what he did. After a few hours sleep every night he rose at 3 A.M. and began a draft of a play taken from the short story. Though he had tampered with the dialogue in many of the plays he had produced, this was in fact the first time that he tried his own hand at an entire play.

When it was finished he had it delivered to Agatha Christie at her London flat. Within a few hours she telephoned him and asked him to tea, which was always an enjoyable occasion in her households. The script lay on a side table and it was not until Peter Saunders rose to leave that Agatha Christie referred to it.

"I may be wrong but I don't think you have written it very well. But you have shown me how it can be done. I will now write your play for you."

Six weeks later the play arrived on his desk—just as she had promised. *Witness for the Prosecution* was to establish Agatha Christie's reputation as a significant playwright from her former lightweight Home Counties scene. All through the rest of her life she maintained that this in fact was the play that gave her the most personal satisfaction.

Wallace Douglas, who had made such a success of *Ten Little Niggers*, was once again asked to direct the cast of thirty. For weeks both he and Peter Saunders used to drop in to the public gallery at the Old Bailey in London to absorb atmosphere. At the time a celebrated and gruesome murder trial concerning a man called Christie was taking place. It is doubtful whether Agatha Christie herself ever went to the Old Bailey although she did closely study a collection of books recalling famous trials. Peter Saunders had also promised her that the script would be vetted by experts for any legal mishaps.

In order to make the set as authentic as possible Michael Weight, the stage designer, produced a startlingly authentic reproduction of the famous No. 1 Court at the Old Bailey, correct in every detail down to the color of the paneling. The set was so arranged that the audience found themselves looking down on the court as though watching it from the public gallery. The co-operation backstage between the resident stage staff and the company technicians was so efficient that a scene change from counsel's chambers back to the elaborate Old Bailey setting took thirty-five seconds.

When he came to direct the play and make it "work," Wally Douglas sat down and in longhand wrote four sides of one-line notes on foolscap paper. This meant that there were something like one hundred points to be discussed. Recalling this, Mr. Douglas remembers: "I found the play was lacking in certain elements and I thought the story-line could be improved. I had read it from the director's point of view as to how the subject was going to appear on the stage to the audience who had paid its money to accept that product."

Wallace Douglas had up until then never met Agatha Christie. "I felt rather impertinent that I should be criticizing her work but on the other hand I felt that if I was to direct the play I had to have confidence."

He telephoned Peter Saunders and told him he had enjoyed the script tremendously but that he did have a number of points

Whenever she accompanied Sir Max Mallowan to the Middle East, Agatha Christie did much of the photographing of the finds from his digs. She not only became very proficient at this, but also helped her husband in the cataloguing of the hundreds of objects that resulted from the three-month expeditions. (Photo credit: Popperfoto)

Greenway, the secluded Georgian home of Dame Agatha Christie. (Photo credit: Popperfoto)

Whenever the sun shone, Agatha Christie took her work into the garden. This picture was taken in the garden of Winterbrook House, her home in Berkshire. (Photo credit: Popperfoto)

"What will Poirot's next move be?" ponders Dame Agatha Christie on the plot of her next book. One of her favorite walks was along the banks of the river Dart at the bottom of the garden at Greenway. (Photo credit: Popperfoto)

Dame Agatha Christie did much of the work plotting her books on long walks alone. "I exist in towns, but I live in the country," she said. (Photo credit: Popperfoto)

Announcement of the opening of *The Mousetrap*, Dame Agatha Christie's play, which holds the record for the world's longest running play. It opened on November 25, 1952, at the Ambassadors Theatre, London.

Agatha Christie attending a rehearsal on the stage set of *Witness for the Prosecution* in 1953. This was the play which was to class her as a serious playwright. *Witness*, with its replica of the Old Bailey set, was an outstanding success in both New York and London, and was later filmed.

Agatha Christie and Peter Saunders greet Richard Attenborough and his wife, Sheila Sim, at the sixth anniversary, in 1958, of the record-breaking run of *The Mousetrap*. (Photo credit: Associated Newspapers)

Dame Agatha Christie "flirts" with John Mills at a party held at the Savoy to celebrate the 2,239th performance of *The Mousetrap*. (Photo credit: Keystone Press Agency, Ltd.)

Agatha Christie, assisted by Peter Saunders, cuts the half-ton birthday cake made in the form of a mousetrap at the tenth birthday party given to celebrate *The Mousetrap*. (Photo credit: *Daily Express*)

Actress Dame Sybil Thorndike and Dame Agatha Christie share a joke at the party to celebrate the tenth birthday of *The Mousetrap*. (Photo credit: Associated Press)

Three theatrical Dames (of the British Empire) enjoy a girls' gossip at Sybil Thorndike's eightieth birthday party in 1962. From left: Dame Peggy Ashcroft, Dame Sybil Thorndike, and Dame Agatha Christie. (Photo credit: London *Express*)

A look of admiration passes between the young Princess Anne and Dame Agatha Christie at the première of the film *Murder on the Orient Express*.

The face of Agatha Christie, at eighty-four years, as seen by Lord Snowden: kindly, wise, and filled with understanding. (Photo credit: Snowden)

One of the last official photographs taken of Dame Agatha Christie when she attended a luncheon party at Thompson House. On her left is the newspaper magnate Lord Thompson and second left is Sir Robert Mark, former Commissioner for the Metropolitan Police. (Photo credit: Thompson Newspapers)

As a schoolgirl, the Queen had read Agatha Christie. Here they meet for the last time at the première of the film *Murder on the Orient Express*, much to the obvious delight of the author. The man in between them is Nat Cohen, chairman/chief executive of E.M.I. Film Productions.

One of the last photographs taken of Dame Agatha Christie. She is seated at her writing desk at Winterbrook House, Wallingford, Berkshire. (Photo credit: Snowden)

Dame Agatha Christie and Sir Max Mallowan in the grounds of Winterbrook House with their dog Treacle. (Photo credit: Snowden)

Agatha Christie seated in the sitting room of her home at Wallingford, surrounded by the flowers and embroidery that she loved. On the work table in front of her is a note pad and on the right the tape recorder which she used in later years when her hands became arthritic. (Photo credit: Snowden)

Dame Agatha Christie and Sir Max Mallowan pictured surrounded by roses in the garden of Winterbrook House. (Photo credit: Snowden)

They were together for forty-five years—Dame Agatha Christie and Sir Max Mallowan, at the garden Gate outside Winterbrook House. When they married in 1930, Dame Agatha gave her age as thirty-seven, three years younger than she was, and Sir Max gallantly wrote his as thirty-one, five years older than he really was. (Photo credit: Snowden)

Dame Agatha Christie and Sir Max Mallowan, in the sitting room of their house at Wallingford. The room is filled with memorabilia and reminiscent of many that she has described in her own detective novels. (Photo credit: Snowden)

Behind Dame Agatha Christie's coffin, as it is carried from the parish church at St. Mary's, Cholsey, walk the three most important people in her life, who shared in the vast fortune she left: Mrs. Rosalind Hicks, her only daughter by her first marriage to Colonel Archibald Christie, Sir Max Mallowan, and behind him Matthew Prichard, the grandson who inherited the rights to *The Mousetrap* when he was a young child. (Photo credit: Popperfoto)

which he felt would improve the play. They met for a couple of hours and finally Peter Saunders said: "Well, I think you should tell Agatha yourself."

A meeting was arranged in Peter Saunders' office in Grand Buildings, Trafalgar Square.

"I was a little surprised at what I saw. It was a dumpy mother-figure and she was very, very sweet. We said "hullo" and the niceties went on and then we finally talked about the play. She asked me, 'What do you think of it?'

"I told her I liked it but that I had one or two things to discuss with her. I then embarked on my list and she listened, interrupting from time to time 'I see . . . yes, yes . . . that's right.'

"I went on relentlessly simply because I felt in for a penny in for a pound, but I could not tell whether she liked what I was saying or not. As far as I was concerned it was just another play for me. It took me something like two hours to get through my list and I ended rather lamely, 'Well there you are. That's all.'

"If I remember she just said 'very good' or something totally noncommittal. Peter asked her when he could expect the amended script. Then it was quite amazing to listen as she thought aloud: 'Well, I'm going to Devon next week, and then the family is coming for a week. I've got those two meetings; and so on. She agreed to do it and said that Peter Saunders would have it on such and such a date.

Just as she was leaving Wally Douglas asked if she would like to take his list with her to remind her of the changes he had suggested.

" 'Oh no, that's not necessary. I can remember it.' "

When Peter Saunders came back from escorting her to the door Wallace Douglas said: "Peter, I think I've overstepped the mark. I'm sorry."

Peter Saunders replied: "Oh, I don't think so. If she says she is going to do it she will."

On the date the script was promised Wallace Douglas could not contain himself and telephoned Peter Saunders to ask if he had heard any news from Agatha Christie.

"Oh yes, it arrived on my desk this morning," Saunders replied.

"Of course I was fascinated to see whether she had embodied

153

everything I had suggested," Wallace Douglas recalls. "When Peter sent the script round I got out the notes she had declined to take and went through every point. Every single one was incorporated. This is a feat which was beyond me," Douglas said.

One thing she flatly refused to do and that was to alter the ending leaving out the final twist. She did not argue but merely said: "This is how I want it to be played and I believe that I am right."

The casting of the play was to prove just as difficult as any previous Christie one. Peter Saunders and Wallace Douglas made a list of thirty-six leading actors who could have played the part of the choleric and patriarchal queen's counsel for the prosecution.

One by one they were approached in numerical order of choice. One by one they turned it down. They found the ending of the play, which was a different one from the short story, so bizarre that Agatha Christie's diabolically clever double double cross at the end had no credence.

Finally Wallace Douglas suggested David Horne who, though a first-class portly character actor, was not star material or a box office draw. The next important role was that of a German woman, which went to Patricia Jessel, whose work had impressed Peter Saunders so much in a former play he had produced, *The Ex Mrs. Y*. When she auditioned for the part she gave such an electrifying performance that both Agatha Christie and Peter Saunders knew that the play would "work." After playing the role for four years in England and in America, Pat Jessel became identified with the role. With passionate intensity she made the whole part so enigmatic that it played a great share in the play's success.

Witness for the Prosecution opened in Nottingham and when asked by the local paper why she chose this Midlands town Mrs. Christie's answer came pat: "Nottingham is so lucky for us [Peter Saunders and herself]. We like it. It sent *The Hollow* and *The Mousetrap* off to a flying start." Then, thrusting out her Margaret Rutherford chin and giving one of her little giggles, she added: "We rather hope to do it every year."

For the opening night at the Theatre Royal Nottingham the shocking pink program contained the warning: "There are no revolver shots in this play." After all it was a family play.

The Nottingham *Evening News* was not so impressed in its review of the opening night. The critic wrote: "For whom else would we sit through a whole evening of average entertainment and acclaim it a success on the strength of the last ten minutes . . . Mrs. Christie tells a clever story but does she lend it probability? The answer is not during this production. The Old Bailey set is impressive, but the scenes there never for a moment capture the thick keyed atmosphere of a trial for murder. There are plenty of dramatics—never drama. Mrs. Christie has sacrificed authenticity for amusement and substituted a string of blithe caricatures for sober men and women."

The play toured Glasgow, Edinburgh, and Sheffield before opening at the 1,640-seater Winter Garden Theatre in London on October 28, 1953. Here the applause was rapturous. The audience rose as one and cheered, stamped and shouted "author" as all thirty of the cast bowed solemnly to a stage box. Sitting well back in the shadows, with the dignity of Queen Victoria, the sixty-two-year-old author beamed behind her tortoise-shell spectacles. Completely stunned by the reception, she bent forward and waved to the audience. Leaning over to Peter Saunders, she whispered; "It's rather fun, isn't it?"

If the Nottingham local paper had not been too impressed, London was. As Eve Chapman of the *Daily Mirror* wrote: "Agatha Christie must be happy this morning. While one thriller *The Mousetrap* is packing them in at the Ambassadors Theatre, another play of hers called *Witness for the Prosecution* opened with great success last night at the Winter Garden Theatre."

Agatha Christie was extraordinarily happy as almost every national newspaper in London gave her a rave notice.

"A thumping good time in court" . . . "An exciting murder trial" . . . "Old Bailey takes a bow" . . . "Agatha's dunit again" . . . "Christie and its Crisp" were some of the headlines.

Only the professional legal magazine *The Magistrate* dared to knock her. "It must be admitted, however, that for educational purposes Miss Christie's Old Bailey is inferior to the real thing, for although she has evidently taken some pains to get her law right she has not completely succeeded . . . counsel are properly counsel-like in manner and mannerisms, but most unrealistically succinct in speech."

As in *The Mousetrap* and several other of her plays with their bizarre endings, the management asked the audience not to give away the final twist and every critic, to a man, was loyal. The magic that this gray-haired, motherly spellbinder shared with her public was quite extraordinary.

"I must say that I did enjoy that first night. Usually it is hideous. I always feel very shy and uncomfortable appearing in public but that was heaven. The play was so well done and there were lots of women waiting for me outside—quite rough types you know—but they welcomed me, patted me on the back, and said: 'Well done, dearie,'" Agatha Christie later commented.

Witness for the Prosecution became a favorite play of royalty. The Duchess of Kent, who was an avid theater goer saw it twice. Princess Margaret, who accompanied her on one occasion, was just twenty-three and wore a velvet New Look dress. When the Duke and Duchess of Windsor returned to London, *Witness for the Prosecution* was the play they chose to see on their first visit since the duke's abdication. As they walked through the theater to their private box there was a ripple of whispering when the audience realized who they were. Suddenly the audience could contain itself no longer and burst into loud clapping. The duke and duchess were obviously affected by the ovation and leaned forward in their box to wave to the crowds. The play was also specially staged years later by the Windsor Repertory Company for the Queen and Prince Philip, who went on stage after the production to meet the cast.

An interesting aspect of the West End stage production of *Witness for the Prosecution* is the fate of three of the leading characters. Patricia Jessel was to die tragically in 1968, her husband in the play, Derek Blomfield (Leonard Vole), and David Horne, who had the role of the queen's counsel for the prosecution, are also dead.

Witness for the Prosecution opened in New York in 1954 a few days after another Christie play, *Spider's Web* had its first night in London. The English actor Ernest Clark was in the role of the prosecuting counsel and went to New York and Patricia Jessel, "the witness," played the part she had so brilliantly created in London. Francis L. Sullivan was cast as the defense counsel and the rest of cast came from America, although Peter Saunders went to great pains to select English actors if he could. Gilbert Miller was co-producer and Robert Lewis, fresh from his success in *Brigadoon* and *Teahouse of the August Moon*, directed.

Mrs. Christie was asked to the opening in New York but declined as this was the time of year when she began preparing for her regular trip to the Middle East with her husband, Professor Max Mallowan.

Audience reaction in New York was even better than in London and Brooks Atkinson of the New York *Times* was laudatory of not only the play but the author as well. Even Francis L. Sullivan, a Christie devotee, had disquietening private thoughts about the play. He was to say later: "I loved the play personally but at the time I had grave doubts about its success in America. I felt it was too English and that might make it difficult to follow especially in the court scenes and it was also dramatic which is supposed to be unpopular here in New York. I need have had no fears. The Duchess of Death has had an even bigger success here in New York than in London and I imagine that the play will run for two years at least." It did.

On May 16, 1955, the New York Drama Critics Circle made their selection for the year. Agatha Christie's *Witness for the Prosecution* was chosen as the best foreign play, *Cat on a Hot Tin Roof* gained Tennessee Williams an award for the best American play, and Gian-Carlo Menotti's *The Saint of Bleecker Street* was the best musical.

Spider's Web was one of the few plays that Agatha Christie wrote especially for an actor or actress. Margaret Lockwood, who had by now made a name for herself as the "wicked lady" of the British film industry, had not in fact ever played in the West End apart from being a beguiling Peter Pan. She was anxious to make a comeback but such was her film success that she was also keen that the play should be a built-in success.

Her agent, Herbert de Leon, therefore approached Peter Saunders with the suggestion that Agatha Christie might be persuaded to write a play specially for her.

Whether in fact Mrs. Christie had ever seen a Margaret Lockwood film is highly improbable but she was an avid newspaper reader, albeit mainly *The Times,* and would certainly have known of her box office success.

Once again Peter Saunders arranged one of his intimate little luncheons, this time at the Mirabelle. Mrs. Christie enjoyed these occasions as a chance to test the menus since, as a non-drinker, the normal cocktail hour meant nothing to her. In her own quizzical way she also needed time to sum up the person under scrutiny and meeting over luncheon was just as pleasant a way as any other.

Margaret Lockwood, with her sparkling personality, has none of the big star personality ego. She is a thoroughly professional trouper with an immense caring for other actors and actresses. She has remained this way until today where she occasionally stars in the British television world as well as the legitimate theater.

The idea for the play was to be a highly sophisticated thriller comedy and Wallace Douglas had been canvased as the possible director.

"Before we met at lunch I realized that although I had read all her stories as a schoolgirl I had no idea what she would look like," Miss Lockwood remembered in a BBC interview. "Like a great many other people I was completely taken by surprise. She was utterly unlike anything I had remotely imagined. She was perfectly charming and we got on very well but I couldn't help thinking of her in the setting of a country vicarage."

During the lunch Agatha Christie had said: "Yes, I would like to do a play for this young lady."

Margaret Lockwood then asked if a part could be written in for Wilfrid Hyde White and if the play could be more of a comedy than a thriller.

Then there came the delicate matter of when Mrs. Christie could deliver so that production could be put into operation. There was the usual discussion of her family plans and future commitments before she gave a date and vanished back to Devon.

Once more Wallace Douglas telephoned Peter Saunders on the day that had been mentioned, three months later.

"Oh yes, I was just going to telephone you. It arrived in the post this morning," Saunders said.

When Margaret Lockwood received her script she immediately sent a telegram to Agatha Christie saying how delighted she was with the part. It was in fact tailor-made for her and there was even a surprise part for a child as Mrs. Christie felt that Margaret Lockwood might like to include her own daughter Julia. It was typical of Agatha Christie's concern for another woman's problem in trying to get her teen-age daughter launched in the career that she wanted to follow.

In every respect this was a play for Margaret Lockwood. It is about the wife of a Foreign Office official who loves to romance and finds her weakness for telling fibs gets her more and more into trouble when a real murder takes place in a country house. Each time Clarissa Hailsham-Brown (she named the role for Margaret Lockwood after her mother's name, Clarissa) told the inspector, "Now I'll really tell you the truth," it was apparent that the audience was going to be taken off on another Christie red herring.

When Wilfrid Hyde White read the script he did not like his role as the heroine's guardian so the part was eventually given to that cultured English actor Felix Aylmer. Margaret Lockwood was then working on a film so the production did not get under way until September 1954.

There was the usual pre-London tryout at the Theatre Royal in Nottingham and though Wallace Douglas had not been too sure about the play he remained quiet, remembering how he had been so critical of *Witness for the Prosecution*.

It was during the final rehearsal in Nottingham that he could contain himself no longer. The play opened with a very long scene in which two elderly men—Felix Aylmer and Harold Scott were talking about butterflies.

"In my opinion," Wallace Douglas remembered, "it did not advance the plot and did not set the scene for what the play was going to be about. I said to Agatha, 'This is too long, darling. This doesn't work.'"

Agatha Christie turned to him and in a voice of finality said: "This will be all right. I know this will be all right."

"In fact she was jolly cross with me," Mr. Douglas recalled.

After the opening night in Nottingham, Agatha Christie went

159

to Wallace Douglas and said: "Wally, you are quite right. I am very fond of that scene but it doesn't work."

Peter Saunders arranged for a room in the hotel and author and director sat down together and worked it out.

"That is what was so very sweet and generous of her. Once she was convinced that she was wrong she was never so discourteous as not to admit it."

One of the reasons that Agatha Christie could produce a script at such short notice, despite her book commitments, was the ease with which she wrote and her enormous reservoir of ideas. Later in her life when Cecil Day Lewis, the poet laureate who wrote detective stories under the *non de plume* of Nicholas Blake, met Mrs. Christie he commented in a lively discussion: "My trouble is that I have a great deal of trouble thinking up my plots."

"That is not my problem. I just hate to put them down on paper," Agatha Christie replied.

To which Cecil Day Lewis countered, "Miss Christie, none of us is getting any younger. I believe you have seventeen plots in hand. Would you sell me a few?"

"Certainly not," Agatha Christie replied. "I intend to write them all myself."

Spider's Web did not on the whole get good reviews but on the other hand it did run for 774 performances. Peter Saunders and Mrs. Christie sat back and chuckled. They had done it again.

In 1956 *Towards Zero* opened at the St. James's Theatre and Mrs. Christie was once more in the stalls as the cast was auditioned. Mary Law had first been asked to audition for the leading lady role but was turned down as the director wanted a star name. It was then suggested that she should understudy.

"I telephoned Vivien Leigh, who was a friend of mine, and we discussed it. 'No, you don't understudy,' she said. 'You auditioned for the part.' Well, a fortnight later they asked me back and I was given the part.

"Mrs. Christie came over to me and said: 'I am so glad. The first day I saw you I wanted you because you are absolutely as I imaged Fay would be so I was determined to have you.' It was absolutely marvelous for me and I do owe a great deal to her.

"She was painfully shy when we met socially. She didn't seem to want to talk to anyone. You'd say, 'It's a lovely day,' and she'd reply, 'Yes.' Then you'd try again. 'It's hotter than yesterday,' and she'd answer, 'Yes.'

"Once we began rehearsing her personality changed. We all found her lines very difficult to say and if someone in the cast said to her, 'Do you mind if I alter this line?' Agatha Christie replied from the stalls: 'Yes, I do mind, I want you to say, 'I hate her, I hate her, I hate her.' "

Not all Agatha Christie plays were a success. Her original play *Verdict*, which was staged at the Strand Theatre in 1958, was booed by the gallery and came off after a run of four weeks.

On the first night the stage management got into such a neurotic state, because of what was happening in the gallery, that they brought the final curtain down forty seconds too soon and cut the closing lines of the dialogue.

When Peter Saunders had to break the news over the telephone of the devastating reviews which the play received, Agatha Christie was typically calm and well mannered.

"At least *The Times* liked it," she replied. "The gallery gave me a rough passage. The critics do not seem to care for it either but you cannot please everyone, can you? I felt sorry for the cast and I came away sad."

Undaunted and unbowed, within a month the sixty-eight-year-old word factory had produced another script, *The Unexpected Guest*, which Peter Saunders rushed into production.

This is a classical rule-breaking Christie, set in Wales, since the audience knows from the beginning who committed the murder. A young man, who has been working with an oil company in the Middle East, is stranded in his motor car on a foggy night. He bursts into a house where a man sits dead in his chair while his wife stands by his side with a revolver in her hand.

As Nigel Stock, who played the role of Michael Stark, explained: "Only two people were involved in the first scene and this meant trying to hold the audience for a long time. It was not easy."

This was one of the few times that Mrs. Christie was not present at the first reading of one of her plays. She sent a message that she was sorry she was unable to be there as she was making raspberry jam.

The reviews were good. Agatha Christie was back in form again. Her public had not deserted her. Despite its non-star cast *The Unexpected Guest* ran for 604 performances at the Duchess Theatre.

Agatha Christie's prolific play-writing period was over by the end of the 1950s. In the next sixteen years she wrote only two more plays, *Go Back for Murder*, (1960) which was based on her novel *Five Little Pigs*, and played at the Duchess Theatre. *Rule of Three*, three original one-act plays, was also performed at the Duchess in 1962.

In America during the 1970s *Spider's Web* was revived. *Ten Little Indians* had been made into a musical which toured under the name *Something's Afoot*.

One of the last pieces of business Agatha Christie completed before she died was to arrange with Peter Saunders for her novel *A Murder Is Announced* to be adapted by Leslie Darbon for the stage.

It opened at the Vaudeville Theater in London on September 21, 1977, with a typical Christie audience and a solid cast which included Dulcie Gray as a subdued Miss Marple. The acting was as serviceable as the dialogue even if Miss Marple is a far cry from Margaret Rutherford's portrayal in the earlier films. Dulcie Gray's interpretation is of a retiring, gray-haired, shabby old thing with a waddling walk and toes that turn in at forty-five degrees when she sits down.

As B. A. Young wrote in the *Financial Times*, "There is no reason, intellectually or dramatic, why the play shouldn't run as long as *The Mousetrap*."

In all there have been nineteen Agatha Christie plays produced; she wrote thirteen herself and six were adapted from her novels. One, *Akhnaton*, written in 1937, has never been performed.

Will Agatha Christie plays stand the test of time like those of Somerset Maugham or Noel Coward? They may date, as indeed have *Murder at the Vicarage*, which has now been running for two years at the Savoy, and *The Mousetrap*, in its twenty-sixth year at St. Martin's. But they do recall a visual nostalgia for a middle-class way of life that will never return to England. Of spacious chintzy country houses, cultivated morning-room talk, impeccable servants, bowls of potpourri, croquet on the lawn, Earl Grey tea poured from Georgian silver, and wafer-thin brown bread cucumber sandwiches.

Perhaps this is what many of us are longing for.

CHAPTER FIFTEEN

Dame Agatha Christie was not at all interested in turning her novels into films and the only reason that she allowed her agent to make those early deals was to extend her reading public. She was never at any time fascinated by the film industry as she was with the legitimate theater. Television interested her even less and in her private life she much preferred an evening of Wagner to watching "the box."

It is a piquant thought that it was in fact the Germans who were the first to see the possibilities of turning Agatha Christie novels into films. As early as 1928 Die Abenteuer G m.b.H (Adventure, Inc.) made *The Secret Adversary* into a film. There existed in Germany at that time a passion for British detective novels, with Edgar Wallace and Sherlock Holmes as top favorites. *The Secret Adversary* made by the producer-director Julius Hagen was reasonably successful so this was followed with *The Passing of Mr. Quinn*. But the first major film made by the same director was *Alibi*, which of course came from the provocative novel *The Murder of Roger Ackroyd*.

The casting of Poirot was the first difficulty and any connection with Mrs. Christie's original conception of a short, egg-shaped Belgian with the finest mustache in England was totally ignored when clean-shaven Austin Trevor was given the role. He was unsuited to the part.

Though she was later to become "heartily tired" of Poirot, when he reached the ripe age of 117 years, having just created him, she was at that stage rather entranced.

Agatha Christie positively hated those early films and vowed that she would never again go and see them as her characters were so badly misinterpreted. She said, "It gives me too much pain."

The first film of any consequence was *Love from a Stranger*, adapted from the play which originated from the now celebrated short story, "Philomel Cottage."

This was filmed twice, the first time with Madeleine Carroll and Basil Rathbone and later with John Hodiak and Sylvia Sidney when the title was changed to *A Stranger Walked In*.

The most filmed of all the early Agatha Christie plays was *Ten Little Niggers* (titled *Ten Little Indians* or *And Then There Were None* in America). The provocative French director René Clair made the first version. This was followed by Harry Allen Towers, directed by George Pollock, and set in the Austrian Alps. Eight years later Towers decided to make another version and this time used the Shab Adah Hotel in Isfahan, Persia, for the setting.

None of these films gave Agatha Christie any pleasure or satisfaction. She was appalled when her play, so rightly set on Nigger Island off the coast of Devon, was jostled to various exotic parts of the world. What was wrong with Devon?

It was not until 1957 when Billy Wilder directed and scripted the film version of *Witness for the Prosecution* that she began to take any personal interest in films made from her books. Though the movie offers poured in for this play after its initial success in London and New York it took eighteen months finally to persuade her to sell the film rights to an American company for £116,000—a record for any British playwright of the day. This delighted her, for despite being a woman of modest tastes in her private life, she was fully aware of her value as a writer. She understood the Italian proverb "money makes money" and was never shy in driving a hard commercial bargain.

Charles Laughton repeated his English stage success in the important role of Sir Wilfred Robarts, Marlene Dietrich played the Austrian wife Romaine, and Laughton's wife, Elsa Lanchester, gave a delightfully witty cameo as Nurse Plimsoll, Sir Wilfred's bossy nurse, who was constantly badgering him to take his heart medicine.

In his biography *Charles Laughton* (W. H. Allen), Charles Higham writes:

"Wilder, acidulous and tough, and Charles, genial and perfectionist, hit it off splendidly. He managed to create a character—in part suggested by his London solicitor Florenz Guedella—at once petulant, childish, and ruthless, seemingly frivolous, but in fact fiercely honest and bent on finding out the truth.

"As conceived by Agatha Christie, the character is impossible. After this great advocate's lifetime of shrewd legalism we are supposed to believe that he can fail to see that his client is guilty, that his client's wife is lying to save his life, or that she is disguised as a cockney in one scene. It says a great deal for Charles's sheer technical skill that he could overcome the manifold deficiencies in the writing."

Whatever Higham feels about the script and its author, both Charles Laughton and Elsa Lanchester were nominated for an Academy Award for their roles in the film.

In an unhesitating voice Agatha Christie has said on many occasions that she did not approve of the four films that were made by M.G.M. in the 1960s all starring that much beloved actress Margaret Rutherford as Jane Marple.

As Agatha Christie said: "I kept off films for years because I thought they would give me too many heartaches. Then I sold the rights to M.G.M., hoping that they would use them for television. But they chose films. It was too awful. They did things like taking a Poirot and putting Miss Marple in it. And all the climaxes were so poor, you could see them coming. I get an unregenerated pleasure when I think they're not being a success. They wrote their own script for the last one—nothing to do with me at all—

Murder Ahoy. One of the silliest things you ever saw. It got a very bad review, I'm delighted to say."

Mrs. Christie had modeled Miss Marple on her great-aunt and her grandmother. She saw Jane Marple as a tall, slender, fragile, pink-and-white lady with silver curling hair and an expression of the utmost gentleness in her china-blue eyes. Although she had led the most sheltered of Victorian lives she was also perfectly capable of going up to the most potent of police inspectors and saying: "I may be what is termed a spinster, but I know the difference between horseplay and murder."

In the 1960s Margaret Rutherford was at the height of her professional trumpeting. As Melvin Maddocks in *The Christian Science Monitor* was to describe her after seeing the first of the quartet, *Murder She Said:* "One has the impression of frumpy hair fringes above baleful eyes and a permanently reproachful mouth. A formidable blocky torso stands draped in a regular tarpaulin of a sweater descending over a tweedy skirt of indefinite length beneath which protrude two dangerously thin legs based hopefully upon sensible walking shoes. The effect is of a warmly bundled English bull-dog."

It was a far cry from Agatha Christie's fluffy old lady, who first appeared in novel form in 1930 in *Murder at the Vicarage,* with her inevitable knitting and strong appetite for the gossip of the local village, St. Mary Mead.

When I was preparing Margaret Rutherford's autobiography for her she was aged and in such a depressive state of mind that her memory faltered. Everyone in the theater who knew this wonderful actress, from Sir John Gielgud down, generously offered to help me with reminiscences.

I wanted to hear Mrs. Christie's version of meeting Margaret Rutherford so I wrote to her, enclosing a note from Margaret's husband, Stringer Davis. I received this brief reply from her secretary: "Mrs. Christie does not give interviews but she has asked me to tell you that while she thinks Miss Rutherford is a fine actress, she bears no resemblance to her own idea of Miss Marple." That was all.

Mrs. Christie may have had her own dissatisfaction about Margaret Rutherford as Miss Marple but it was nothing compared to the horror that this delightfully gentle actress expressed when she was asked to play the part. It also took several years and a great deal of persuasion to tempt her at all. Had she not needed the money and been in arrears with her tax it is doubtful whether she would ever have consented to play Miss Marple.

"I never wanted to play Miss Marple. I never found murder amusing. I don't like anything that tends to lower or debase or degrade," she told me shortly before her death in 1972.

Margaret Rutherford had talked it over many times with her agent, Dorothy Mather of Film Rights, and a close friend, writer Alison Uttley. Mrs. Uttley came up with the piquantly logical explanation. She said that playing the role of Miss Marple was in fact a question of art, just as murder is in a morality play. If played well it could be pleasing and entertaining and it did have moral values of a particular kind.

It was quietly spoken, film director George Pollock, who finally persuaded Margaret Rutherford by explaining that Miss Marple was not so much concerned with crime, but that she was more involved in a game—like chess—a game of solving problems ahead of the police. Murder was just one of the ingredients to make it entertaining.

As Dame Margaret explained to me: "Miss Marple was undoubtedly a good woman and helped people. It was Christmas Day 1960 that I finally took the plunge and telephoned George with my answer: 'Yes, I will be Miss Marple.' He seemed delighted and said that it was his best Christmas present."

A salient point is the similarity in the private lives of Agatha Christie and Margaret Rutherford. Both had introverted childhoods and were left a great deal to their own devices of making up stories and filling their small worlds with imaginary people. Both believed in goodness and kindness and miracles and to the very end of their lives had the ability of being able to enter a child's mind.

Both were large women who were acutely conscious of their size.

"Oh to have been born an O.S. (outsize)" Agatha Christie constantly wailed.

"If you have a face like mine the thing is to learn to live with it and come to terms with it . . . I really have lost count of the number of chins I have. At the last count there might have been four or five," Margaret Rutherford told me.

In their private lives they were gentle, beautifully mannered women living in their own sheltered worlds but professionally they could be truculent, demanding, and oftimes irascible. Each preferred tramping the moors in comfortable old tweeds and brogues to standing around at cocktail parties with a glass of apple juice in their hands. Both had in their own way perfected a technique of shedding themselves of bores. A kind of comatose descended on them as they quietly moved on to pastures afresh. They were both made Dames of the British Empire—Miss Rutherford in 1967 and Mrs. Christie in 1971—in reward for giving pleasure to millions of people the world over.

Finally they both found complete contentment and marital happiness with men younger than themselves. Professor Mallowan was fourteen years younger than Dame Agatha Christie and actor Stringer Davis was seven years junior to Dame Margaret Rutherford.

Author and actress were to meet only once, in 1962 when Mrs. Christie visited the set of *Murder at the Gallop*. There was an instant rapport. As Margaret Rutherford said: "This delightful woman came down to see me on the set and when we met face to face we instantly clicked. I completely overcame my first tentative prejudices about Christie crime and became most fond of Jane Marple."

Later in the same year Agatha Christie dedicated *The Mirror Crack'd from Side to Side*, a detection novel about a famous actress, to "Margaret Rutherford in admiration."

If Mrs. Christie herself was not happy with this film version of Jane Marple, Margaret Rutherford fans were delighted. They flocked to cinemas all round the world. Not one critic raised a voice in protest, and a whole new generation of readers switched on to reading Christie books.

Alexander Walker of the *Evening Standard* and one of Britain's most erudite critics summed it up:

"The answer is that Margaret Rutherford fills the spinster's tweeds of her renowned detective Miss Marple splendidly. She is hugely enjoyable. With chin wagging like a windsock on an airfield and eyes that are deceptively guileless, she clumps her way through lines, situations and disguises that would bunker an actress of less imperial aplomb."

As late as 1974 Dame Agatha was still in a relentless mood when she criticized the casting of Margaret Rutherford as Miss Marple. This brought a sharp reply back from Jack Seddon of Pinewood Studios, who had the scripts of the M.G.M. films.

"It is quite true, as Miss Christie says, that the screen Miss Marple was nothing like her own creation. This is because she wasn't intended to be. The Miss Marple of the books struck me as snobbish, unkind, and cold, with a stealthy, almost reptilian eye.

"The intention with the screen Miss Marple was to create a person of warmth and gusto and, as portrayed by the late Margaret Rutherford, it seems that intention was achieved.

"That Miss Christie 'would never advise anyone to go and see them' comes a little late, as millions already have, no doubt to the great financial benefit of the principal parties concerned—including I should have thought Miss Christie."

It was Nat Cohen, chairman and chief executive of E.M.I. Film Productions, who was brave enough to try again and to woo Dame Agatha to agree to another film being made from one of her novels.

"I had a feeling that the Agatha Christie novels, particularly the Poirots, had a great attraction for the public. I then got in touch with Lord Brabourne, who is an outstanding producer. We felt that *Murder on the Orient Express* would be the ideal thing to get the ball rolling."

It was in fact Lord Mountbatten who made the approach to Dame Agatha Christie. He told me:

"I knew that my son-in-law John Brabourne would handle it quite differently from the Margaret Rutherford films, which I knew had infuriated her. I then wrote to her and said that since we have been in correspondence about *The Murder of Roger Ackroyd*, when she used my idea for the plot, I wondered if she would see my son-in-law to discuss his making a film. As I told her: "I know that you do not like films being made from your books but he would do it quite differently.'"

Dame Agatha agreed to meet Lord Brabourne and turned up for luncheon at the Savoy Grill with the usual family retinue. He then told Dame Agatha about all the films he had made, one or two of which she seemed to know about, particularly the entrancing film made in conjunction with Richard Goodwin and the Royal Ballet from *The Tales of Beatrix Potter*. The film had been an outstanding success not only commercially but also artistically.

Once Dame Agatha indicated that she would quite like to see a good Poirot film made, the rest of the family, including Mathew Prichard, her grandson, weighed in too.

"It was fairly clear though that if she hadn't said 'yes' nobody would have agreed," Lord Brabourne said to me.

Over the next eighteen months they all met several times at the Savoy Grill for luncheon and the discussions continued. Lord Brabourne remembers: "She had very little small talk but we were discussing definite subjects—we were talking about films and how to treat stories and so on. She was knowledgeable, particularly about the characterization. It is amazing the way she does it because you sit there thinking what an extraordinary mind and wonderful ideas."

Even the financial arrangements for the film were discussed at the luncheons with Dame Agatha, then a woman of eighty-three, who sat there making shrewd observations. All the film rights are owned by the family firm and according to Mr. Cohen, "I think Agatha Christie, Ltd., has received more money for the rights of this film than any other film that has been made in Britain, mainly because the company is on a participation of profits. This is the most successful British financed film that has ever been in the history of film making. There have been films made in England with American finance but although they are British films I do not describe them as a 'British financed film.'"

Richard Goodwin joined John Brabourne as producer and the charismatic Sidney Lumet of New York was appointed director.

Once again the dialogue proved to be difficult to adapt and veteran British screen writer the late Paul Dehn was called in to make it "work" and supply a great deal of the additional dialogue necessary.

Throughout this period, too, Lord Brabourne and Agatha Christie corresponded fairly regularly. She always wrote in her own handwriting, which was round and bold and not too easy to decipher. Lord Brabourne has kept most of the letters.

"The sad thing is that the most interesting letter by far is missing," he commented. "It was the one when she talked about *Death on the Nile,* which she turned into a play, and why she had taken Poirot out of it simply because she did not want him to appear on the stage as he was such a difficult person to cast.

She was also kept advised of the casting of the various characters in *Murder on the Orient Express* and was delighted at the all-star selection. Apart from Albert Finney, who played Hercule Poirot, there was Lauren Bacall, Martin Balsam, Ingrid Bergman, Jacqueline Bisset, Jean-Pierre Cassel, Sean Connery, John Gielgud, Wendy Hiller, Anthony Perkins, Vanessa Redgrave, Rachel Roberts, Richard Widmark, and Michael York. Mike Todd had used this technique in *Around the World in 80 Days* and proved that if you pack in the big names, no matter how small the part, the star-struck public will keep the box office busy.

As Hercule Poirot was to be the real star, she had her agent, Edmund Cork, send John Brabourne the portrait painted in the mid-twenties by W. Smithson Broadhead on commission by the *Weekly Sketch.* She felt it could be a guide for Albert Finney, a considerably younger man.

Charles Parker, one of the world's top make-up artists, together with hair stylist Ramon Gow, who had previously collaborated in *The Great Gatsby,* were responsible for the physical transformation of Finney into Poirot. It took the tall, slender, thirty-eight-year-old actor two hours to become the short, stocky Belgian detective. During this time he acquired padded cheeks, a false nose, and thirty pounds of body weight.

The final result was that, to most people who saw the film, Albert Finney did look remarkably like Broadhead's drawing of Poirot though with decidedly more "little gray cells." But not to Agatha Christie.

She found only one glaring fault with the film. "It was well made except for one mistake I cannot find in my heart to forgive. It was Albert Finney as my detective Hercule Poirot. I wrote that he had the finest mustache in England—and he didn't in the film. I thought that a pity. Why shouldn't he have the best mustache?"

As Finney was appearing in a play in the West End of London every night, his own reddish-brown hair could not be dyed; besides this would have been contrary to Poirot's own methods of keeping his hair sleekly black with "tonic" and not "dye." The final solution was for Finney to coat his hair every morning with black powder, which took four shampoos each night to make it clean enough for his evening performance.

It is generally accepted that Poirot's English is deliberately imperfect and liberally interspersed with phrases literally translated from the French: "Do not derange yourself, I pray you, monsieur." But when the case has been solved and Poirot is about to make his devastating pronouncement his English miraculously improves as if his accent had been sharpened along with his wits during the solving of the crime.

Albert Finney's wife, French film actress Anouk Aimeé, coached him with his accent and Finney himself mentally set Poirot as an Edwardian as he had made his first appearance in literature in *The Mysterious Affair at Styles* as far back as 1920 when he was already retired from the Belgian police force.

Agatha Christie was fascinated with the immense care that was taken to produce an exact replica of the Orient Express, which made its maiden voyage on October 4, 1883. She had regularly made the three-day trip from Calais to Istanbul while traveling to the Middle East with her husband, Sir Max Mallowan.

In *Come, Tell Me How You Live* she wrote: "I used to be fascinated by the sight of the Orient Express at Calais and longed to be travelling by it. Now it has become an old familiar friend, but the thrill has never quite died down. I am going by it. I am *in* it. I am actually in the blue coach, with the simple legend outside: Calais-Istanbul."

She told how she liked its tempo, which began allegro con fuore, gradually slowing down in a rallentando, and proceeding eastward definitely legato.

173

One fanatic reader of *Murder on the Orient Express,* which was first published in 1934, and titled *Murder in the Calais Coach* in the American edition, was so anxious to confirm whether Mrs. Christie had got all her change points correct that he took the train himself and made the trip from Calais to Istanbul just to check for himself. She had—of course.

For the film of *Murder on the Orient Express* Tony Walton, the production designer, managed to borrow pieces of the old Orient Express from the Wagon-Lits Company's museum in Paris and meticulously assembled them like a nostalgic jigsaw on the sound stage of E.M.I. Elstree Studios outside London.

The result was an exact replica of the gleaming dark blue carriages with their fittings of solid oak and mahogany, silk damask curtains, seats of velvet with Brussels lace antimacassars and hand-cut glass separating the sleeping compartments from the outside aisle.

The engine used for the exterior shots of the film made in a snow drift at Pontarlier in eastern France, and in the reconstruction of the Istanbul station of 1934 in a railway yard in Paris, was an SNCF "F" Class "Pacific" locomotive No. 230 G353.

Mrs. Christie had hoped to visit the set purely for nostalgic reasons but a painful broken hip precluded this. She was, however, kept informed about the film's progress by Lord Brabourne and heartily approved of the attempt to create the authentic atmosphere of her story. The location shots were filmed in England, France, and Turkey.

When the film was ready for distribution, Nat Cohen arranged that a private showing of it be given to its author and her family in the E.M.I. cinema in London.

"Knowing of Agatha Christie's reputation for frankness we felt it would be the wrong thing to invite her to the press showing because if she had not liked the film she would have told the press so. Instead we asked her to come along with a party of her family and friends.

"I did not go into the theater as I felt it would be wrong for me or anyone else connected with it to be there. We wanted her to make her own decision."

It was an anxious little party of E.M.I. executives who waited outside their own private cinema while the film was shown.

When the door was opened Dame Agatha walked out tardily on the arm of her husband, as her hip still troubled her. Finally she reached Nat Cohen and John Brabourne, who were waiting to greet her.

She looked up into their faces and said very slowly and quietly: "I think it is a delightful film. This is one of the happy moments of my life, knowing that at last one of my subjects has been put into a film that I am delighted with."

Agatha Christie was not the sort of person to enthuse too much about anything and this was praise indeed. E.M.I. had been confident themselves that they had made a first-class film but had she not approved, apart from any other embarrassment, there could have been difficulties in negotiating for any more of her books to be turned into film scripts in the future, which E.M.I. hoped to do.

Lord Brabourne swept Dame Agatha and Sir Max off to a celebration luncheon.

"It was great fun," Lord Brabourne recalls. "She was in terrific form. We talked a lot about her books and what she thought of them. She told me which ones she had liked, others that she felt could be made into films, and some that she couldn't remember at all. She thought that *Passenger to Frankfurt* might make a good film but I don't actually think she was right." One must agree with Lord Brabourne because in this genre Agatha Christie was never a match for Ian Fleming and here she was clearly out of her depth.

The première of *Murder on the Orient Express* was a glittering show business occasion in London with several members of the royal family present.

Although she had been taken into the theater in a wheel chair, when it came time for Dame Agatha to be presented to the Queen she was determined to stand, and a photograph was taken as the Queen bent over the fragile eighty-four-year-old lady whom she had last talked to a few years before at one of her own private luncheon parties at Buckingham Palace. Dame Agatha refused to sit down and remained standing as Princess Anne moved nearer to congratulate her.

"Dame Agatha was just so old and tired," Lord Mountbatten

recalls, "but she had keyed herself up for this great night and did it marvelously."

When the film finished to rapturous applause many of the people concerned with the making of it had been invited by E.M.I. to a party at Claridge's.

"Dame Agatha and Sir Max were like excited children," Lord Brabourne remembers. Lord Mountbatten sat next to Dame Agatha at the guest of honor table. During the evening the stars of the film each came over to her table to be presented to the Duchess of Death. Dame Agatha's eyes, now shrunken with age, scanned the vast ballroom as if she were memorizing the whole scene.

It was well past midnight when Lord Mountbatten wheeled her in a chair to a waiting car amid the greatest ovation that the film industry in London had ever seen. It was to be Dame Agatha's last big public appearance.

Incidentally, had it not been for the foresight of a quick-witted French railway porter, Agatha Christie may not have lived to write *Murder on the Orient Express*. Just before beginning to work on the book she slipped on the icy platform at Calais and fell underneath the stationary train. Seeing her plight, a porter quickly pulled her off the rails just before the train began to move.

After Dame Agatha's death Lord Brabourne negotiated with Agatha Christie, Ltd., for the purchase of *Death on the Nile*, her own favorite foreign travel novel. Again Lord Mountbatten was brought in as mediator, this time between the film company and President Sadat of Egypt. *Death on the Nile* was the first foreign film to be made in Egypt for many years. Its cast included Maggie Smith, David Niven, Angela Lansbury, Olivia Hussey, Mia Farrow, Bette Davis, Jane Birkin, and Peter Ustinov as Hercule Poirot. It omens to be even more successful than *Murder on the Orient Express*.

As long as the present mood for nostalgia remains, the rich storehouse of Christie novels that are suitable for turning into films could stretch far into the twenty-first century.

CHAPTER SIXTEEN

IT IS A TANTALIZING thought that if Dorothy L. Sayers had not abdicated from the world of detection writing and projected herself into the rarefied atmosphere of translating Dante and writing religious poems and plays, Agatha Christie might not have emerged as the undisputed Queen of Crime. For a period in the 1930s Mrs. Christie was only shoulder high to Miss Sayers, who was intellectually the superior writer.

The difference in the technique of the two writers is interesting. The publication of a Dorothy L. Sayers book every second year was a major literary event. Agatha Christie left her mark by churning out two books a year and getting her name recognized among the mass of the ordinary reading public.

Mrs. Christie's switch over to Collins in 1924 was an inspired piece of timing as she arrived there at the moment when Sir Godfrey Collins, uncle of Sir William, was beginning to build up a crime list. Six years later he had the ingenious idea of forming Collins' Crime Club. *Murder at the Vicarage* was in fact to be the first Christie published under the Crime Club label. The introduction of Jane Marple as an amateur detective in a full-length novel was another piece of shrewd reasoning on Mrs. Christie's part, as this was to bring in a whole new field of housewife readers who recognized a little part of themselves in this snooping village spinster.

By the mid-thirties the impact of the crime list of Penguin paperback, founded by Agatha Christie's old friend Allen Lane, was also considerable. Now she was not only forcefully promoted by Collins, her hardback publishers, but by Penguin, which had become a vogue among all classes of the reading public. People began collecting walls of Penguins and their attractive green and white covers became a feature of young intellectual middle-class homes. Two early Christies, *Murder on the Links* and *Murder at the Vicarage*, were among the fifteen original titles; Agatha Christie and Dorothy L. Sayers were both being represented with two books each.

The real building up of Agatha Christie's sales did not begin, however, until 1935 when the figures for *Three-Act Tragedy* (*Murder in Three Acts* in America) reached the best-selling ten thousand.

Penguin's records were lost during the war years so it is to Elizabeth Walter, who has been an editor at Collins since 1961, that I turn for a correct picture. Writing in her contribution to *Agatha Christie, First Lady of Crime*, she explains: "It was not until 1943 that Agatha Christie reached 20,000 with *Five Little Pigs* [*Murder in Retrospect* in America] . . . perhaps a result of wartime dependence on the printed word for entertainment. Thereafter she never looked back and the Agatha Christie phenomenon becomes the Case of the Escalating Sales with *Sparkling Cyanide* [*Remembered Death* in America]—1945—selling 30,000 within twelve months and *The Hollow* [in America *Murder After Hours*], touching 40,000 in the following year. By 1950, when her fiftieth book, *A Murder Is Announced*, was published the first printing was 50,000 and her subsequent crime books have never sunk below that figure."

In a surprisingly short time Agatha Christie had the astonishing experience of seeing 1,000,000 paperback copies of her books published on one day. In England she is published in paperback by Penguin and Collins' own firm, Fontana, and in America by Dell and Pocket Books.

Who are these readers and did she have any contact with them? The famous names who read Agatha Christie are legion and as varied as President Charles de Gaulle and the former British Prime Minister Sir Clement Attlee. There is scarcely a British diplomat who does not travel abroad even today without his Brigg umbrella, Bowler, and Christie.

All her life Dame Agatha preferred to keep her readers at a distance. There was never any question that she could be persuaded to autograph copies of her books in leading bookshops, appear on television, in book programs, or do promotion tours.

With her books now translated into 103 languages her daily post bag came from all over the world. The irrelevant letters were quickly sorted from the genuine ones, which she made every attempt to answer.

Discussing this aspect of her work, she told Lord Snowden: "Well, I think first of all I like to make sure that the letter really has something to do with writing or literature. A great many are just silliness really. They want information, 'What are your favorite colors in dress,' and something else, and a lot of things that are your own business and nobody else's. And that I do dislike very much. But if someone wants to know about writing and asks how would I begin, how would I do it, I would give the best advice I could from my own memories. That I have no objection to doing."

One reader that Dame Agatha was delighted to sit next to at Crime Writers' luncheon on several occasions was Sir Robert Mark, who until he retired a few months ago was Britain's top policeman. He has been an Agatha Christie admirer since he was a boy of twelve years of age in Manchester.

Dame Agatha and Sir Robert were to meet three times over the years at various Crime Writers' Club occasions and they must have made an incongruous pair at these parties—the tall immaculate policeman and the little old lady with the kindly eyes of a wise old elephant.

"Well, she was very old of course but she was quite lively. We were both saying the polite things to each other. I told her I had read her books since I was a small boy and this seemed to give her pleasure. She muttered the usual platitudes back to me."

Sir Robert invited me to tea at New Scotland Yard to discuss his acquaintance with Dame Agatha. I was ushered into his large office on one of the top floors, which looked more like a sitting room in a Christie country house than the hot seat for crime detection that it really was. Tea was brought in and Miss Marple could not have faulted the charming way it was served by a young woman police secretary. We talked for three and a half hours as the years drifted back to Sir Robert's boyhood in Manchester, before the 1914–18 war.

"The first book I ever read was *King Solomon's Mines* and I must have read it a dozen times. My brother had told me the story first in bed and then I joined the local library."

Why Didn't They Ask Evans? was the first Agatha Christie that he read and from then on he solemnly plowed through every copy of her books the library had.

"If you use public libraries, as I have all my life, you are suddenly thrilled to find an author and you devour everything that this author has written. I did the same thing with Edgar Wallace and Henry Rider Haggard. I hope Dame Agatha would not have been offended to be included in that particular trio because it was people like them who encouraged young people in my generation to read as well as work. They formed the reading habit. I'm an avid reader, I read anything at all. In fact I think it's probably true to say that I've got more pleasure out of books, including rubbishy books, than any single thing, but you have to acquire the art of reading when you are young. You have to look upon reading as something that you want to do and you discover and enjoy it."

Henry Rider Haggard and Edgar Wallace I could understand, but why would a vigorous, tough boy from the Midlands choose Agatha Christie?

Sir Robert explained: "Oddly enough without the effect of television in those days it was much easier to accept the vicarage party, French windows out to the croquet law, and wafer-thin cucumber sandwiches to be a natural middle-class background. People were less well informed and perhaps in a way it was easier for somebody of my age to read Agatha Christie and accept it as being almost a realistic pattern of life."

There is one question that every Agatha Christie reader wants to know and here was the chance to have it answered from the very top. Could Agatha Christie stories ever relate to reality?

"I don't mean this unkindly but in a way her tales are fairy tales. They all relate to a dream world. It's a world that I am rather fond of where all the characters are either amusing or intriguing, and there is very little real vulgarity or obscenity. A world in which nobody ever mentions the shortage of policemen or the problems arising from urban crime and this kind of thing. In real life police work is totally different. Never in the whole history of criminal investigation in this country has there ever been an amateur involved in the process of crime detection with any significance. I think I'm probably right in saying that not since 1829 when the paid professional police were first established has there ever been a single case in which you could say that a private person like Miss Marple, Hercule Poirot, or Sherlock Holmes has ever been involved.

"Has it ever occurred to you that in almost every crime novel the crisis is over when the identity of the wrongdoer has been made known? There is usually never a word about the problems of the police in gathering the evidence necessary to obtain a conviction in the present-day climate of criminal justice."

There have of course been specialist plays and novels like *Anatomy of a Murder* which illustrate this. Sir Robert claims that 98 per cent of all crime novels are devoted to solving the crime and the technical details as to police procedure are not the concern of the author simply because the whole purpose of detection writing is to entertain.

We discussed the current vogue for "private eye" series like *Columbo*, where a fascinating serial has been built around one man's inquisitive brain.

"I doubt very much whether you could have done in print with *Columbo* what you could do on a cinema screen. His was the visual image," Sir Robert commented.

As a final question I asked Sir Robert what he thought about Dame Agatha's strange disappearance story fifty-one years ago.

181

"I feel it was just a reaction of her wounded pride and this leads some people to a kind of blind unreasoning. After all not everybody in this world reaches the conclusion through experience that anger and hatred are self-defeating. It can be a painful lesson to learn. Hate and envy and those kinds of obsessive emotions are fearfully self-destructive and all you can feel for a person who suffers from them is intense sympathy."

All her adult life Agatha Christie had read *The Times* and it is from their reportage that she kept abreast of world events. Even sitting out in a tent in Baghdad in heat rising to 120 degrees F. she could be found doing her crossword puzzle from this paper. It seemed natural therefore to ask the views of three gentlemen from *The Times* who had read her prolifically at some stage of their lives.

Firstly there is Iverach McDonald, the former foreign editor, who made twelve trips to Russia during his career. A fervent Agatha Christie fan, wherever he travels he always takes his batch of paperbacks.

As he told me: "I was always especially careful to see that I had plenty with me on my trips to Russia. They were wonderfully popular among the young Russian Intourist guides who always asked very correctly, 'Do you have any Agatha Christies you could spare?'"

In his entertaining autobiography A *Man of the Times* (published by Hamish Hamilton) he told of his blond traveling companion of three weeks—Lydia Ivanovna—who acted as his official Russian guide. They spent a couple of weeks together traveling from the Iranian frontier to Moscow and McDonald managed to keep her extremely happy with his stock of Agatha Christies.

I asked Iverach McDonald about the language of Agatha Christie's books because as a charming and sophisticated writer himself his opinion was valid. "I find it very direct English with a wonderfully economic way of depicting her characters in a sentence or two." As a seasoned traveler he gave this piece of advice to anyone traveling to the Middle East or crossing through the Iron Curtain.

"You can't go wrong with an Agatha Christie. It is the best and the cheapest present that I know."

Bernard Levin, Fleet Street's controversial middle-aged prodigy, has a different view, which cannot altogether be because of the twenty years' difference in age. Levin, who never minces his words, recently wrote an article in *The Times* which stirred up blood pressures all over the country.

"I am happy to say that the critical perception of even the infant Levin was sufficiently keen to discern that the detective stories of Dorothy Sayers were bilge even by the exceptionally low standard of the form; has anybody else, in any kind of novel, ever created a hero who was at once so unconvincing, ridiculous and nasty as Lord Peter Wimsey? The same critical perception began work very early in the case of Agatha Christie, for although there is no doubt that she was the undisputed champion of keeping the readers guessing to the end, her prose is of such unredeemed badness that I soon found her books quite unreadable."

I do not know exactly how Agatha Christie would have reacted to Levin's comment. She could let unpleasant incidents wash over her and I am sure that in her younger days she would have rebounded just as she did when she had bad reviews in 1958 for her play *Verdict*, which was taken off after a month. She would have set about writing a novel that Levin would have enjoyed. So much more so as they had one common passion—the music of Wagner.

Dorothy L. Sayers would have been furious at Levin. "What can you expect of a fellah who leaves the L. out of my name?" is a likely retort.

I finally spoke to the reviewer of crime books on the *Times*, H. R. F. Keating. He is the author of *Murder Must Appetize*, a study of the detective stories of the 1930s, and of a series of crime novels featuring Inspector Ghote of the Bombay CID. Ghote was described in the New York *Times Book Review* as one of the great characters of the contemporary mystery novel. With Ghote's first appearance in *The Perfect Murder* in 1964 Keating was awarded the Golden Dagger for the best crime novel of the year. In April 1977 he edited an omnibus to which well known writers contributed called *Agatha Christie, First Lady of Crime*.

"Agatha Christie wrote about the generally accepted image of England so that Americans and people all over the world were delighted and in a way I really think was one of her secrets. She handled her stock responses superbly. She, being an ordinary person, thought in these terms and therefore produced books which ordinary people all over the world like and want to read.

"If you read, as I do for my sins, a fair amount of not-so-good crime writing where other people do produce ordinary characters and write in an ordinary way but fluff it slightly, you see the difference. She didn't fluff at all. When she wanted to paint a character of a perfectly ordinary guy she really did hit him exactly right and said just enough about him but never too much. I honestly think that very seldom did she ever deviate in telling a story. There's a terrible temptation if you are writing for an audience, which is somewhat below you intellectually, to put in your little clever bits of whatever, but she didn't do it. It was interesting, too, to see how her tastes changed over the years and how she kept up. It is curious because she wasn't intellectual—but she was intelligent."

Typical of the young people who have been captivated by Agatha Christie is Martin Phillips, who works in the London offices of Harold Fielding, a company that distributes manuscripts of Agatha Christie plays. His interest goes back to his school days and in his bedroom at Raynes Park he has shelves packed with over three hundred international editions of Agatha Christie. In addition to this he has kept up a comprehensive scrapbook over the years.

When I asked him why and had he ever met her, he replied: "No, I never did but I just like to keep everything about her." It was almost as though he was speaking about a favorite aunt.

The youngest Agatha Christie fan that I came across was Matthew Woolard, a seven-year-old Londoner, with an I.Q. of 155.

Matthew began his reading habit as a baby of eighteen months when he first recognized words on the buses. By the time he was seven he had collected and read over fifty Christies which he had bought with his own pocket money at charity fêtes or on the 5p shelf outside secondhand bookshops.

His mother had read Agatha Christie and talked about the

books so it was a natural transition that he became interested, especially after he had seen the film *Murder on the Orient Express*. When I discussed the books with Matthew and why he preferred them he said: "Well, what I like about them is that you don't know the murderer until the end. They give you just the right amount of clues and not too many. The murders are done in a good way and they've been properly done, if you know what I mean."

His favorites were *Nemesis,* 1971, and *Death in the Clouds* (America, *Death in the Air*), 1935, where he assured me, "I guessed the murderer." Matthew is now nine years old and has progressed from reading Christie to political geography and the history of tobacco.

In India Poirot is the favorite, New Zealand prefers Miss Marple, but in Honolulu Mardi Strode prefers Ariandne Oliver. "I think that Dame Agatha invented that character so she could be in her own books," she wrote me.

Mrs. Strode is right as in *The Pale Horse* (1961) Agatha Christie reveals a very clear picture of herself on one of her more frenzied working days in the character of Mrs. Oliver.

The story of Geri Courtney of Chicago is not a particularly happy one but it does pinpoint the problems of writer-reader relationship, the fanatical devotion Agatha Christie inspired and the unconscious demands made of her.

Geri became infatuated with Agatha Christie during her teens after she had seen the film *Witness for the Prosecution*. This began a fervor which lasted for well over ten years and all her pocket money went on buying Christie paperbacks.

"I'd buy them as I didn't like to go to the library because there were not my books. So I used to go down to the small secondhand shops where you could pick them up for practically nothing, but it meant going through a couple of thousand books and I'd be thrilled after six hours if I found just one Agatha Christie that was old and battered. Sometimes you'd get them home and find that you already had that book under another title.

"One day I looked up Agatha Christie's address in *Who's Who* and I thought well I'm cheeky enough and I've got the nerve of the devil so I wrote her a letter and asked if she could possibly send me a list of all the books that she had written and if she knew any title variations. I got a letter back from her—that would be September 1963 [Agatha Christie was seventy-three at the time]. Geri was so delighted to be in correspondence with her favorite author that she telephoned from Chicago a couple of times.

"I really thought it was worth the money because at that time it was about nine dollars. First her husband answered one call and then she came to the telephone but it was quite clear that she mistook me for someone else. So she said she hadn't been feeling well and that she must go and hung up."

Undaunted, Geri then made a financial arrangement with London's leading bookshop that as every Agatha Christie was published a copy would be sent to the author for autographing, who then returned it to the bookshop, which finally sent it to Geri in Chicago to add to her collection. This worked well for several years enabling the girl to begin an amazing cross-reference index system of cards concerning the various books, their characters, and her own thoughts about them.

When I met Geri in London, where she now lives with her Irish husband and small son, it became clear to me the almost paranoiac fanaticism that Agatha Christie had inspired could have had its drawbacks for the author.

Right from the beginning it almost spelled disaster. Each book was read and dissected from a personal viewpoint. After Geri had read *4:50 from Paddington* (American title, *What Mrs. McGillicuddy Saw!*) she immediately wrote to British Railways to get a timetable to check that there was a train at this time and to work out "where the darned thing was going to."

Agatha Christie also received a letter about the book. "I used to write to her just as if I was talking to you now. I always told her when I didn't like any of her characters. I remember asking her who did Lucy finally choose in the *4:50 from Paddington* because there were two guys she had her eye on."

On May 4, 1968, Agatha Christie wrote back explaining that though she was Lucy's creator she did not know what Lucy's reactions would be as she was a girl who always kept her thoughts to herself. Miss Marple seemed to be quite certain whom Lucy would choose but the matter was left purposefully uncertain. Agatha Christie herself had a leaning toward Bryan Easterbrook, as Lucy certainly liked him best, but Cedric was by way of being a challenge to her talents since he was obviously an extremely difficult character.

By now Geri had become so intoxicated with England as seen through Agatha Christie books that she announced to her husband—no Christie fan—that she was leaving for England.

"She reminded me so much of my grandmother that I just wanted to come to England and sit down and have a quiet chat with her and tell her how much I enjoyed her books. Another reason I decided to come was that I realized how old she was and that her health was getting progressively worse so I wanted to be here when she died. I don't know why, I just did. I felt that England wasn't going to be the same and I wasn't going to get as much out of it if she was already dead."

Geri did not see Agatha Christie on that trip or on any other. Back home from her Christie mission, her marriage broke up. She decided that she must return and make her home permanently in England to be near Agatha Christie. An unfortunate incident happened at this time. Sir Max Mallowan sent a letter in error to Geri which was obviously meant for a Mrs. Livingstone of Chicago whom he had met on one of his archaeological digs. It took Geri just twenty-four hours before she had tracked down the rightful owner at an oriental museum in Chicago. In thanking Geri for her trouble Sir Max wrote that if they ever returned to Chicago, where they once visited, he hoped they would meet.

Geri continued to write Agatha Christie twice-yearly letters and after the breakup of her marriage sent a letter to announce that she would be returning to England. Sir Max answered that he hoped that when she came it would be possible to arrange a brief meeting although neither he nor Dame Agatha had been well for some time and were cutting down on their engagements. He then gave her their telephone number at Wallingford, inviting her to ring when she arrived.

A few months later, her marriage over, Geri was back in England for an indefinite stay. One of the first things she did was to hire a car and drive down to Wallingford, where she called at the police station and asked for the way to Winterbrook House. On the opposite side of the big brick wall in front of the house is a public telephone booth. Trembling with excitement at the thought of meeting Dame Agatha at last, she telephoned the number Sir Max had given her. He answered, listened, and hung up. Geri had made the cardinal mistake of intruding on their privacy. Shortly afterward a woman appeared from the house and shut the gates to the driveway.

Geri returned to London, heartbroken. She remained in England, remarried, and suffered a terrible accident that has left her minus a leg and with a badly damaged body. Few people would have survived it. Today her face is vital and pretty and mindful of Judy Garland in her twenties.

Geri made one further attempt to contact Dame Agatha by letter but was told by Sir Max in a reply that he and his wife "did not see strangers." From that June day in 1970 she locked away all her memories of Agatha Christie until I met her and we talked.

"No, I didn't go to her memorial service. I was no longer interested. But I have so much to be grateful to her for. She gave me my unquenchable thirst to live in England. She made it all so interesting and even though some of the people were downright nasty you still had the feeling through her books that English people were basically very good, very honest, and the type of people that would be behind you if they were your friends. I think she did more for putting across the English people, like in those war films of the forties, than anyone else.

"She gave you the feeling that they would plod on no matter what the circumstances were and how tough things got and would always end up seeing their way through. I just felt I loved the English people and it was all because of Agatha Christie. Besides if it hadn't been for her I wouldn't have been here; I wouldn't have met my lovely husband and had my son."

CHAPTER SEVENTEEN

MANY PROFESSIONAL writers develop their own individual routines which give them the most suitable conditions to work under. Trollope said in his autobiography that "three hours a day will produce as much as a man ought to write." Somerset Maugham stretched himself to four hours, but not a minute longer. Others find that with the help of an electric typewriter they can do more and with a dictaphone perhaps even longer.

But as Agatha Christie freely admitted the actual writing is tiring. Tiring both to the mind, which has to concentrate, and to the back and fingers when typing. After she had broken her wrist and had twinges of arthritis in her hands she would get cramp in the fingers and found it difficult to continue with her three-finger typing.

About three quarters of her books were dialogue and this is where her strength was. She once wrote to her Swedish admirer, Professor Frank Behr, that she hoped he would go on "listening to my characters for many years more and not grow tired of doing so."

To Lord Snowden, who had a long talk with her during a day taking photographs at her home in Wallingford, she agreed that her books came from an oral experience rather than a literary one. On her walks she spoke aloud the dialogue of her characters so that they grew up naturally around her. They thus developed themselves in her mind though she had to contain them professionally. She gave them great freedom and allowed them to talk away without worrying about their formal polish or finesse.

Dame Agatha became tired of the question repeatedly asked of her: "I suppose you take your characters from real life?"

"No, I don't," she replied. "I invent them. They are *mine*. They've got to be my characters—doing what I want them to do, being what I want them to be—coming alive for me, having their own ideas sometimes, but only because I've made them become *real*."

Professor Behr pointed out to me that what her characters say may be misleading or false but the way in which they say it is real, true, inevitable. The narrator's role is to listen to their conversation and type it down on paper. He mentioned how Agatha Christie told him that when she had to dictate a story to her secretary, due to the broken wrist, the conversation of her brain children threatened to swell beyond the stipulated number of pages.

Professor Behr, who is now emeritus but before his retirement was professor in English first at Stockholm University and later for thirteen years held the Andrew Carnegie chair at Gothenburg, is one of that valiant band of people in the world who has read everything Agatha Christie has written.

His major work, *Studies in Agatha Christie's Writing*, published in 1967 in *Gothenburg Studies in English* is based on the source material of sixty-seven volumes of Agatha Christie's works of which fifty-eight were full novels and 9 short stories. He checked the frequency of certain words which were used in fifty-nine volumes containing 4,200,000 words.

Agatha Christie wrote her books without literary ambition. Like all professionals she certainly had monetary gains in mind but here she was in good company as it was Dr. Johnson who said, "No man but a blockhead ever wrote, except for money." If it had not been for the lure of money how much would Charles Dickens have written or Bernard Shaw for that matter? Money can be a healthy incentive.

That Agatha Christie had no ambition to create a literary style of her own was also her strength. She did not get involved in elaborate descriptions of scenery and nature but her narrative came in the language which was natural for her.

"When reading her books I have a pleasant, not to say nostalgic, feeling of listening to the easy flow of the talk of ordinary people whom I met in British homes during my young days spent at Oxford University. My academic colleagues in England generally talk in a different style. This cannot interest you very much because as a native you distinguish between the two types without knowing what you are doing. But to foreign speakers and to linguistics generally it is important," Professor Behr told me.

"The great thing about writing is that you can do it anywhere. All you need is a chair, a table, a typewriter and a bit of peace," Agatha Christie once said when discussing her work.

During the six weeks that she took to write a novel, when she was working at her peak form, she shut herself away from anything that could distract her.

"I have to be firm with everybody. I explain clearly that it is quite impossible for me to get on with my dead body if a live body is moving, breathing, and in all probability talking, in the near vicinity."

This professional approach was the key factor to her steady productivity right up to her eightieth birthday. Wherever she happened to be whether it was Baghdad, Brighton, or Banff she churned out "a Christie for Christmas," which became a familiar jingle in the publishing world.

In order to have a book out each December she worked through some of the winter for delivery in March. When that book was safely delivered to the publishers she immediately began planning the next one, which would not be written for perhaps another five or six months.

Whatever critical readers may have found to dislike in Agatha Christie's books she could not be faulted on her ingenuity and supreme plot making and this is exactly what kept her at the top of her profession for all those years. It was also her incredible meticulous attention to detail in her detection novels. Whereas Dorothy L. Sayers got her servants all wrong Agatha Christie's could not be faulted, simply because she knew the domestic scene through and through.

While discussing this aspect of her work with Lord Snowdon she told him: "When you first start to think out a book the nicest thing to do is to go for a long walk somewhere, and my first book —*The Mysterious Affair at Styles*—came to me walking about on Dartmoor when I had a fortnight's holiday from the hospital in Torquay. I had of course been thinking about the plot for a long time.

"My sister occasionally used to say to me, 'You really look like an idiot walking along the street talking to yourself.' My answer to that was that you very often forget things if you don't hear them aloud."

All through her life this is exactly the way she planned her books. In the summer if the weather was good she would go into the garden and walk around with notebook in hand. After several weeks she had usually filled half of it with carefully planned moves and the occasional diagram to remind her of a salient point. It was only after this routine had been completed, and all the complicated plot changes worked out, that she got down to "the awful chore of writing."

An illustration of the way she thought was explained by Peter Saunders—The Mousetrap Man—when he once inquired how she was getting along with a certain play.

"That's all finished," she replied.

When he asked when he would be able to see the script she replied airily: "Oh, I've only finished it in my head. I still have to put it down on paper."

Agatha Christie did most of her typing on dull wet days.

"Indoors is the place to get down to work," she said. "Flowers and trees within sight make me want to play truant. It is a shame to waste the weather. I stoke up energy when the flowers are out."

Agatha Christie was a woman of simple, uncomplicated truth. A woman who was not afraid to say that what she really enjoyed was "to sit in the sun with my feet up."

During most of her writing career she claimed that she never mentioned her work until it was finished. It was almost that she felt in talking about it that something of its strength may have evaporated.

Disraeli said that "an author who speaks about his own books is almost as bad as a mother who talks about her own children." Agatha Christie's views were that "the moment you have talked about a thing you are rather dissatisfied with it. Later I may try it on a couple of people and perhaps take advice. I can't often put anything over on my daughter—she always guesses."

In later years this was to change as she admitted that she often spoke to her husband, Sir Max Mallowan, no mean author himself, about her work. Although he had never read a detection novel until he married Agatha Christie she persuaded him to read every one of hers. She herself enjoyed reading other detection writers if they were sufficiently interesting and it was not unusual for her to go back and read some of her own favorites that she had written.

One thing is certain, that it was Dame Agatha, and she alone, who controlled the destiny of her characters and decided even the most minute details such as what Poirot would be eating for dinner that night in a particular situation. This part of her work she found thoroughly enjoyable.

"You can't do anything until you have got your characters, until you feel that they are real to you. I go walking up and down the garden with them talking to Miss Marple, the vicar, and so on. Perhaps Miss Marple is having difficulty in her garden and her broad beans have not come up properly that year. You can feel it all happening and that's right. It isn't hard work. It is the moment that you begin to type or dictate you get tired because your mind has to concentrate on it. I mean it is like writing a long letter to someone.

"You are taking hold of something in yourself which is creative but having done that you are as tired as a keen gardener who comes in from digging up the peas or digging up something else . . . you would come in and ache."

Another approach she had to working out her plots was to take a humdrum household chore, such as washing up, and then let her mind wander.

"An idea just jumps into your head like a jack-in-the-box. That's the pleasant part. You think it is good and just hang on to it."

Some of her better ideas even came while lying in the bath.

"I dream them up while lying in the bath and I eat apples and drink cups of tea and have bits of paper and pencils around. Unfortunately today's baths are not made with authors in mind. Old-fashioned baths with nice wooden ledges are the best. Now they are all modern and slippery."

In talking to Cecil Wilson of the *Daily Mail* in 1962 when she was still a prolific writer, Agatha Christie explained that the real hell of writing detection stories was having to tie up all the loose ends in the last chapter. "By the time you have done it you are sick of everyone in the book."

Just as Dame Agatha Christie wished her private life to be kept a secret when she was alive so her family wish it to remain after her death. Sir Max Mallowan consequently refused to see me until a contact was made through Sir Patrick Reilly who, like Sir Max, is a Fellow of All Souls in Oxford. Sir Max Mallowan made it quite clear to me that it was only because of this that he had consented to see me at all. He was then working on his autobiography and was under such pressure that when he invited me the invitation was for tea eight weeks later.

It was a blustery, cold November day when I arrived at Winterbrook House. Although Dame Agatha had lived in the large house behind the long brick wall on the road to Cholsey for over forty years few people knew precisely where she lived, and fewer still had ever met her.

Mrs. A. Wheeler, who had lived next door for over forty years, did not see her very often as in the early days Agatha Christie was abroad a great deal and in later years she did not leave the house. Winterbrook House with its twenty green acres is surrounded by brooding ewe trees and is Georgian in architecture. The spacious grounds run down to the river Thames.

I arrived at Winterbrook House at 4:30 P.M. precisely. Mrs. Honeybone, who had been secretary to Dame Agatha for many years and now assists Sir Max Mallowan, showed me into the sitting room. One felt HER presence immediately in the highly organized clutter of this room from the past. There was a large comfortable sofa and wing-back chairs covered with a pale magnolia brocade. The mantelpiece was cluttered with porcelain—delicate figures of birds, ornate vases, small porcelain boxes. On either side of the fireplace were candelabra lights and an oval mirror in white Dresden china fringed with flowers.

The sofa was draped with several pieces of crewel needlework —Braque-like birds in flight and a colorful square in a floral pattern. On the fireside table stood a Victorian immortelle of dried flowers under a glass dome. The Persian rug on the wooden floor glowed with color in the softly lit room. There was the unmistakable smell of potpourri—musty and sweet. It was a collector's room in contrast to that of an interior decorator. One felt that each object was there simply because of itself; each brought back memories of some experience, some strange encounter, and here they were, all jostled together, in a room which had been arranged entirely for the pleasure of the people who lived in it.

Sir Max Mallowan came into the room. A white-haired man of positive character. I tried to picture him as the keen young archaeologist of the fresh pink cheeks and penetrating eyes whom the buxom, middle-aged Agatha Christie had fallen in love with. He had her dog Treacle on a lead . . . a snappy little dog who was devoted to his mistress. There were always dogs in Agatha Christie's life. Treacle made several abortive attempts to close in on my ankles, which made the introduction somewhat chaotic.

Even the tea, which Mrs. Honeybone brought in, was just what I had hoped for—cucumber sandwiches, fluffy homemade jam sponge, and Earl Grey tea.

Although he declined to discuss his wife as a person we did speak about how she worked.

"My wife always wrote the last chapter first. In this way she was able to gather up all the clues and neatly tie the parcel. It was only after she had done this that she went back to the beginning and worked her way through," he explained.

We then spoke about how she had helped in his expeditions. Not just with her companionship but also her robust physical help photographing and mending broken objects.

As she once said: "You can imagine the thrill of rubbing away dust and dirt to find, say, an amulet worn 7,000 years ago."

One felt the deep devotion this husband and wife had for the ancient cities of the Middle East and their concern should the lack of money or the world political situation prevent further excavations being made so that the modern world might be denied a better understanding of life as it was lived in the desert cities thousands of years ago.

It has also been said that Dame Agatha gave financial help to the expeditions over the years but if she did it is something that she herself would never have spoken about.

As Sir Max Mallowan talked I had a fleeting glimpse in my mind of the Khatūn, as the Arabs called her, in blazing heat whipping up lemon curd and vanilla soufflé over a kerosene stove while a saucer-eyed kitchen staff watched these miracles of creation. And when in her nervousness she dropped an egg on the floor so complete was their confidence in her that they felt it was all part of the Khatūn's own special magic.

It was now after 6 P.M. as Sir Max escorted me out into the cold night. The sky had cleared and was speckled with bright stars. Treacle yapped at his side as he waved me off. It had been a most enjoyable experience.

One would have thought that with such assured sales and her world-wide readership Agatha Christie would have become immune to the tribulations that many other authors suffer. But she was never afraid to disclose her own doubts and worries.

"When you write a book you get very tired. I should say about halfway through. You begin to feel that this book is no good I am sure. You will have to read it again to see if it has gone wrong anywhere. You know perfectly well where your stories are going but when you feel it has nearly got there it is as though you were running into Paddington station and you think, very soon I am going to finish."

For her eightieth birthday present William Collins gave Agatha Christie a dictaphone. Whereas most octogenarians would have quailed at taking on a new gadget at that time of life she set about learning how to use it and rather enjoyed the result.

"I must say that since I broke my wrist and began using a dictating machine I rather enjoy speaking the dialogue in my books," she commented. Words much more applicable to a girlish in-génue than a seasoned and famous old lady.

All Agatha Christie's novels published under the name of Mary Westmacott were written at much greater speed than her detection books. This she attributed to the fact that they were a holiday for her and had to be done in a very short time. It was during this period of her life, too, that she became enchanted with the writings of T. S. Eliot and longed to take titles from his books, *The Time of the Rose* and *Time of the Yew Tree*. What she did in fact was to amalgamate the two into one title, *The Rose and the Yew Tree*.

Agatha Christie strongly objected to any personal questions put to her but was generous in her advice to anyone who seriously wanted to know how to go about it, willingly passing on the advice that Eden Phillpotts had given her so many years before.

"If you really want to write you must decide what kind of style you want to work in and then read books that have the same style. You will have to put up with a lot of publishers returning books that you have written or magazine articles and that is very depressing. Everything in life is partly hard work and partly luck. And luck is really the important thing.

"People think that writing must be easy for me. It isn't. It's murder. I've never yet written a book I haven't abandoned in disgust halfway through. I never have much faith in my writing—I am always scared that people will find out that I really can't write."

These are not profound words but they have a great deal of common sense about them and it is interesting that an author of such acclaim and experience should have the humility to admit to the same agony that overtakes almost every writer in the business.

Even in her choice of names for her characters Agatha Christie had her own set of rules and gave them a great deal of thought. It was no idle matter that she chose Mrs. Posselthwaite, General Arlington, Colonel Luscombe, the Dean of Chistlehampton, Philip Lombard, Emily Brent, Anne Beddingfield.

In discussing the choice of names for her characters with author Ernest Dudley he mentioned Raymond as a first name and said that it gave him the image of "a slimish dark sort of chap, rather foreign—but especially dark."

"No . . . no," Agatha Christie protested. "No . . . the name Raymond to me means a very fair-haired, blond man, not at all dark or foreign-looking."

Agatha Christie was intuitively ahead in her thinking when she gave her characters names that take a little trouble getting used to so that in time they become firmly entrenched in the reader's mind. It is a technique used in television detective series in America—Starsky, Hutch, Kojak, and Columbo. It is unlikely that Dame Agatha gave much thought to changing techniques, she was always the gifted amateur in that sense. At least that was the impression she liked to give. Or again was this merely a mask for her shrewd ability?

Why did Agatha Christie continue to write until her total numbered ninety-four books in all? It could not have been for financial gain as she had never been a desperately struggling writer. When Mrs. Miller died in 1926, despite living in reduced circumstances, she left her daughter Agatha not only the family home, Ashfield, but an estate the net value of £13,527 16s. 8d., which was a considerable amount of money in those days.

The explanation is a much simpler one. She always sunk her capital into houses and writing had become a way of life for her, even if she did not admit it publicly. When once asked if she could give up work she replied stoutly: "If I won the football pools and could pay off all my back income tax. Yes, of course I could. No one ever enjoys writing. It is far too much an effort of concentration. In the evenings you feel dead. If the day has gone well you feel played out and if it has not you feel broody. My husband and I always try to write our books at the same time in different parts of the same house and then we get the whole business over in one chunk."

There is a story that I like to believe is true that in 1970 when Dame Agatha was eighty years old there was some conjecture whether or not she would be able to deliver a "Christie for Christmas." Her health had not been good, with a reoccurrence of an old heart illness. Her publishers, Collins, approached her and suggested tactfully that if it was not possible then they would produce a Ngaio Marsh that Christmas.

The book was finished and delivered within a couple of weeks.

Somerset Maugham predicted that in the near future the police novel (as he called detection writing) would be studied in colleges and universities throughout the world and that "aspiring aspirants for doctoral degrees will shuttle the oceans and haunt the world's great libraries to conduct personal research expeditions into the lives and sources of the masters of the art."

Agatha Christie will surely top the list for the ability to be able to mesmerize her readers when she was developing a story line. As Professor Behr, disarmingly says: "I should admit at once that the choice of Agatha Christie's production as text material for a linguistic study would not have occurred to me if I had not during the past few years devoted a good deal of my spare time to reading her books for pleasure and relaxation."

Professor Behr not only studied Agatha Christie's writings but made a comparison between hers and a corpus of other books chosen at random—P. G. Wodehouse, Somerset Maugham, James Joyce, Joyce Cary, and Angus Wilson.

Though he is now over eighty years old the professor has a vivid memory of the day he and his wife were invited to tea by Dame Agatha at 48 Swan Court, not far from the King's Road in Chelsea.

They were ushered into a sitting room which was scantily furnished with "an old chest of drawers, a table, an old sofa for two with much worn upholstery and seriously damaged springs, a side table with immortelles under glass, which made me think of the room of the two sisters in one of her novels. The atmosphere was adequate and inspiring."

The Swedes were offered tea or coffee, and they chose coffee owing to the inadequacy of the coffee at their hotel. Dame Agatha got up from the depths of the sofa with not a little difficulty and when Mrs. Behr made an attempt to help her she declined the offer saying "This is good for me." She then disappeared into the adjacent kitchen and closed the the door. After some time she reappeared with coffee, sandwiches, and cakes.

"I clearly remember that there was also some kind of pastry to cut pieces from, a rounded affair with white on top, probably cream. It tasted good," the professor continued. "The coffee was also good and the first thing my wife said when we came out was 'What nice coffee' and she was very particular about coffee."

The conversation that followed was almost exclusively about Agatha Christie's books and writing generally. She spoke simply without pretense or mystification, about finding subject-matter, constructing plots, and varying the theme from book to book. She told the professor that once these matters had been adequately settled she sat down to write the story and develop the plot through the medium of the talk of her characters. Her answers to the professor's questions were straightforward and precise. There were no literary or psychological extravagances and absolutely no padding.

"When I was talking to her I had to sharpen my wits and try to match her by not saying anything simply to fill up a vacuum. At first I felt a bit nervous but having this kind and modest old lady in front of me and seeing my wife enjoying every minute of it all, as if it was the most natural thing in the world for her to share a ramshackle sofa with the Queen of Crime, my nervousness passed off."

Agatha Christie also asked the professor how long he thought her books would be read after her death.

"She was not altogether indifferent to that question. I did not have to be polite when saying that I could see no time limit to the popularity of her stories."

"Fashions change," she replied, and then with a glimmer of amusement in her eyes, "Think of Shaista's knees."

In the Christie novel *Cat Among the Pigeons* Poirot had suspected all along the French actress who impersonated Shaista. It was her elderly knees that gave her away.

Agatha Christie's facial expression hardly changed during the hour-long visit. As Professor Behr remarked: "She ought to have been a good card player. But this is not strictly true as she looked at my wife from time to time—Signe was a very good-looking woman—and patted her once or twice on the back. I then noticed

a faint glimmer of light spread over her face and make it beautiful.

. "That is how I remember her and think of her. To judge from
pictures in newspapers she had changed a great deal in the last
few years of her life."

Agatha Christie's occasional experiments with different detection writing formulas as in *Endless Night* (1967) and *Passenger
to Frankfurt* (1970) were perhaps not altogether happy but her
public bought them as loyally and enthusiastically as ever and
they did serve to illustrate her continued alertness to social trends.

"I am frightened by young people being involved in crime . . .
Having dealt in dishonesty all these years I can only say that honesty will always be the best policy. And I am more convinced of
that with every book I write."

Over the years Dame Agatha not only up-dated her plots but
adapted her language to present-day living. It is commendable
that this eighty-year-old Dame was able to write in *Passenger to
Frankfurt* (1970), "Safe is a four letter word but not the kind of
four letter word that people are interested in nowadays."

And even more pungently: "Don't you go arseing around with
the Russkies again."

Well how about that Miss Marple?

CHAPTER EIGHTEEN

I<small>T IS SELDOM</small> that the death of an author makes headlines in the financial pages. But Agatha Christie certainly did this. The London *Financial Times* devoted half a page on January 19, 1976, to "the intricacies of the commercial legacy left by Dame Agatha Christie," which would have baffled even Hercule Poirot and Jane Marple. The headline over six columns read "The Mystery of the Christie Fortune."

On May 9, 1976, the London *Sunday Times* wrote over six columns "How Dame Agatha Made Her Killing." She was "the richest writer Britain has produced" and "One of the Top Money Making Writers of All Times," commented another London paper.

The estimated figures for Agatha Christie's earnings during her sixty-odd years of writing varied from newspaper to newspaper. They only agreed on one point—namely that her financial arrangements are and remain one of the many Agatha Christie mysteries and one which may never be solved. Her literary agent told the *Financial Times*: "Don't ask us for any figures; we have not got them."

It is a fair assumption that even if Mr. Cork did have the figures computed up to date he would not have passed them on. Agatha Christie cast a spellbinding loyalty over all her close associates, assuming that she did share with them all her financial secrets. The details of her affairs were known only to herself, her closest family, her advisers, and of course the tax inspector.

During all her long life Dame Agatha Christie was as elusive and secretive about her finances as she was about most aspects of her personal life. She was born of an age and class that considered it exceedingly vulgar to disclose information of a personal nature. She felt that her responsibility to her readers was merely to entertain them for two to three hours through the characters she created. She herself wished to remain an enigma. Her relations and her husband, as well as her advisers, solicitors, and agents have been no less close-lipped since her death.

Many British authors and artists since the war have sought refuge abroad for fear of the deathly demands of the British Inland Revenue. There is hardly a month passes that some well-known name slips from these shores. But not so Dame Agatha.

All her life she was fond of foreign traveling, especially with her husband to the Middle East, but it is highly unlikely that she had ever contemplated moving abroad permanently. In spite of her American father the English scene was as much part of her life as she became part of it. Devon, Oxfordshire, and London, they were her settings where she moved freely about from the one home to the next as the seasons and moods demanded.

At the same time there are now indications that she did not need to live abroad for tax purposes simply because with infinite shrewdness many years ago she had taken every conceivable precaution to safeguard her fortune wherever the law left an opportunity. Hercule Poirot himself could not have done better.

It has been said that she was not interested in or cared about money. This is not correct. She cared greatly and she would painstakingly go through the statement and contracts from her publishers and point out any mistake however small and seemingly unimportant.

Agatha Christie's personal needs were not extravagant for a woman in her financial position. The only Rolls-Royce in the family was bought by Sir Max Mallowan for a couple of hundred pounds but sold again when he realized how it ate up petrol. Otherwise there were no flashy limousines, racing stables, jewelry, or expensive clothes. Two sisters, the Misses Olive and Gwen Robinson of the small town of Dartmouth in Devon, made some of her dresses for some time and only gave up when they became too elderly to continue their dressmaking business. Dame Agatha lived much in the same style as her characters in her books—comfortable but not ostentatious.

She did, however, endeavor to provide for her family and several carefully chosen charities through the various trusts that were set up. She made no secret that she loathed paying more tax than necessary and she was once quoted as saying that she had to write one book a year to pay her tax but she also stringently limited it to one simply because if she wrote more she would "enlarge the finances of the Inland Revenue, who would spend it mostly on idiotic things." That she wrote at least one book a year prevented her in fact from taking advantage of almost the only loophole the British tax laws give authors—that they can spread the income from one book over three years for tax purposes.

Agatha Christie cannot have missed out on much else and it looks on paper as if it was finally a draw between her and the tax inspector. While her earnings were estimated to have been in excess of £12,000,000 to £14,000,000 she left net only £106,683.91p on her death.

Apart from a bequest of £10,000 to her husband and various small legacies such as £1,000 to her son in-law Anthony Hicks, £500 to her sister-in-law Mrs. Dolores Mallowan, £3,000 to Mrs. Lily Betson, £500 to her godchild Jennifer Oates of Cambridge, the sum of £150 to her gardener Frank Lavin (who was later given an additional £50 in a codicil), £500 to an elderly gardener, W. Cox, who still tends the household at Wallingford, £250 to the faithful secretary, Mrs. Daphne Honeybone, the bulk of the estate was left to her daughter Rosalind, Mrs. Anthony Hicks.

To her agent and friend, Edmund Cork, she left a black bust of

Mercury and "my Damascus pearl inlay chest of drawers with the name Agatha Christie inlaid on top," while *The Mousetrap* producer, Peter Saunders, was given her bust of Mrs. Siddon, the actress, and twenty-five volumes of *British Theatre*. Both these gentlemen have earned a great deal of money from Agatha Christie's writings over the years and will continue to do so for a long time to come. Taken that a literary agent's fee is 10 per cent of an author's earnings Mr. Cork's small firm must have received an income in excess of one million pounds.

With what infinite care she distributed, what to the outside world must seem as trivialities, among the people who surrounded her is shown in a codicil to her will made out in 1975, a few months before she died and four years after she had signed her main will. She then revoked the previous bequest of her collection of Stevengraphs and Tunbridge Ware and the stone figure of Buddha to her son-in-law Anthony Hicks and the green Venetian glass fish and her souvenirs of *The Mousetrap* play to her grandson.

One wonders what emotions that Buddha figure and glass fish had aroused in her that she should go to the trouble and expense in her eighty-fifth year to take such fanatic care of their future fate? And why would her only grandson, Mathew Prichard, be denied *The Mousetrap* souvenirs as he has been the legal owner of the play since he was a child when his grandmother gave it to him?

Old people are apt to develop an almost paranoiac passion for their special possessions and Agatha Christie of the clear, cool, logical brain was no exception. One wonders what fit of pique overcame her so that she bothered to add these changes. This is another secret that remains locked in the family.

Apart from being a curio, Dame Agatha Christie's will is of no importance since it does not give one clue to the decades-old mystery of her financial spider web. The will was in effect just one way of tidying up the petty cash.

The mystery not only concerned Agatha Christie's earnings when she was alive but also the disposal of her posthumous royalties, which can be assumed to be enormous and perhaps even larger than her total income during her lifetime.

The copyright to *The Mousetrap*, which is still running leisurely and in good form, and far from being even slightly out of breath, belongs to her grandson Mathew Prichard. The copyright to *Curtain* and *Sleeping Murder*, the last of her books to be published by Collins in England and Dodd, Mead in America, also remain in the family. The American advance on *Curtain* alone was $1,000,000 and it is expected to become one of the biggest earners of what was described as her "money-making machine." The United Kingdom and Commonwealth first hardback printing was 120,000 copies and both in the United States and Great Britain it stayed on the best-seller list for many months.

Agatha Christie's English publisher, Collins, claims that her books will go on selling long after everybody now working for the firm is buried and gone. In a normal year 5,000,000 Agatha Christie paperbacks are sold in the United States alone and nobody expects this to stop as the sales will be bolstered by further film successes and future generations will grow into Agatha Christie fans. As long as the copyright is still valid—fifty years—the earnings will continue well into the coming century. Apart from anybody else, the British Treasury will benefit greatly.

Agatha Christie's books were not immediately a financial success in the 1920s and neither were they handled with the business acumen which became so evident later. Her first book brought the disastrous income of £26.0.—not a sum to instigate complicated tax schemes. This was *The Mysterious Affair at Styles*, published in 1920.

Nor have her solicitors been more communicative. John Wollen, who is one of the partners of the Torquay family firm, gave, however, a vague clue as to what happened to the hidden treasures. Agatha Christie died at a great age, he said, and she had therefore "plenty of time to make such disposals as she thought fit . . . she disposed of a great number of copyrights. She gave *The Mousetrap* to her grandson. We knew everybody would be astonished at the low value of her estate but she was also well advised over the years."

One piece of advice she followed in June 1955 was to create a limited company—Agatha Christie, Ltd. This company handled virtually all her manuscripts after this date but not the books and plays that she had written previously. She had a contract with the company for life and was paid a salary and expenses. The directors of the company were Dame Agatha herself, her daughter, Mrs. Hicks, and the perpetual Mr. Cork, her agent. The visible assets were her ingenuity and her work force and she became in effect both the rider and the horse. Both performed equally well over the country of finance and detection.

After a certain point the tax on the income of such a private company will be taxed at a much higher rate than normal. This is to prevent rich people being able to siphon their top supertaxed earnings off and covert them into capital. It was therefore a logical move for Agatha Christie in May 1968 to sell 51 per cent of the share capital to Booker McConnell, Ltd. This £25,000,000 international group had four years earlier diversified from its rum, sugar, and engineering activities into literature through a subsidiary they called Booker Books, Ltd.

The first author they took over in this was Ian Fleming, the creator of James Bond, whom they paid £100,000. Later they added to their list Dennis Wheatley, Georgette Heyer, Robert Bolt, Harold Pinter, John and Penelope Mortimer, and others. How much Booker McConnell paid for its 51 per cent stake in Agatha Christie is not known. It did not need to disclose the sum as it was less than 5 per cent of its net assets. It is, however, supposed to be well in excess of the £100,000 paid to Fleming.

Agatha Christie manuscripts before 1955 were of course not included in the deal but it is understood that a part of her pre-1955 production has since been taken over by the company and thus Booker McConnell on her death controlled the vast majority of her books as well as some plays.

Between 1968 and Agatha Christie's death in 1976, Booker McConnell had increased its share holding to 64 per cent. The remainder was owned by Mrs. Hicks—2 per cent—and the much favored grandson, who had 16 per cent—and the rest was invested in various family and charitable trusts.

If it was not a bad deal for Dame Agatha it certainly was not for Booker either, as by 1974 the company's net assets were £900,199. The financial press made a point of this, and commenting on Booker's interim results, which shot the share prices up from 8 pence to 114 pence, the headline read: "Dame Agatha Gives a Boost to Booker." In the annual report of Booker McConnell, Ltd., for 1975, the chairman, Sir George Bishop, made this exceptional statement to his shareholders: "To our great regret Agatha Christie [no Dame in this cold world of figures] died on January 12, 1976. Our association with her began in May 1968 when we made an investment in the company which bears her name and in which we now own 64 per cent of the equity. She had an unsurpassing ability as a storyteller and her creative vigor was sustained until the end. Her latest book *Curtain* topped the best seller list both here and in the United States for many weeks. Few authors have given so much enjoyment to so many readers around the world."

So there she was—the little girl from Devon with all her complexities, her shyness, her daydreaming, and her strong secretive family feelings. There she was at the end of her long and productive life classified in cold naked figures in the chairman's annual report alongside the sugar and barrels of rum.

It is odd and strange that the English socialist-inclined society, which is against unearned incomes and wants the workers to get the full harvest of their labors, through their twisted legislation forces this creative and endlessly hard-working laborer to share the fruits of her lonely efforts with anonymous shareholders who for purely speculative reasons, had invested in rum and sugar. The first of those commodities at least had not been appreciated by her during her long life.

The annual returns of Agatha Christie, Ltd., must by law be filed at Somerset House in London and be available to anyone who cares to see them. They do, of course, only give the minimum of information but they show over the last few years Booker McConnell, Ltd., has increased its shareholding in Agatha Christie, Ltd. On January 1, 1973, it owned the same 51 per cent as it began with but during the year it bought for an unknown sum a further 700 shares from the trustees, represented by Mr. Cork who also transferred 1,600 shares to the grandson, Mr. Prichard, and 200 to Mrs. Hicks. In 1975 the trustees then sold Booker Books, Ltd., a further 600 shares so that Booker now had 6,400 shares, which represented 64 per cent; Mrs. Hicks had 201, Prichard

1,600, and the trustees 1,798, the remaining shares being held by Edmund Cork as a director.

Neither Dame Agatha nor Sir Max Mallowan had any shares in their own name but they may of course have benefited under the trust. Apart from directors' fees of £10,000 divided among the six, the company paid a dividend which could vary from 70 per cent to 80 per cent plus.

The profit has risen steadily and sharply and by 1973 it was £239,101—£125,000 after taxes. The 1974 figures were £283,000 and after taxes £172,000. In 1975 there was a huge jump as the profit went above £1,000,000 and after taxes £490,000, which was probably due to the film *Murder on the Orient Express*. From £10,000 the working capital had increased to £1,790,000. The grandson's share of this alone would be £286,400.

The question, however, remains. How did Agatha Christie pay her bills? She remarked on one occasion during the last years of her life, "I am not a rich woman. My income is tied up in such a way that I only have access to a certain amount of money."

One reason for the reticence surrounding Agatha Christie's finances since her death is supposed to be that negotiations were under way for selling further parcels of shares and early works to Booker. Before Booker came into the picture Agatha Christie had, however, made a sensational deal with Metro-Goldwyn-Mayer when she sold the television rights to her books for a fantastic £1,000,000 in the sixties.

Mr. Lawrence Bachman, who was then chief European representative for M-G-M, has stated that the deal was done on his initiative. Edmund Cork said that they had been pressed for years to sell the rights and that complicated negotiations had been going on for some time. Bachman explained further that M-G-M hoped to get several television serials from these rights and that they expected Agatha Christie would help with the preparation as "she has a wonderful power of analysis." They made no arrangements for her further works, nor was it mentioned what she would be paid for her assistance in the preparations.

For M-G-M it was perhaps not as clever a deal as it was for Agatha Christie. The scripts were turned into cinema films which were not particularly successful despite the presence of Margaret Rutherford, and Agatha Christie disliked them intensely. But now at least she had got her own back for the miserable deals on her early books. It may have quietly pleased her that she had brought the harvest in at last.

Murder on the Orient Express has grossed in excess of £20,-000,000 and is the most profitable all-British financed film ever made, but E.M.I. has taken the obligatory Christie vow and is not telling either to whom the royalty is paid nor how much. Another film, *Murder on the Nile*, has completed production and is expected to make yet another fortune. The Christie financial empire seems limitless and must be a delightful headache for her agent to keep track of this profitable jigsaw puzzle.

Just a few figures from 1976 will give a vague, but tantalizing, idea about what amounts are involved. *Curtain* brought as mentioned an American advance for the paperback rights of $1,000,000 plus $300,000 for the hardback in the United States and United Kingdom royalties of £60,000. The same year the *Orient Express* sold 3,000,000 paperbacks in the United States and earned $300,000 in royalties. It seems that the only place that the *Orient Express* is not running is on the rails to the Orient.

In the United Kingdom 2,000,000 paperbacks were sold worth £800,000 in the shops and earning royalties of £70,000. This was the income so far for 1976—the year of her death—£930,000. And I have not included the earnings for the best-selling film *Murder on the Orient Express* nor the constant trickle—or floods —of royalties from the twenty-eight countries where her books are still sold, one of the most enthusiastic being Japan. How much further can you get from Devon, Oxfordshire, and Chelsea?

If her income in the later years became enormous Dame Agatha was no less concerned with the accounts than when they were modest in the beginning of the 1920s.

From Banff Springs Hotel, Banff, Canada, she wrote on September 26, 1922, to Mr. Basil Willett of The Bodley Head, which was then her publisher, thanking him for a check of £47 18s. 10d. —about $216 at the time—and immediately on her return to Ashfield in Torquay she wrote again on December 6 and asked him to send her accounts, which she had asked to be held over until her return.

From her London flat at 8 Addison Mansions W14, she wrote again to Mr. Willett, pointing out that while he had taken the selling price of *The Secret Adversary* in America to be 7s. 6d. it was actually $1.75 and as the average exchange had been $4.45 to the pound, she had due to her from The Bodley Head 1,258 copies at $1.75 equals $2,201.50, of which the royalty equaled £49. 9s. 5d. less 8 per cent income tax £3. 19s. 2d. equals £45 10s. 3d. instead of the £43 8s. she had received—a difference of £2. 2s. 3d., which is less than $10. She added that it was a very small difference but that it all helps in these hard times.

From her other house, Styles, Sunningdale, Berkshire, she wrote again to the much suffering Mr. Willett, May 25, 1962, that there had been a mistake in the accounts for *Poirot Investigates*. Although the royalty generally was 10 per cent there had been sold twelve copies at 7s. 6d. and she thought that the royalty should have been 20 per cent, which would make a difference in her favor of 7s. 6d. or $1.50. Nothing was too small to escape her scrutiny and thus it always was.

Although it was to be Mrs. Miller who influenced her daughter's character throughout her life, Mr. Miller's arithmetic lessons, learned in the schoolroom at Ashfield, were to prove no less important. They left an indelible print and healthy respect for money that stayed with Agatha Christie all her life.

Within a few months after her death Agatha Christie manuscripts had become possible collector's items. In 1977 the manuscript of the novel *A Murder Is Announced* was advertised by Christie's in a sale of nineteenth- and twentieth-century books and manuscripts. It was a typewritten script but there were many amendments and corrections in Dame Agatha's own handwriting. A few weeks before the sale it was mysteriously withdrawn. Christie's was secretive in its reply to my enquiry, saying that the present owner had withdrawn the manuscript from the sale as the owner did not wish to sell it. It seems more than likely that hearing of the sale Agatha Christie, Ltd., stepped in and claimed ownership.

It seems unlikely that any will even be on public sale as they are now all in the possession of the Agatha Christie Trust.

The manuscript would probably have only fetched a few hundred pounds but it is indicative of the strong hold that Agatha Christie's family is keeping on all her possessions, even after her death.

CHAPTER NINETEEN

IN THE LONDON SUBURBS of Kensington and Hammersmith are eighteen Harrison Homes where old ladies of limited means live in great contentment. They could have come straight from the pages of an Agatha Christie—nannies, cooks, parlormaids—all good women who have given of their best in domestic service. With the present-day conditions of smaller houses and increasing expenses families are no longer able or willing to keep them in their last days.

Suddenly after fifty or sixty years in service they find themselves thrown out into a harsh world. Most of them have no relatives or children of their own. They are totally alone . . . and often defenseless. These then are the ladies who have found a new life in these cheerful, attractive houses.

The old ladies provide their own furniture, buy and cook their own food, and draw their own pensions. They live an independent life but as part of the Harrison community they are expected to be good neighbors.

Although the homes were founded in 1869 they were not put on their present financial footing until the 1960s. It was at that time that Dame Agatha heard about them through her friend, Miss Mary Fisher, who did part-time secretarial work for the homes.

Sitting in one of the cozy rooms the Honorable Lady Sachs, the vice-chairman, told me how Dame Agatha came to be involved.

"They were once a penny-picking Victorian charity . . . I mean run by awfully nice Kensington ladies with feather boas in summer and musquash coats in winter, but little idea of organizing funds for the homes. Miss Dorothy Webb, daughter of the Victorian architect Sir Aston Webb, was Victorian authority. I am sure her heart was in the right place but the old ladies were in awe of her when she arrived and poked her umbrella into this or that. They dared not answer back.

"This was the atmosphere we wanted to change. Over the years we have found, thanks to education and the social services, that finance is not usually the main consideration in admission. It is loneliness, inability to find accommodation they can afford, ruthless landlords who make their lives an absolute hell."

For many months in her astute way Dame Agatha had probed Mary Fisher about the homes. There was no immediate rush. It was all done very quietly.

First of all her son-in-law, Anthony Hicks, and other members of the family trust arrived. "They literally went through everything with a fine-tooth comb—the finances, our terms of reference, all things that went back to the 1860s. They left no stone unturned," Lady Sachs continued.

The first gift, given in 1965, was the sum of £10,000, which Dame Agatha wanted used for "bricks and stones and improving the buildings."

"It was the Dame Agatha's money that gave us the courage to start a new wing. We turned five houses inside out and put in a lift, a club room, and a laundry in the building we are sitting in now. And then we did a complete rethinking about the interiors of the rooms and gave each one an electric refrigerator and cooker."

During the next few years Dame Agatha was to give another

£50,000 to the Harrison Homes, which literally "saved our lives."

It was not until the rebuilding had been completed that Dame Agatha accepted an invitation from the Harrison Homes Council to go and see what her money had done. She was invited on her first visit to unveil the plaque that was placed in the clubroom to commemorate her gifts to the homes and officially reopened the newly built block.

She meticulously inspected each room, noting the carefully planned work units, and was especially interested in the height of the working surface, which had been specially designed to avoid unnecessary bending.

Though she appeared shy and slightly withdrawn with the council, once she got among the old ladies her whole demeanor changed. She understood them completely, for these were like the characters she had been talking to in her books for over fifty years.

"Oh, you have a problem with hearing," she said. "There are some good hearing aids these days. . . . Does your rheumatism hurt you? Mine hurts here. . . . You were in service in Suffolk. No, I don't know Lord X but I do know the house—a lovely part."

"She was an absolute dear the way she went round and talked to each one. Very few of them had actually read her books though they all knew who she was," Lady Sachs recalled.

Every Christmas a different old lady was selected to write to Dame Agatha. No one interfered with what she wrote—it was merely to be a letter representing all the grateful old ladies and telling any news. Dame Agatha always replied in her own handwriting with a chatty letter.

There was a great deal of sadness at the Harrison Homes when they heard of Dame Agatha's death. As one old lady said to me: "You know she gave us so many lovely useful things. We shall never forget her."

Old age and its misfortunes were never far away in Dame Agatha's mind, and her sympathy was always practical. When she heard of one old lady in her own village who could not manage on her money she ordered a box of groceries from the village shop to be delivered every week for as long as the old lady lived. It was from the same village shop where Lady Mallowan's housekeeper did all their own shopping. Dame Agatha always preferred to use small family shops and disliked supermarkets. She was terribly upset when she heard that paperbacks of her books were being sold in some of the larger chains.

"What next? They will be selling them in butcher's shops soon," she commented waspishly.

During the thirty years that she lived in Wallingford few people ever saw Lady Mallowan personally. The mayor, Mrs. Pat Ashton, is an admirer of her books but said on her death: "To my knowledge I have never seen her, although I believe she used to walk by the river near here. She was not involved in town work, but I'm sorry about her death—Wallingford has lost a celebrity, and we have few of them."

P. C. Gordon Bartlett had been a police officer at Wallingford for twenty-three years but met Agatha Christie only once. This was when a lorry crashed into the brick wall outside her home.

"While I was there I explained that my son enjoyed her books, and she agreed to sign some of them for him. He was really thrilled," he recalled.

Wallingford Library has most of the Agatha Christie books. Mrs. Maureen Page, assistant librarian and town councilor, said that they were among the most popular books there. "But I think that is because people enjoy them rather than because she lived here."

If the residents of Wallingford wanted to catch a glimpse of Lady Mallowan, as she was known locally, the best way was to book seats for the Sinodun Players Christmas pantomime. For twenty-six years she had been president of this local amateur dramatic group, which put on three shows a year. Though she may not have been able to attend the productions during the year because she was abroad Dame Agatha always tried to see the pantomime, which included such classics as *Cinderella, Robinson Crusoe, Jack and the Beanstalk, Sinbad the Sailor, Little Red Riding Hood, Puss in Boots, Snow White,* and *Aladdin.* In 1952 in honor of Agatha Christie becoming president the Sinodun Players staged *Peril at End House* and presented her with an album of photographs and a program signed by all the cast and technicians.

After each performance she usually made a point of asking to see the cast and congratulating them on their performance.

Two years ago the Players decided to find a permanent home for their activities, which had up to now been staged in the Masonic Hall, and tried to raise sufficient money to buy the historic old Corn Exchange in the center of the town.

The aim was to raise £35,000 for the purchase of the building and transform it into a theater, conference hall, lounge, and bar. This could also be used by other amateur and professional touring companies.

All the businessmen in Wallingford were approached and many contributed but when the director, John Atwell, wrote to Dame Agatha, who had never been approached to help in any way before, and asked whether they could "count on your financial support" he received a reply from Sir Max Mallowan rejecting this. He explained that his wife was involved in many charitable trusts and was particularly interested in old people's homes and in any case she did not approve of the Corn Exchange project.

He also explained that at the same time he was trying to raise money for the British Archaeological Institute, which also had a gap of £30,000. Clearly the dramas of 6,000 years ago were of more importance in the Mallowans' lives than those presented by the local drama players.

There may be another explanation. As a professional woman who had worked hard all her life she had no time for amateurs . . . no time for people who did things just for pleasure.

A check did arrive however for £150 after Dame Agatha's death, which has been earmarked for new costumes for the Christmas pantomime. John Atwell feels that at least Dame Agatha would have approved of this.

Children have always played an important part in Agatha Christie's life. One of her lesser known interests is the Agatha Christie Trust for Children. Set up in 1969 it was formed to help deprived and physically handicapped children. A house was bought in Abergavenny by the trust, which also supports the Medical Research Fund for the University Hospital of Wales.

When *Murder on the Orient Express* was premièred in Wales in December 1974, as Prince of Wales, Prince Charles attended this first royal cinema occasion for Wales. The three charities which shared the proceeds were the Agatha Christie Trust for Children, the National Advertising Benevolent Society, and the Variety Club of Great Britain, which all have strong connections with Wales through their work.

Though Dame Agatha was unable due to ill health to play a very active role in the running of her children's home this is competently handled by her grandson, Mathew Prichard, who lives nearby.

The children of Galmpton Primary School, in the nearest village to Greenway, Dame Agatha's Devonshire home, were another interest in her life. As the chatelaine of Greenway she was automatically appointed to the Board of Managers of this state-aided Church of England primary school. One of the first things she did was to give the school a twenty-foot-high silver birch tree for Christmas in 1940. She had decorated the tree with colored lights and on lighting-up day had a present for every child in the school.

A few years later she introduced what was to become a yearly event, the Mallowan Literary Prize, to encourage the children in the art of writing. Each year Dame Agatha set the subject matter, which ranged from A *Trip Abroad to The Sea, My Idea of a Hero, If You Were Not Yourself Who Would You Like to Be,* or *My Favorite Character from the Bible.* She insisted that the children entering should use pseudonyms as she explained to the headmaster, Mr. Fellingham, she "knew many of the children by name and therefore it would not be fair." One year the children were given the names of English counties, Kent, Sussex, Surrey, and so on, another year they were called after animals, and again flowers. One of the conditions of the competition was that the essay had to be done in school and the subject matter was not to be announced until the event took place.

It took Lady Mallowan three weeks each year to read through the essays and after she had whittled them down Sir Allen Lane of Penguin Books joined her for the weekend to select the winners. The results were always sent to the school with an accompanying letter giving an explanation for her choice.

After reading the essays on the Bible, Lady Mallowan wrote to the headmaster that it was quite clear that the children were interested in their scripture classes. She also added that her husband, Sir Max Mallowan, said that the shocking low standard of his university students' English was partly due to the fact that they had not been brought up to read the Bible.

As she told Mr. Fellingham: "I try not to be influenced by better writing and spelling, which one has a tendency to do. If they are read aloud, one revises one's opinions quite differently. A test I make is to put them in cold storage and after a fortnight see which one of the essays has stuck in my memory."

On one occasion she left the choice of title to the headmaster and when he came up with the idea of "A Dwarf, a Musical Instrument, and a Whale," she was ecstatic.

"Forty-two versions of that idea arc quite a challenge to stimulate our budding brains," she told him. "I can hardly hold myself back from competing with an entry."

As the headmaster explained: "It was quite interesting to note that Lady Mallowan's ideas about story writing and using good English were not always in line with what the teachers thought. I suppose we were nearer the grindstone. A teacher initially begins by encouraging a child to use his or her powers of description and imagination whereas an author, who is more used to the demands of the literary market is more concerned with precise, clear, uncluttered English."

If she was not able to be present Lady Mallowan always sent a letter to be read aloud to the children. In this she explained very carefully why she had chosen the winners and added solid common sense advice.

One year she wrote that "Sussex has written a delightfully gay account of herself as the Loch Ness monster which made good reading but that she had a slight tendency to substitute description for dramatic content."

On an even more practical note Lady Mallowan used to cajole her various publishers into donating large parcels of reference and classical books to supplement the school library. As she explained to the headmaster: "The school ought to have plenty of new books at frequent intervals if you want children to grow up literate and to enjoy reading."

Her mind was always thinking up new and amusing ways to stimulate the children. In 1971 she wrote to Sir William Collins and suggested that he send the school a copy of a very handsome book on birds which had just been published. She then contacted the headmaster asking that the book should be inscribed with the words that it was a reward for the industry of the children who had taken so much trouble that year to compete. "So you see in a way it is their presentation to the library," she explained.

It was not until her eighty-fifth year that Dame Agatha wrote to the present headmaster, Godfrey Heywood, saying that she felt it was time she handed over her position on the Board of Managers to her daughter, Mrs. Hicks.

In the last few years Mrs. Hicks has in fact resurrected an old custom that dates back to the foundation of the school in 1870. Every year the whole school of about 150 children is invited to Greenway for a raspberry tea and Morris and country dancing on the lawn. In the days before the 1920s the children used to arrive in wagons but after this the visits were stopped.

A new extension to the school in memory of Dame Agatha was recently opened. Both she and her daughter, Mrs. Hicks, had previously donated a few hundred pounds for a new classroom, which was opened by Dame Agatha in 1971. The memorial classroom has been built above the previous one and was opened by Sir Max Mallowan last March. Not everybody in the village of Galmpton was pleased when they received a letter asking for donations.

"She certainly didn't profess enough interest so far as I saw in the general life of the school to warrant having a memorial in her name when someone else has had to raise the money," Mr. Fellingham told me. "There are many people around here who feel that the family could have given more financial help than they have. So when I hear that they are calling it the Agatha Christie memorial classroom it sticks in my jaw a bit."

During the years she spent at Greenway, Agatha Christie and her family always turned up at the local Brixham Flower Show. For visitors they were as much an attraction as the rows of prize-winning vegetables.

Every show day the family would arrive with their flowers and containers and various bits and pieces and stand alongside the other village exhibitors arranging their vases. Mrs. G. R. Hatley, who was the secretary for many years, remembers Lady Mallowan's exhibits clearly.

"She began exhibiting in the fifties and I would say that we were then in the beginning of the free-style Constance Spry era. Each flower was especially placed so that it showed to its best advantage as opposed to the Victorian idea of just plonking them in. I would say that Dame Agatha was not completely Victorian yet not of the modern school. She would bring a big round bowl and perhaps use water lilies in a conventional flat arrangement whereas now we raise them a bit, build the arrangement up or elongate it."

When asked once what was the secret of the success of her garden Dame Agatha replied: "My gardener." She was not far wrong because she had a remarkably good gardener.

Year after year Greenway scooped almost all vegetable prizes and the onions grown by the gardener, Frank Lavin, were the pride of the village. In the end after years of winning, Mr. Lavin tactfully withdrew from entering. Today at the gates of Greenway he runs for the Hicks family a well-stocked nursery. But any visitor hoping to catch a glimpse of the house where Agatha Christie lived will be disappointed as it is hidden well away behind a bank of formidable trees.

Every year there is a steady stream of visitors from America who visit Galmpton and who wish to see anything associated with Agatha Christie, but like everything else in her life there is little evidence that she ever lived there.

Few of the people who worship in the Parish Church of Churston Ferrers are aware that the magnificent stained-glass window at the east end of the church was donated by Agatha Christie in 1957.

Up until the time of her death she was to remain as much an enigma to the people in her local village as she was to the world at large. And this is exactly what she wished.

CHAPTER TWENTY

Although she died in her Berkshire home, and is buried nearby, Dame Agatha Christie belonged in spirit to Devon. With its tradition for thick cream, buttercup-yellow butter, lonely sea-washed coves, and the warm west wind, Devon is not only one of England's most beautiful counties but has produced some of its finest writers.

When Agatha Christie was a child of two years of age in 1892, to "escape from the sins of the flesh" in London, Oscar Wilde took his wife and two children to Devon where he rented the home of the Dowager Lady Mount Temple, high on Babbacombe Cliff. During his stay there he completed A Woman of No Importance and also supervised the rehearsals of Lady Windermere's Fan, which opened at the Theatre Royal in Torquay. Wilde would have liked to remain in Torquay but the call of London and Lord Alfred Douglas proved too strong to resist.

Although she was bedridden, that beguiling Elizabeth Barrett Browning did much of her writing during the days she lived in

Torquay hoping to cure her chronic illness. The Victorian author Edward Bulwer-Lytton, who wrote *The Last Days of Pompeii*, lived on Walden Hill for some years.

A regular summer visitor was Benjamin Disraeli, Earl of Beaconsfield, who stayed with his rich patron, Mrs. Brydges-Williams, on Mount Braddon. She was to leave him the handsome sum of £50,000 in her will, which was a considerable fortune at the time.

Richard Blackmore set his romantic novel *Lorna Doone* in the wild and barren Exmoor country. Robert Herrick, the poet, and Sara Coleridge, daughter of Samuel Coleridge, both lived in Torquay. In Barton Road where Agatha Christie grew up were no fewer than four authors. The Misses E. and H. Ormerod lived at St. Mary's, Sir John Bailey at Rooklands, and Short Towers was the home of Miss Sybil Keighley, who on her return from India wrote a most engaging memoir, and of course Eden Phillpotts lived round the corner.

Francis Brett Young, author of *My Brother Jonathan* and *Deep Sea*, practiced as a doctor in nearby Brixham from 1907 to 1914. In later years Paul Gallico spent some time near Torquay before going to live in the South of France. Elizabeth Goudge lived at Marldon where she used the local folklore to create her novel *Gentian Hill*.

Sean O'Casey moved to St. Mary Church in Torquay so that his children could be educated at the liberal-thinking Dartington Hall. Today Henry Williamson, *Tarka the Otter*, delights in the countryside of Torbay, Ethel Mannin lives in retirement in nearby Shaldon, and Christopher Milne, the original *Christopher Robin*, has a pleasing book shop in Paignton.

When Dame Agatha Christie turned eighty-one years, the West Country Writers' Association invited her to be the guest of honor at one of their conferences. Christopher Fry, president of the association, thanked her for creating Hercule Poirot and for her astonishing inventiveness which had continued unflagging for as long as he could remember in the novel and in the theater where she had discovered "the secrets of perpetual motion."

Actor-writer Robert Speaight proposed the toast with these eloquent words: "To Dame Agatha, who for many years has enjoyed our gratitude and now basks in our congratulations. We are proud to touch the fringe of her laurels."

There are two schools of thought as to why Dame Agatha Christie was never accorded the honor of being given "the freedom of Torquay." One is that a die-hard core of reactionaries who still remembered the notoriety of her first marriage were against it and the more likely second explanation is that Dame Agatha herself would not have wanted it. She was much too modest and genuinely shy to have wished for this honor for herself.

Edmund Crispin, the detection novelist, has made his home in the hills behind Totnes. He was one of the few writers ever to be invited to Greenway, as he and Agatha Christie were old friends from the Detection Club days.

"The visits to Greenway were very agreeable and very informal. There was a massive dining room and you never knew what you were going to get. You might be eating off Georgian silver or something from Woolworths. You might be pouring wine from an eighteenth-century port decanter or drinking from some cheap glasses that Agatha had found when shopping. There were children and dogs and always amusing talk. Both Sir Max and Agatha had such beautiful manners that they put everyone at ease."

Edmund Crispin feels that Agatha Christie was much more amusing as a person than her writings would lead one to believe. He recalled once giving her a lift home after she had been to dinner with the Crispins.

"Well, Edmund," she said, "you have not written anything lately."

"That's quite right," he admitted.

"Why not?" Dame Agatha persisted.

"I can't think of a plot," Crispin replied.

"I wouldn't have thought," she commented, "that this would have worried *you*."

He told me of another occasion when by chance he met Dame Agatha at Paddington station where they were both catching the same train back to Devon. She complained to him that she couldn't find anything to read on the journey. This seemed to him quite ridiculous so he went over to the bookstall and found himself staring at row after row of Agatha Christies. He settled for a cookbook by Elizabeth David instead.

One of Edmund Crispin's most amusing memories of Dame Agatha Christie was at a dinner party given by the Detection Club. Suddenly there was a pause in the conversation as Dorothy L. Sayers boomed out: "I get sick of Lord Peter Wimsey, Agatha. Do you get sick of Poirot?"

"Yes, I do," Agatha Christie replied. They both lapsed back into silence.

In fact Agatha Christie often commented how tired she was of Poirot and there is at least one quote when she said she positively "hated him." But she was saddled with him since "I cannot afford to kill him off."

To other writers Dame Agatha's Wallingford home was even more interesting than Greenway as apart from her library of five hundred paperback crime books by other writers she had a fascinating collection of reference books—the Koran, textbooks on the Chinese language, works on Persian art, and a wide bibliography on poisons. In separate cases there were rows and rows of her own books in every kind of language which formed part of the decoration of the living room.

Though in her younger days Dame Agatha enjoyed London with its theater and concerts, in later years she preferred to stay at home in the evenings "reading other people's detective stories and listening to classical music."

In July 1971, while in London to finalize the publication of her eighty-first novel, *Nemesis*, Agatha Christie fell and broke her hip, but such was the character of the woman that she hobbled round for a week in great pain in the belief that it was only badly bruised. Back at Winterbrock House the fracture was discovered and she was whisked off to the Nuffield Orthopedic Center at Stoke Gabriel.

Though the leg was to mend, friends say that this accident more than anything else hastened the final decline in her health.

In the last years of her life there were days when her mind was as lucid and crisp as ever, and she continued to do her *Times* crossword puzzle and reread some of her earlier books, but it was apparent to everyone around her that Dame Agatha was nearing the end of her life. Though she suffered no destroying, ugly illness, due to old age, a bad heart, and arthritis she had become mentally and physically frail.

When Sir William Collins—who died a few months after Dame Agatha—realized that there would be no Christie for Christmas in 1975 he went to see her to try and coerce one of the two manuscripts she had written in the early days of the war which had been lying in the vaults of a bank for over thirty years. *Curtain*, which she wrote first, in which Hercule Poirot died, was made over formally by deed of gift to her daughter Rosalind and *Sleeping Murder*, later published in 1976, was given to her husband, Sir Max Mallowan.

At first Dame Agatha was adamant that both books should remain unpublished until after her death but Sir William could be remarkably persuasive. His trump card was that unless Hercule Poirot was killed off by her own hands, after her death other writers might try and keep him alive. Had not Kingsley Amis written a James Bond novel round Ian Fleming's character?

She listened but was still very thoughtful. Sir William continued silkily: "And what about someone having the cheek to finish Jane Austen's unfinished novel *Sanditon*."

It was his final taunt that unless quick action was taken one might even see Hercule Poirot in an ice extravaganza or guest star in a spaghetti Western. This was too much! Dame Agatha froze, but gave permission for *Curtain* to be published.

For the faithful followers of Agatha Christie *Curtain* is an oddly nostalgic book and takes M. Hercule Poirot, now crippled with arthritis and his face lined and wrinkled, back to *Styles* where we first found him. Only the patent-leather black hair (now alas out of a bottle) was there to remind one of the glory that was Poirot. How could any reader who had followed the gallant Belgian through fifty years not shed a tear when he informed Hastings that he had moved the amyl nitrate ampoules away from beside his bed? He preferred to leave himself in the hands of the *bon Dieu*.

Miss Marple fared better than Poirot in her terminal case, *Sleeping Murder* (Collins; Dodd, Mead in America, 1976).

Agatha Christie left her favorite character as sharp-witted, wise, and shrewd as ever to continue busybodying in the village of St. Mary Mead.

Christmas 1975 was a time for the last family gathering at Winterbrook in Wallingford. It was a happy time for Dame Agatha, who knew and understood, as few other women do, everything about family unity. Just before Christmas she insisted on being carried downstairs and placed on the sofa in the drawing room where she received Holy Communion for the last time.

Dame Agatha was a deeply religious woman. She gained strength and comfort from prayer during her lifetime. By her bedside she kept the copy of *The Imitation of Christ* by Thomas Kempis which her mother had also done in her lifetime. On the flyleaf under her name, "Agatha Mallowan," she had written an extract from St. Paul's Epistle to the Romans.

> Who shall separate us from the love of Christ? Shall tribulation, or distress, or persecution, or famine, or nakedness, or peril, or sword? . . . For I am persuaded that neither death, nor life, nor angels, nor principalities, nor powers, nor things present, nor things to come, nor height, nor depth, nor any other creature, shall be able to separate us from the love of God, which is in Christ Jesus our Lord.

On January 12 Dame Agatha Christie Mallowan's life ebbed away. She died gently as her husband wheeled her in a chair to the drawing room after luncheon. Theirs had been an uncommonly sound marriage as there was no personality struggle—each respected the necessity of mental independence and privacy in marriage. Apart from their work they had also shared many merry hours in each other's company.

Agatha Christie exposed her love for all the world to see in a poem entitled "To M. E. L. M. in Absence" in *Road of Dreams* (1924) and republished by Collins and Dodd, Mead in 1973.

Twenty months after his wife's death Sir Max Mallowan married a mutual archaeological friend of theirs, Miss Barbara Parker. It had always been the wish of Dame Agatha that should she die before him her husband would remarry.

The evening after Dame Agatha died London's theater world paid its own special tribute to her. It is an honor reserved for the great names who have given their talents to make the English theater as vital as it is. All over the West End between 10 P.M. and 11 P.M. the theaters dimmed their lights to honor this exceptional woman while inside the performances went on—just as Agatha Christie herself would have wished.

Four months later to the day in St. Martins-in-the-Fields, the actors' own church near Trafalgar Square, people from every facet of her life came to pay their tribute to Dame Agatha. There were the actors and actresses who had played in her films and plays, scholars from the Oxford world of Sir Max Mallowan, friends who had been associated with the Mallowans in their archaeological expeditions, and frail old ladies from the Harrison Homes mingling with members of the Detection Club and the Crime Writer's Association. The church was packed.

Dame Agatha's favorite psalm, Number 23, "The Lord Is My Shepherd," was read in quiet, measured tones. Sir William Collins, who had known Dame Agatha for fifty years, gave the address. He spoke about her modesty totally unspoiled by her fame.

"In her own genre of literary work we must accord her the title of genius, although she herself would never have admitted to any deep-seated literary pretensions. But she possessed in supreme measure one mark of literary greatness, the art of telling a story."

When asked once what she would like to be remembered for one hundred years hence she replied: "Well, I would like it to be said that I was a good writer of detective and thriller stories."

Despite her beguiling tea-cozy looks and old-fashioned manners Dame Agatha Christie's personal life had not always been placid. There was a period when it was racked with passion, anger, and anguish. But the essence of her character never changed. It was a rare combination of complicity, tenacity, insight, sensitivity, suspicion, professionalism, and a fanatic craving for personal privacy.

What more applicable way to end this life than with one of Dame Agatha Christie's own favorite quotations.

"Life is a pure flame and we live by an invisible sun within us."

APPENDIX
Agatha Christie Titles

1920 *The Mysterious Affair at Styles*
1922 *The Secret Adversary*
1923 *Murder on the Links*
1924 *The Man in the Brown Suit*
1924 *Poirot Investigates* (short stories)
1925 *The Secret of Chimneys*
1926 *The Murder of Roger Ackroyd*
1927 *The Big Four*
1928 *The Mystery of the Blue Train*
1929 *The Seven Dials Mystery*
1929 *Partners in Crime* (short stories)
1930 *The Mysterious Mr. Quinn* (short stories)
1930 *Murder at the Vicarage*
1931 *The Sittaford Mystery*
1932 *Peril at End House*
1932 *The Thirteen Problems* (America: *The Tuesday Club Murders*)
1933 *Lord Edgware Dies* (America: *Thirteen at Dinner*)
1933 *The Hound of Death* (short stories)
1934 *Why Didn't They Ask Evans?* (America: *The Boomerang Clue*)
1934 *Murder on the Orient Express* (America: *Murder in the Calais Coach*)
1934 *Parker Pyne Investigates* (short stories) (America: *Mr. Parker Pyne—Detective*
1934 *The Listerdale Mystery* (short stories)
1935 *Three-Act Tragedy* (America: *Murder in Three Acts*)
1935 *Death in the Clouds* (America: *Death in the Air*)
1935 *The A.B.C. Murders*

1959 *Cat Among the Pigeons*
1960 *The Adventure of the Christmas Pudding and Other Stories*
1961 *The Pale Horse*
1961 *Double Sin and Other Stories*
1962 *The Mirror Crack'd from Side to Side*
1963 *The Clocks*
1964 *A Caribbean Mystery*
1965 *At Bertram's Hotel*
1966 *Third Girl*
1967 *Endless Night*
1968 *By the Pricking of My Thumbs*
1969 *Hallowe'en Party*
1970 *Passenger to Frankfurt*
1971 *The Golden Ball and Other Stories*
1971 *Nemesis*
1972 *Elephants Can Remember*
1973 *Postern of Fate*
1974 *Poirot's Early Cases*
1975 *Curtain*
1976 *Sleeping Murder*
1977 *An Autobiography*

AGATHA CHRISTIE MALLOWAN TITLES

1946 *Come, Tell Me How You Live*

TITLES UNDER THE PSEUDONYM MARY WESTMACOTT

1930 *Giant's Bread*
1934 *Unfinished Portrait*
1944 *Absent in the Spring*
1947 *The Rose and the Yew Tree*
1952 *Daughter's a Daughter*
1956 *The Burden*

AGATHA CHRISTIE POEMS

1924 *The Road of Dreams* (republished 1973)

AGATHA CHRISTIE CHILDREN'S BOOK

1965 *Star Over Bethlehem*

1928 *Alibi* (England)
1932 *Alibi* (America)
1930 *Black Coffee* (England)
1936 *Love from a Stranger* (England)
1936 *Love from a Stranger* (America)
1937 *Akhnaton*
1940 *Peril at End House* (England)
1943 *Ten Little Niggers* (England)
1944 *Ten Little Indians* (America)
1945 *Appointment with Death* (England)
1946 *Murder on the Nile* (England)
1946 *Murder on the Nile* (America)
1949 *Murder at the Vicarage* (England)
1951 *The Hollow* (England)
1952 *The Mousetrap* (England)
1953 *Witness for the Prosecution* (England)
1954 *Witness for the Prosecution* (America)
1954 *Spider's Web* (England)
1956 *Towards Zero* (England)
1958 *Verdict* (England)
1958 *The Unexpected Guest* (England)
1960 *The Mousetrap* (America)
1960 *Go Back for Murder* (England)
1962 *Rule of Three* (England)
1975 *Murder at the Vicarage* (England)
1977 *A Murder Is Announced* (England)

INDEX

239

243